"Dr. Pierce has w̲... scriptures to bring ... cannot live a life of following Jesus without being Wise @ Heart. From the ER to the scriptures, this life-applicable book will serve as a useful reference for the reader for years to come."

> —Dr. Keith J. Hamilton, President, Alaska Christian College

"*Wise @ Heart* is a powerful prescription for anyone in search of God's wisdom for a more fulfilling and healthier spiritual life."

> —Frank Baker, Media Director, Saddleback Church

"I like to think that I know my husband better than anyone else. But this book has humbled me into seeing that God not only knows him better, God is the author of my husband's exciting and extraordinary life. This book allows us to see into the very hearts—both spiritual and physical—of ordinary people like you and me. It teaches us about humanity through the wisdom of God himself. It is a book for all time, to read over and over, to study, and to turn to through the different seasons of your life when you need to seek wisdom.I consider this book the prescription for every heart."

> —Diane Pierce

"It had me at 'take a piece of corn out of a toddler's nostril!' Please buy this book and give one to everyone you know. My college tuition depends on it!"

> —Hannah Pierce, author's daughter, age 17

"I began reading this book today with the intention of reading one chapter and ended up getting through the fourth before I had to put it down so I could do homework. It's great, very engaging, bu⟋

I think its greatest strength is the convenient organization of scripture. I can't imagine anyone in ministry turning it down, simply because it will be such an easy resource. The ER stories also provide a great parallel between the physical and spiritual heart."

—JACOB PIERCE, author's son, student and worship leader at Liberty University

# WISE @ Heart

### DR. KENNETH B. PIERCE

HighWay
A division of Anomalos Publishing House
Crane

HighWay
A division of Anomalos Publishing House, Crane 65633
© 2009 by Kenneth Pierce
All rights reserved. Published 2009
Printed in the United States of America

09  1

ISBN-10: 0982323557 (paper)
EAN-13: 9780982323557 (paper)

A CIP catalog record for this book is available from the Library of Congress.

Cover illustration and design by Patty Findley

All scripture verses are from the HOLY BIBLE: NEW INTERNATIONAL
VERSION®. NIV®. Copyright © 1973, 1978, 1984 by International Bible
Society. Used by permission of Zondervan.

# Dedication

This book is dedicated to my family. To my dad, for helping me to believe that it is possible to achieve excellence, and to my mom, for helping me to believe that it would be worthwhile. To my kids, Jacob, Hannah, and Emily, who provided a great laboratory for me to observe how much God has blessed me. To my wife, Diane, who encouraged me to write this book and then gave me the space to do it. I love you all more than you can ever know.

Mahalo to my church family at Kauai Christian Fellowship. You have been there through all of the ups and downs and shared many moments of laughter and tears with me and my family. I look forward to spending an eternity in heaven with you all.

Finally, I thank my fellow Christian, good friend, medical school classmate, anatomy lab partner, and Emu roundup accomplice, Dr. Mark Crouch. I owe you a debt of gratitude for sharing the audio recordings of the Book of Proverbs made by your father, the late Dr. Norman Crouch. Your father was a great example of a faithful Christian, husband, father, and physician. It was a privilege to know him in life, and his wisdom lives on through his teachings…as wisdom always does.

# CONTENTS

# ABOUT THIS BOOK

The typical Emergency Room (ER) is a unique environment in which to observe human behavior. An ER is pumped full of emotion and adrenalin, dripping with trauma, blood, and noise. It is fast-paced and hectic. It is a snapshot of life on fast-forward. On other occasions, time seems to stand still when a patient takes their final breath. Simultaneous with that last gasp, the person's spirit escapes their body, leaving a palpable silence like a vacuum. To the awareness of those observing, time, indeed, seems to stop just for a moment. For those of us who work there, it is *controlled* chaos. For an outsider, I suppose it is just chaos. Depending on my level of fatigue, a shift in the ER is either energizing or exhausting. It is always, always hard work.

During my nearly twenty years as an ER doctor, I have seen more trauma, tragedy, violence, bloodshed, death, and abuse than any person should ever have to witness. I have saved some lives as well as provided comfort and care to many others. I have never questioned whether or not the work I do matters—because it does. On a busy weekend night shift, it would not be unusual, in the course of twelve hours, to care for a gunshot victim, deliver a baby, comfort a grieving family member, take a piece of corn out of a toddler's nostril, suture a stab wound, crack open a chest to do open heart massage, pronounce someone dead, shock someone's heart back into a normal rhythm, diagnose appendicitis, treat a child with meningitis, give a clot-busting drug to treat a heart attack, sedate a combative drug abuser, cut a hole in a neck to open an airway, and drain fluid from the abdomen of someone with liver failure. That is life in an ER through my eyes.

I am not a Bible scholar. I am just a Christian who is struggling to make sense of this world and serve God to the best of my abilities. And, I am failing miserably on both counts. The world often does not make sense to me and, well, I usually serve myself better than I serve God.

About twenty-five years ago, I began a simple process of studying the Bible, which became a routine and is now a habit. I read a chapter of the book of Proverbs each day. I also read Psalms, Ecclesiastes, and James on a regular basis. These books are often referred to as the "Wisdom Literature" in the Bible. I take notes when I read the Bible or anything else for that matter. That is a habit. I read every book with a pen in my hand, underline words and phrases that appeal to me, and write notes in the margins. This pretty much makes every book that I read unreadable for anyone else. I have underlined my way through about ten Bibles so far. I get a new one from my wife or one of my kids for Christmas about every two years.

I started creating my own "restructured" version of the book of Proverbs by collecting verses together based on related topics. After a few years, I began to add references from other books of the Bible that related to each topic. There were fifty plus topics defined arbitrarily by me. I accumulated hundreds of pages of notes. It dawned on me that I had created something that might be helpful to others. At the very least, I could pass it on to my kids and other family members. Even if not terribly useful to others, I would, at least, have something to show for the time that I spent on my back lanai in the dark hours before dawn, drinking strong coffee and listening to seventies rock and roll while hunched over my Bible.

My life has not been boring. I was raised in the Republic of Panama where my father was employed by the U.S. government. My mother was born and raised in Panama. I attended English-speaking schools, played most sports, and spent a lot of my youth in jungles and on beaches. After high school, I attended Purdue University for three semesters before transferring to Lamar University in Beaumont, Texas. Here, I earned a Bachelor of Science degree in Psychology and was the Captain of the weightlifting team. I then went on to complete my medical degree at the University of North Texas Health Science Center in Fort Worth, Texas. I completed my internship in San Diego, California and began the full-time practice of emergency medicine. After practicing emergency medicine for twelve years and while serving as the Medical Director for an emergency department, I completed a Masters of Science in Medical Management from the University of Texas at Dallas School of Management. In my last employed position before starting a consulting business, I served as the CEO of a large multi-specialty medical group. As a management consultant, I now help individuals and organizations to be more effective in achieving their goals.

I have been married for over twenty-five years to Diane, my high school sweetheart and best friend. Diane is a very talented nurse, life coach, Bible teacher, public speaker, and the best wife and mother that I know. We have three amazing children who all know and love the Lord. My son, Jacob, has chosen to serve God as a Worship Leader and will soon complete his degree in Worship at Liberty University in Lynchburg, Virginia. He recently married *his* high school sweetheart. Like his father, when he sees something he wants, he goes for it! My daughter, Hannah, will soon enroll as a student at the Savannah College of Art and Design in Savannah, Georgia. My youngest daughter, Emily, will graduate from high school in a couple of years. This book is mostly for my kids. I want to share the wisdom that I have learned through my study of the Bible and through life experience with them. I hope that they find it helpful.

The purpose of this book is to promote the search for wisdom, which I believe is the foundation for the life that God intends for *all* people. Regardless of your current situation, God's desire is that you become *wise*. It is through the acquisition of wisdom that we develop the ability to discern God's will for our lives. God has promised us that wisdom is ours for the asking. The corollary is that if we lack wisdom, then it is because we have failed to seek it and ask God for it.

It is when we allow wisdom to enter our *heart* and become woven into the very fabric of our soul that we can truly "test His good, pleasing and perfect will" (Rom. 12:2). The key to living a life of godly purpose, then, is to live a life driven by the pursuit of wisdom. Those who seek wisdom with all their heart will find it; they will become *Wise @ Heart*. This is God's will for each of us.

All of the stories in this book are based on true events and my personal experiences. The names have been changed to protect identities. I hope you enjoy the peek behind the curtain of my life as an emergency physician and physician leader. It has been a very rewarding experience for me, and I consider it a privilege to work as a doctor and provide care to people who are ill or injured. It is also an honor to be asked to lead people as well as have the opportunity to impact their individual development and an organization's performance.

To get the most out of this book, I recommend that you read it with pen, pencil, or highlighter in hand and with your Bible open.

Write your own comments and ideas in the margins. Underline or highlight the areas that are meaningful to you. Feel free to email me your thoughts and any suggestions for improvement. I recommend that you purchase a copy of the Life Application Study Bible, published by Zondervan, in whatever translation appeals to you. My favorite is the NIV translation. The footnotes, tables, and cross-references have been immensely helpful in guiding my study over the years. I welcome your comments and suggestions. My prayer is that God bless you in this life and by His grace because of your belief in Jesus Christ with eternal life in His presence. And, may you seek to become *Wise @ Heart.*

# WISE @ HEART AND THE WILL OF GOD

*My son, if you accept my words and store up my commands within you, turning your ear to wisdom and applying your heart to understanding, and if you call out for insight and cry aloud for understanding, and if you look for it as for silver and search for it as for hidden treasure, then you will understand the fear of the Lord and find the knowledge of God.*

—PROVERBS 2:1–5

You have been given the opportunity to make an investment that will yield returns above and beyond your wildest dreams. God has given you the opportunity to make an investment that will return greater riches than gold, silver, or precious gems. In God's economy, *wisdom* is of greater value than any other earthly treasure. God wants you to have all of the wealth—spiritual and physical—that He has set aside for you; just for you. It is God's will that you have this treasure. The choice to receive this treasure is yours to make.

# CHAPTER ONE

# THE BATTLE FOR YOUR HEART

My father-in-law, Jake, died suddenly and unexpectedly. My educated medical guess is that his heart suddenly developed an abnormal rhythm, quivered, and stopped. He was the picture of health. He was seventy-four years old, active, on no medications, with no known chronic medical conditions, and recently pronounced "fit" after a physical examination by his doctor. He was not negligent about his health. He did not smoke and he rarely drank alcohol. He was fairly active. Just prior to his death, Jake was out working in his meticulously maintained yard. That is where his symptoms began.

He thought it was indigestion and felt a little lightheaded. He went in to lie down for a while and told his wife, Jeneth, that he was not feeling well. He suspected that the lunch he had recently eaten was the cause of his symptoms. A few minutes later, Jeneth heard him make a choking sound. She rushed into the bedroom and saw immediately that he was unconscious. Unlike the miraculous recovery or resuscitation that you may have seen on television, this story has a sad ending. Jake is dead. He was a loving, loyal, and generous husband, father, grandfather, and friend. His family misses him dearly. Jake's heart simply gave out. It failed him.

As a veteran ER doctor with nearly twenty years in practice, I have seen more tragedy and trauma than any person should have to see in a lifetime. I have cared for victims of gunshots, stabbings, car wrecks, blunt trauma, rape, physical abuse, substance abuse, heart attacks, strokes, cancer, infections, and a few shark attacks. I have delivered babies and saved a few lives. And, too many times, I have witnessed death. Sometimes, death comes suddenly and unexpectedly as it did with Jake. At other times, I have witnessed the slow painful death caused by diseases like cancer, diabetes, kidney failure, liver failure, or serious infections. The most common cause of non-accidental death in America, and one that I see frequently, is heart disease.

All humans come equipped with two hearts—a *physical* heart and a *spiritual* heart. Most of us are quite aware of our physical heart, which is the muscular organ slightly to the left of center in our chest that is about twice the size of your fist. It circulates blood by pumping an average of seventy times per minute, over one hundred thousand times per day, and more than 36 million times per year. I estimate that Jake's heart beat more than 2.6 billion times in his lifetime. Despite the efforts of the best minds in medicine, man has not been able to produce an "artificial" heart that can come anywhere close to the miracle of the human heart created by God. Our spiritual heart, also created by God, is even more amazing. It never stops beating. It will live on in eternity long after your physical heart has ceased to function.

Physical death is inevitable for all of us. The average life expectancy in the U.S. today is between seventy-five and eighty years. Healthy living will generally prolong your life, and unhealthy living will generally shorten your life. However, whether it is through illness or accident, we eventually will die. Despite all of the miraculous advances in medicine, sooner or later, we will all die a physical death.

On the other hand, there is no spiritual death. Our spirits live on after our physical body has died. That is the good news. The bad news is that while some spiritual hearts will spend eternity in the presence of God in heaven, other spiritual hearts will spend eternity separated from God in hell. The cause of eternal separation from God is spiritual heart disease, also known as sin.

There is an antidote for spiritual heart disease that will guarantee that our spiritual hearts will spend eternity in heaven. That is good news because, according to the Bible, all of us have spiritual heart disease. Romans 3:10–12 says, "There is no one righteous, not even one; no one seeks God. All have turned away, they have together become worthless; there is no one who does good, not even one." And Romans 3:23 continues: "...for all have sinned and fall short of the glory of God." Without the antidote for spiritual heart disease we are doomed. The dire need for an antidote is often encountered in our physical lives as the following story illustrates. I do not remember where I first heard, or read, this story. Here it is to the best of my recollection:

A large city experienced a sudden epidemic that threatened to wipe out its entire population. The symptoms experienced by the victims were much like the flu but much more serious. The first cases were reported in a local high school and rapidly spread throughout the city. Within a week, the first deaths were reported and, within two weeks, it appeared that the infection had 100 percent mortality in those infected. An antidote was desperately needed.

Doctors and scientists worked frantically to contain the infection and find a cure. The city was quarantined. No one could get into or leave the city. It appeared that nearly all of the population was infected and over half had died before the end of the first month. Infected healthcare workers began to die. Then, it was discovered that one young man, Joshua, aged fifteen, appeared to be immune to the infection. He was showing no signs whatsoever of illness despite having close contact with many infected individuals.

Joshua was taken to a hospital where multiple tests were conducted that determined that his blood contained an antibody that would both prevent and cure this deadly infection. The word of this spread and the city rejoiced. A cure had been found! There was just one problem. The antibody could not be separated from Joshua's blood. His actual blood was required for injection into an individual to be effective. Joshua was an average-sized fifteen-year-old with a blood volume of about seven liters. It would take all of his blood to treat the infected citizens of the city.

The public health authorities of the city presented this dilemma to Joshua. They explained carefully to Joshua that he was their only hope but that it was his decision alone to donate his blood. He could donate some of his blood to save a few, all of his blood to save all, or none of his blood. The choice was his. Joshua made his decision quickly. He chose to donate his blood—all of it—to save the lives of the citizens of the city. He gave his life in order to save others—most of them complete strangers. He gave his life so that others could live.

This story is fictitious, but there is a true story that is even more dramatic than this one. Jesus, the Son of God, gave his life willingly for us as payment for our sins—our spiritual heart disease—so that all who believe in him would receive everlasting spiritual life in the presence of God. John 3:16 says, "For God so loved the world that he gave his only Son, that whoever believes in Him shall not perish but have eternal life." Romans 10:9–10 says, "...if you confess with your mouth, 'Jesus is Lord' and believe in your heart that God raised him from the dead, you will be saved. For it is with your heart that you believe and are justified, and it is with your mouth that you confess and are saved." Jesus is the only antidote for spiritual heart disease. All who accept Jesus as their savior will be saved.

Those of you reading this book that have not made a heartfelt and vocal confession of Christ, I hope that you will choose to do so now. Those of us that have made this confession have an important question to ask ourselves: "What is an appropriate response when someone gives their life to save yours?" Here is another story that is true. Some details have been changed to protect identity.

One day, Jerry, a muscular black man in his mid-thirties, came to the emergency department with a fever and a cough. He was an otherwise healthy individual who worked as a physical education teacher and coach at a local high school. He came to the ER late one evening because the football team that he coached had practiced late that day and they were leaving early the next morning for a football game in a neighboring town. He did not appear particularly ill, so I anticipated that I would be able to take care of him fairly quickly with an examination and a prescription.

When I had Jerry take off his shirt so that I could listen to his lungs, I saw a scar along his left flank and back, extending around to his abdomen. When I asked him about the scar, he told me a touching story.

Jerry played football in college and was a likely candidate for the pros. His college football career was going well when he learned that one of his brothers, who suffered from severe diabetes, was in need of a kidney transplant. Jerry volunteered to be evaluated as a possible donor. He was the only suitable match among all his family members. Jerry donated one of his kidneys to his brother so that his brother could live. If not for Jerry, his brother likely would have died awaiting a donor. There just are not enough organ donors available to meet the needs of those awaiting donation. However, as a result of donating his kidney, Jerry was required to give up his football career. Jerry is a hero in anybody's eyes. When I asked Jerry how his brother was doing, Jerry said that his brother was alive and well and enjoying raising his two small children—children who would have lost their father if not for Jerry's selfless sacrifice.

What is the appropriate response for an individual who is the recipient of this type of a gift? Ephesians 5:1–2 tells us that, as a result of Christ's love and sacrifice for us, we are to be "imitators of God" and "live a life of love" just as Christ did. We are cautioned in Ephesians 5:15–17 to "be very careful then, how you live—not as unwise but as wise, making the most of every opportunity, because the days are evil. Therefore do not be foolish, but understand what the Lord's will is." In 2 Timothy 2:15, we are instructed to "do your best to present yourself to God as one approved, a workman who does not need to be ashamed and who correctly handles the word of truth." This is the appropriate response for those of us who are the recipients of Christ's sacrifice and God's grace: To present ourselves to God as workmen who will live out the truth of God's love; to live as wise, not as unwise. We are to be imitators of Christ in our life of love and sacrifice. Jesus affirmed that the greatest commandments are to love God and to love others (Matt. 22:37–40). However, the choice is ours.

It is possible to receive God's gift of spiritual salvation through Christ and yet be saved as "only as one escaping through the flames." We do this when our response to God's grace is other than that described above. It says in James 2:24, 26 that "you see that a person is justified by what he does and not by faith alone...As the body without the spirit is dead, so faith without deeds is dead." Our profession of faith in Jesus Christ must be accompanied by a life of worshipping God and service to others. We are saved by grace and not by any act other than professing our faith in Christ (Eph. 2:5). Our only appropriate response to this grace is our undying love for God and service to others in His name. In order to serve God and others effectively, we must have a healthy spiritual heart.

If you are going to attend to the health of your spiritual heart, it is helpful to know some facts about your spiritual heart. Your spiritual heart:

- Is where our knowledge of God and the Holy Spirit reside (Deut. 6:5; 1 Kings 9:3–4; Ec. 3:10–11; Jer. 17:5; 24:7; 29:13; Matt. 5:8; 22:37; John 5:41–42; Rom. 2:15; Eph. 5:19; Col. 3:1; Heb. 8:10; 1 John 3:19–24).
- Is where wisdom resides (Ps. 90:12; Prov. 10:8; 14:33; 15:14; 16:21; 16:23; 18:15; 22:17–21; 23:12; 23:15–16; 24:30–34; Ec. 8:5).
- Is where foolishness resides (Prov. 12:23; 15:7; 19:3; 22:15).
- Is where God wants us to keep his Word (Deut. 11:18; Prov. 3:1–2; 4:4; 4:21; 6:21; 7:3; Heb. 8:10).
- Can be controlled by God (Ex. 4:21; Prov. 21:1; Ez. 36:26; Mal. 4:5–6; Acts 16:14; Rom. 2:29; 2 Cor. 1:21–22; Eph. 1:18; Heb. 8:10; 1 John 3:19–34).
- Is where our plans are devised (Prov. 6:16; 16:1; 16:9; 19:21; 24:1; Ec. 8:11).
- Is where our motives and purpose reside (Prov. 20:5; Matt. 6:21).

- Is where our emotions reside (Lev. 19:17; Prov. 12:25; 13:12; 14:10; 14:13; 14:30; 15:13; 15:15; 15:30; 17:22; 24:17–18; 25:20; 27:9; Ec. 5:20; 7:3–4; 11:9–10; John 14:1; Col. 3:15).
- Is where our character resides (Prov. 3:3–4; 16:5; 18:12; 21:4; 22:11; 27:19; Matt. 12:34; Col. 3:23–24).
- Is revealed by our speech (Prov. 10:20; 12:23; 15:7; 15:28; 16:23; 17:20; 22:11; 22:17–21; 24:1; 26:23–26; Matt. 12:34; 15:18).
- Must be carefully guarded (Prov. 4:23).
- Should strive to be like God's heart (1 Sam. 13:14).
- Is what God looks at rather than at outward appearances (1 Sam. 16:7; 1 Chron. 28:9; Prov. 15:11; 17:3; 20:27; 21:2; 24:11–12; Jer. 17:10; Luke 16:15; 1 John 3:19:24).
- Is where righteousness and wickedness reside (Prov. 6:16; 6:25; 7:25; 10:20; 11:20; 12:20; 15:28; 17:20; 20:9; 23:17–21; 23:26–28; 26:23–26; 28:14; Ec. 7:7; 7:26; 8:11; 9:3; Jer. 17:9; Ez. 18:31; Matt. 15:18; James 3:13–18; 4:8).

As you can see, our spiritual heart is *who we are*. Our spiritual heart is what is seen by God and by someone who is spiritually wise (Prov. 20:5). Spiritual wisdom equips us with another set of eyes—the eyes of our heart (Eph. 1:18). The eyes of our heart allow us to see others more clearly as God sees them. That is, we are able to see them as they are inwardly—in their spiritual heart—rather than focusing on outward appearances (Prov. 20:5). These spiritual eyes also enable us to see into our own hearts as God sees us. Most importantly, these spiritual eyes help us to see the path of wisdom that would otherwise be very faint, dimly lit, and overshadowed by the well-traveled super-highway to destruction paved by sin and rebellion against God.

Some of you may be suffering from spiritual heart failure. Most likely, this is due to sin in your life that is straining the capacity of your spiritual heart. It is unlikely that you will become spiritually well until you deal with the source of your spiritual heart disease. The prescription for spiritual heart failure is Jesus Christ: "But he was pierced for our transgressions, he was crushed for our iniquities; the punishment that brought us peace was upon him, and by his wounds we are healed" (Is. 53:5). The beauty of this prescription is that the treatment is not only curative, but it is also preventative. A spiritually healthy heart helps us to withstand the assaults of our sinful world and the temptations to sin that we all face. God and Satan are battling for our spiritual heart. Each wants control of our spiritual heart. The choice is ours.

It is God's desire that we become *Wise @ Heart* (Prov. 23:15–16) so that we live "as wise, not as unwise." As we love God with all of our heart (Deut. 6:5) and seek him with all of our heart (Jer. 29:13) we will grow in the wisdom and knowledge of God (Prov. 2:1–5). That is the process of becoming *Wise @ Heart.*

In addition to the numerous verses included above, there are many more verses that make reference to our spiritual heart. I have included many of these verses in **Appendix A** at the back of this book. A few of my favorites are included below. As you read this book, I hope that you will reflect on the health of your spiritual heart and commit to becoming *Wise @ Heart.*

Here are some verses to consider:

- Deuteronomy 6:5—"Love the Lord your God with all your heart and with all your soul and with all your strength."
- 1 Samuel 16:7—"But the Lord said to Samuel, 'Do not consider his appearance or his height, for I have rejected

him. The Lord does not look at the things man looks at.
Man looks at the outward appearance, but the Lord looks
at the heart.'"

- 1 Chronicles 28:9—"And you, my son Solomon,
acknowledge the God of your father, and serve him with
wholehearted devotion and with a willing mind, for the
Lord searches every heart and understands every motive
behind the thoughts. If you seek him, he will be found by
you; but if you forsake him, he will reject you forever."

- Psalms 14:1—"The fool says in his heart, 'There is no
God.'"

- Psalms 51:10—"Create in me a pure heart, O God."

- Proverbs 3:1–2—"My son, do not forget my teaching, but
keep my commands in your heart, for they will prolong
your life many years and bring you prosperity."

- Proverbs 3:3–4—"Let love and faithfulness never leave
you; bind them on the tablet of your heart. Then you will
win favor and a good name in the sight of God and man."

- Proverbs 3:5–6—"Trust in the Lord with all your heart
and lean not on your own understanding; in all your ways
acknowledge him, and he will make your paths straight."

- Proverbs 4:23—"Above all else, guard your heart, for it is
the wellspring of life."

- Proverbs 5:12—"How my heart spurned correction."

- Proverbs 16:1—"To man belong the plans of the heart, but
from the Lord comes the reply of the tongue."

- Proverbs 16:5—"The Lord detests all the proud of heart.
Be sure of this: They will not go unpunished."

- Proverbs 16:9—"In his heart a man plans his course, but
the Lord determines his steps."

- Proverbs 16:21—"The wise in heart are called discerning, and pleasant words promote instruction."
- Proverbs 16:23—"A wise man's heart guides his mouth, and his lips promote instruction."
- Proverbs 17:3—"The crucible for silver and the furnace for gold, but the Lord tests the heart."
- Proverbs 17:22—"A cheerful heart is good medicine, but a crushed spirit dries up the bones."
- Proverbs 18:12—"Before his downfall a man's heart is proud, but humility comes before honor."
- Proverbs18:15—"The heart of the discerning acquires knowledge; the ears of the wise seek it out."
- Proverbs 19:3—"A man's own folly ruins his life, yet his heart rages against the Lord."
- Proverbs 19:21—"Many are the plans in a man's heart, but it is the Lord's purpose that prevails."
- Proverbs 20:5—"The purposes of a man's heart are deep waters, but a man of understanding draws them out."
- Proverbs 27:19—"As water reflects a face, so a man's heart reflects the man."
- Proverbs 28:14—"Blessed is the man who always fears the Lord, but he who hardens his heart falls into trouble."
- Ezekiel 11:19–21—"I will give them an undivided heart and put a new spirit in them; I will remove from them their heart of stone and give them a heart of flesh. Then they will follow my decrees and be careful to keep my laws. They will be my people, and I will be their God. But for those whose hearts are devoted to their vile images and detestable idols, I will bring down on their own heads what they have done, declares the Sovereign Lord."

- Ezekiel 36:26–27—"I will give you a new heart and put a new spirit in you; I will remove from you your heart of stone and give you a heart of flesh. And I will put my Spirit in you and move you to follow my decrees and be careful to keep my laws."
- 1 John 3:19–24—"This then is how we know that we belong to the truth, and how we set our hearts at rest in his presence whenever our hearts condemn us. For God is greater than our hearts, and he knows everything. Dear friends, if our hearts do not condemn us, we have confidence before God and receive from him anything we ask, because we obey his commands and do what pleases him. And this is his command: to believe in the name of his Son, Jesus Christ, and to love one another as he commanded us. Those who obey his commands live in him, and he in them. And this is how we know that he lives in us: We know it by the Spirit he gave us."

# CHAPTER TWO

# BECOMING
# WISE @ HEART

Darcy, a ten-year-old girl, arrived at the ER by ambulance. She was attempting to ride her bike down a flight of cement stairs and had a horrible crash in the process. The paramedics had correctly diagnosed that Darcy had broken her right femur—the thigh bone. In fact, the X-rays that I ordered showed that her femur was shattered. She was going to have to have surgery to repair the damage.

It was obvious that Darcy was in severe pain, so a nurse quickly placed an intravenous line so that I could administer a strong pain reliever directly into her blood. Darcy was just about to receive this medication when her parents arrived in the ER. That is when trouble began.

After I described Darcy's injuries to her parents, I explained that she was going to need surgery to fix her broken femur. I also assured them that she would be made comfortable by the pain medication that I was about to administer to her. Much to my surprise, Darcy's parents informed me that they were not in favor of Darcy having surgery and also did not want her to receive any medication. They wanted to take her home immediately. I was stunned.

Darcy's parents informed me that "they don't believe" in western medicine. Darcy had only received "natural" medicine her whole life. Darcy's parents had been born and raised in the United States. They were not immigrants or the children of recent immigrants. They were not raised in a foreign or Native American culture that practices traditional healing techniques. They were not members of a religious sect that precludes the use of western medicine. Their beliefs were theirs alone. These were intelligent, educated people so I suspect that they had carefully researched the various alternative medical practices that they used. Darcy had not received the childhood immunizations that pediatricians currently recommend. And, while I acknowledge that current western medical practices fall short in the treatment of many diseases, orthopedic surgery for a shattered femur is undisputedly better than watchful waiting or herbal remedies. Darcy would likely die or be severely deformed or crippled without surgery.

Fortunately, with the help of the orthopedic surgeon and several nurses, I was able to convince the parents that surgery was the best course for Darcy. They were suspicious, but, in the face of such unanimous opposition, they gave in. Darcy did very well after surgery and recovered full use of her right thigh and leg with only a slight limp, which would most likely disappear over time.

Darcy's parents, while well-meaning, loving, and caring parents, were about to make a terrible mistake because of their ignorance. They were not malicious, just ill-informed. Without intending to, they could have seriously harmed Darcy, the child that they obviously loved so much.

We often engage in this same kind of faulty logic when we make decisions about our spiritual health. We concoct our own opinions about spiritual matters of great importance rather than seeking God's wisdom in these matters. At times, the Bible—the Word of

God—will conflict with our beliefs. We risk serious spiritual damage when we stick to our beliefs rather than accept God's teaching even when it seems paradoxical. What may "feel right" to us may not actually be right. Our feelings and faulty beliefs can lead us down the path of destruction.

Perhaps you, like me, have spent a considerable amount of time, effort, and energy trying to discover God's will for your life. Perhaps, also like me, you have become frustrated by this endeavor. I hope that, as you read this book, you will come to believe, as I have, that becoming *Wise @ Heart* is God's will for each of us. In order to properly serve God and others, we must have a clear understanding of God's principles and instruction. Becoming spiritually wise—*Wise @ Heart*—is the process of becoming spiritually mature.

Throughout this book, I will do my best to provide scriptural support for this conclusion. It is my belief that there is overwhelming evidence for this premise. You must ultimately decide for yourself. You may believe that God has a specific, individualized, and detailed plan for your life. If so, you are in good company since many people, including some very bright scholars, believe this. I can find very little evidence in the Bible or through my own anecdotal experience that this is the case. Since this is such a hotly contested issue, I will forego any lengthy theological discussion of the matter.

If you desire to engage in a formal study of this subject, there are quite a few books written on the subject of finding your "purpose" in life or discovering God's will for your life. For my part, it has been quite liberating to settle on the belief that God has a generic desire for all individuals. God's ultimate desire for each of us is that we all become *Wise @ Heart*. This generic purpose becomes individualized when we apply God's wisdom by uniquely using our talents, time, opportunities, relationships, and wealth to honor God and serve others.

This may not be comforting to those of you who believe that God has a specific plan for your life—that there is a specific individual that God intends for you to marry, a specific school that God expects for you to attend, or a specific career that God has chosen for you to pursue, and so on. If this is what you believe, then I hope you will suspend this belief long enough to finish this book. You may change your mind or, at least, open your mind to an alternative view.

I believe that our purpose here on this earth is to live in obedience to God by submitting to all that He requires of us. This is a *generic* purpose that applies to all of us. This obedience is expressed in our *individualized* commitment to grow in spiritual wisdom and maturity. The life decisions that we face are opportunities to exercise spiritual wisdom. The consequences that we face as a result of those decisions are also opportunities to grow in wisdom.

When making a decision, God expects us to view each choice through a single lens—wisdom. The question we ask, when facing a decision, should not be, "What will make me happy?" or, "What will make me the most money?" The question we should ask before making any significant decision is, "What is the *wisest* choice among those that are available to me?" The only way that we can know the answer to this question is to search the scriptures for an understanding of God's generic principles that we can use to determine the wise course we should take. We can also appeal to the wisdom of godly individuals who have been where we want to go who can serve as mentors.

The shear number of verses listed below provides compelling evidence, I think, that God desires that you become *Wise @ Heart*. I encourage you to read each verse carefully and consider the many rewards and benefits that are available to those who seek to become

*Wise @ Heart.* Here is an abbreviated list of some the benefits of becoming *Wise @ Heart* that you will find in the verses included below:

- Blessings and favor from God;
- Wealth;
- Good health;
- Effective leadership;
- Knowledge;
- Prudence;
- Discretion; and
- Honor.

Of course, these are principles and not necessarily promises. In general, if you live according to God's principles of wisdom, then these blessings are available to you. Would you like to experience these blessings? Is this what you desire for your life and for the lives of your loved ones? The prescription for you, then, is to become *Wise @ Heart.*

Becoming *Wise @ Heart* embodies all of what God desires for us and all that God expects of us. For example, if we are *Wise @ Heart,* then we will worship and serve God wholeheartedly. This wholehearted service of God implies obedience to all of God's commands. If we are *Wise @ Heart,* then we will worship God in spirit and in truth. If we are *Wise @ Heart,* then we will serve others and understand their needs. If we are *Wise @ Heart,* then we will be good managers of the wealth (time, money, talents, and opportunities) that God has given us. If we are *Wise @ Heart,* then we will work to seek and save the lost. If we are *Wise @ Heart,* then we will minister to other members of the body of Christ. The list goes on. Obedience to God's commands is always the *wisest* course.

Let's look deeper into what the scriptures teach us about wisdom. My hope and prayer for you is that you will see the importance and value of focusing on developing spiritual wisdom. First, we will examine the process described in the scriptures for becoming *Wise @ Heart*. In Job 28:28, God says that "the fear of the Lord—that is wisdom and to shun evil is understanding." King Solomon, the writer of the book of Proverbs and the wisest man who ever lived, instructs us in Proverbs 9:10–11 that, "the fear of the Lord is the beginning of wisdom, and knowledge of the Holy One is understanding. For through me your days will be many, and years will be added to your life." The "fear" that is referred to here is the type of fear that leads to respectful obedience.

Fear of God develops when you acknowledge the absolute authority of God. And, this fear, according to Proverbs 2:1–5, develops as a result of first seeking His wisdom: "My son, if you accept my commands within you, turning your ear to wisdom and applying your heart to understanding, and if you call out for insight and cry aloud for understanding, and if you look for it as for hidden treasure, then you will understand the fear of the Lord and find the knowledge of God." James instructs us, "If any of you lacks wisdom, he should ask God, who gives generously to all without finding fault, and it will be given to him." In these verses, we are instructed that, as we seek wisdom, we grow in our fear of God, which leads to greater wisdom.

The wisdom referred to in the verses above is God's wisdom, not human wisdom. This is an important distinction since there are significant differences between the two. First of all, if you are a follower of Christ, then the Holy Spirit lives in you and provides you with the ability to know and understand the wisdom of God. In 1 Corinthians 2:12, it says, "We have not received the spirit of the world but the Spirit who is from God, that we may understand what

God has freely given us. This is what we speak, not in words taught us by human wisdom but in words taught by the Spirit, expressing spiritual truths in spiritual words. The man without the Spirit does not accept the things that come from the Spirit of God, for they are foolishness to him, and he cannot understand them, because they are spiritually discerned. The spiritual man makes judgments about all things, but he himself is not subject to any man's judgment."

There is another message here beyond the comforting news that the Holy Spirit will guide us in developing spiritual wisdom. That is, as you grow in spiritual wisdom, you will find yourself in greater conflict with what the world considers "common sense." You will find that God's wisdom often conflicts with human wisdom. For example, the instruction that God's wisdom is more valuable than riches (Prov. 8:11) is contrary to what our culture teaches.

God's desire is that we become *Wise @ Heart*. This holds true for all races, cultures, genders, and generations. If you are a man, then there is no need to be concerned about how your masculinity, intelligence, wealth, or achievement measures up to the current "cultural" standards of success. For, as we see in Ecclesiastes 7:19, "Wisdom makes one wise man more powerful than ten rulers in a city." If you are a woman, then there is no need to fall into the cultural trap of obsessing about your appearance and appeal to men since wisdom is the most attractive feature you could ever hope for (Prov. 31:10–31). If you are a child or teenager, then there is no need to strive to fit in with the "cool" crowd or wait until you are "grown up" to start the process of being obedient to God's will for you. Choose your friends wisely. God's principle is that you will grow wise (Prov. 13:20; James 1:5–8). All of us, everywhere, have the same purpose in God's plan—to become *Wise @ Heart*.

In 1 Kings 3, there is an account of an interaction between God and King Solomon. God appeared to Solomon in a dream and said,

"Ask for whatever you want me to give you" (verse 5). If you have read this story you know that Solomon proceeded to ask for "a discerning heart to govern your people and to distinguish between right and wrong" (verse 9). The text continues: "The Lord was pleased that Solomon asked for this. So God said to him, 'Since you have asked for this and not for long life or wealth for yourself, nor have you asked for the death of your enemies but for discernment in administering justice, I will do what you have asked. I will give you a wise and discerning heart, so that there will never have been anyone like you, nor will there ever be. Moreover, I will give you what you have not asked for—both riches and honor—so that in your lifetime you will have no equal among kings'" (verses 10–13).

Look now at what King Solomon wrote later in his life. This passage is found in Proverbs 8:1–36 and, in my Bible, is entitled "Wisdom's Call": ·

> Does not wisdom call out? Does not understanding raise her voice? On the heights along the way, where the paths meet, she takes her stand; beside the gates leading into the city, at the entrances, she cries aloud: "To you O men, I call out; I raise my voice to all mankind. You, who are simple, gain prudence; you who are foolish, gain understanding. Listen, for I have worthy things to say; I open my lips to speak what is right. My mouth speaks what is true, for my lips detest wickedness. All the words of my mouth are just; none of them is crooked or perverse. To the discerning all of them are right; they are faultless to those who have knowledge. Choose my instruction instead of silver, knowledge rather than choice gold, for wisdom is more precious than rubies, and nothing you desire can compare with her.
>
> "I, wisdom, dwell together with prudence; I possess

knowledge and discretion. To fear the Lord is to hate evil; I hate pride and arrogance, evil behavior and perverse speech. Counsel and sound judgment are mine; I have understanding and power. By me kings reign and rulers make laws that are just; by me princes govern, and all nobles who rule on earth. I love those who love me and those who seek me, find me. With me are riches and honor, enduring wealth and prosperity. My fruit is better than fine gold; what I yield surpasses choice silver. I walk in the way of righteousness, along the paths of justice, bestowing wealth on those who love me and making their treasuries full.

"The Lord brought me forth as the first of his works, before his deeds of old; I was appointed from eternity, from the beginning before the world began. When there were no oceans, I was given birth, when there were no springs abounding with water; before the mountains were settled in place, before the hills, I was given birth, before he made the earth or its fields or any of the dust of the world. I was there when he set the heavens in place, when he marked out the horizon on the face of the deep, when he established the clouds above and fixed securely the fountains of the deep, when he gave the sea its boundary so the waters would not overstep his command, and when he marked out the foundations of the earth. Then I was the craftsman at his side. I was filled with delight day after day, rejoicing always in his presence, rejoicing in his whole world and delighting in mankind.

"Now then, my sons, listen to me; blessed are those who keep my ways. Listen to my instruction and be wise; do not ignore it. Blessed is the man who listens to me, watching daily at my doors, waiting at my doorway. For whoever finds me finds life and receives favor from the Lord. But whoever fails to find me harms himself; all who hate me love death."

My hope is that it is becoming clear to you that God places a high value on wisdom. In the following chapters, we will be examining the wisdom found in the scriptures as they relate to various important topics. Supporting biblical references are included to assist in your understanding and to guide your further study. These references are not intended to be exhaustive, and you may choose to supplement your learning with more in-depth study. As we engage in this journey together, let us always remember that the purpose of this journey—and God's desire for you and for me—is to become *Wise @ Heart.* I have included some of my favorite verses on wisdom here. You will find more in **Appendix B** at the end of the book. Here are some wisdom verses to consider:

- Job 12:12—"Is not wisdom found among the aged? Does not long life bring understanding?"
- Proverbs 1:7—"The fear of the Lord is the beginning of knowledge, but fools despise wisdom and discipline."
- Proverbs 3:7–8—"Do not be wise in your own eyes; fear the Lord and shun evil. This will bring health to your body and nourishment to your bones."
- Proverbs 3:13–18—"Blessed is the man who finds wisdom, the man who gains understanding for she is more profitable than silver and yields better returns than gold. She is more precious than rubies; nothing you desire can compare with her. Long life is in her right hand; in her left hand are riches and honor. Her ways are pleasant ways, and all her paths are peace. She is a tree of life to those who embrace her; those who lay hold of her will be blessed."

- Proverbs 4:6—"Do not forsake wisdom, and she will protect you; love her and she will watch over you."
- Proverbs 4:7—"Wisdom is supreme; therefore get wisdom. Though it cost all you have, get understanding. Esteem her, and she will exalt you. She will set a garland of grace on your head and present you with a crown of splendor."
- Proverbs 4:11—"I guide you in the way of wisdom and lead you along straight paths. When you walk, your steps will not be hampered; when you run, you will not stumble."
- Proverbs 9:9—"Instruct a wise man and he will be wiser still; teach a righteous man and he will add to his learning."
- Proverbs 9:10–11—"The fear of the Lord is the beginning of wisdom, and knowledge of the Holy One is understanding. For through me your days will be many, and years will be added to your life."
- Proverbs 9:12—"If you are wise, your wisdom will reward you; if you are a mocker, you alone will suffer."
- Proverbs 10:1—"A wise son brings joy to his father, but a foolish son grief to his mother."
- Proverbs 10:19—"When words are many, sin is not absent, but he who holds his tongue is wise."
- Proverbs 11:2—"When pride comes, then comes disgrace, but with humility comes wisdom."
- Proverbs 13:10—"Pride only breeds quarrels, but wisdom is found in those who take advice."
- Proverbs 13:20—"He who walks with the wise grows wise, but a companion of fools suffers harm."
- Proverbs 14:1—"The wise woman builds her house, but with her own hands the foolish one tears hers down."

- Proverbs 15:20—"A wise son brings joy to his father, but a foolish man despises his mother."
- Proverbs 15:33—"The fear of the Lord teaches a man wisdom, and humility comes before honor."
- Proverbs 16:23—"A wise man's heart guides his mouth, and his lips promote instruction."
- Proverbs 17:16—"Of what use is money in the hand of a fool, since he has no desire to get wisdom?"
- Proverbs 17:28—"Even a fool is thought wise if he keeps silent, and discerning if he holds his tongue."
- Proverbs 19:8—"He who gets wisdom loves his own soul; he who cherishes understanding prospers."
- Proverbs 19:11—"A man's wisdom gives him patience; it is to his glory to overlook an offense."
- Proverbs 19:20—"Listen to advice and accept instruction, and in the end, you will be wise."
- Proverbs 28:26—"He who trusts in himself is a fool, but he who walks in wisdom is kept safe."
- Proverbs 29:11—"A fool gives full vent to his anger, but wise man keeps himself under control."
- Ecclesiastes 7:10—"Do not say, 'Why were the old days better than these?' For it is not wise to ask such questions."
- Ecclesiastes 7:11–12—"Wisdom, like an inheritance, is a good thing and benefits those who see the sun. Wisdom is a shelter as money is a shelter, but the advantage of knowledge is this: that wisdom preserves the life of its possessor."
- Ecclesiastes 7:19—"Wisdom makes one wise man more powerful than ten rulers in a city."
- Ecclesiastes 8:1—"Who is like the wise man? Who knows

the explanation of things? Wisdom brightens a man's face and changes its hard appearance."

- Ecclesiastes 9:17—"The quiet words of the wise are more to be heeded than the shouts of a ruler of fools."

- James 1:5–8—"If any of you lacks wisdom, he should ask God, who gives generously to all without finding fault, and it will be given to him. But when he asks, he must believe and not doubt, because he who doubts is like a wave of the sea, blown and tossed by the wind. That man should not think that he will receive anything from the Lord; he is a double-minded man, unstable in all he does."

- James 3:13–18—"Who is wise and understanding among you? Let him show it by his good life, by deeds done in the humility that comes from wisdom. But if you harbor bitter envy and selfish ambition in your hearts, do not boast about it or deny the truth. Such 'wisdom' does not come down from heaven but is earthly, unspiritual, of the devil. For where you have envy and selfish ambition, there you find disorder and every evil practice. But the wisdom that comes from heaven is first of all pure; then peace-loving, considerate, submissive, full of mercy and good fruit, impartial and sincere. Peacemakers who sow in peace raise a harvest of righteousness."

# CHAPTER THREE

# THE BUILDING BLOCKS
# OF WISDOM

On an already busy day in the ER, I received a radio call from paramedics, informing me that they were five minutes out from the hospital with a twelve-year-old girl who was hit by a car a few blocks away. She was crossing a street near her school and was hit by an SUV. She was in critical condition. I immediately mobilized our trauma team and we were ready to receive the patient upon her arrival. I knew from much experience that these cases often end poorly even with the best of care. My prayers for this little girl started at that moment.

When she arrived, it was obvious that she was very seriously injured. She was comatose due to a head injury as well as had internal bleeding and multiple broken bones. My team and I worked hard to stabilize her enough to get her into surgery where the cause of her internal bleeding was identified and corrected. An orthopedic surgeon was called in to set her broken bones. A CT scan of her head showed bleeding around her brain. Since we did not have a neurosurgeon available at our facility, she was transferred to a major trauma center for further care. A couple of years later, I saw this girl at a soccer game. She came up and thanked me for the care that I had provided for her in the ER that day. She appeared to have completely recovered from her injuries. My prayers for her had been answered.

In medicine we like lists. We like algorithms and protocols that break things down into steps or procedures. This helps us to be efficient, to be complete, and to provide better care. Most of all, it helps to think clearly about what we are doing. The case that I described above had a good outcome largely because every member of the team acted "by the book" quickly and efficiently, which was exactly as we had been trained to do. There is a training course in trauma care entitled, "Advanced Trauma Life Support (ATLS)," that most ER doctors and trauma surgeons take. ATLS provides protocols (a series of steps) that, when followed, have been shown to increase survival—reduce death—due to major trauma. These protocols are so highly regarded that a trauma physician will very rarely depart from them.

I find it helpful to think of spiritual wisdom in a similar fashion. God has provided us with His "protocols" for our life that are contained in the Bible. Wisdom is made up of a series of steps, or building blocks, which can be examined individually. It is hard to describe wisdom unless you can break it down into the elements that form the building blocks of wisdom. When you examine these building blocks individually, you can see how they fit together.

Here are building blocks of wisdom that you will find in the Bible: Knowledge, Understanding, Discernment, Judgment, and Prudence. When I think of a wise individual, these are the characteristics that I see demonstrated in their lives. When I observe a wise decision, these are the elements that appear to be involved in that decision. When linked together, like building blocks or steps in a protocol, we are able to use these elements to construct an image of what we define as wisdom.

Let's start with *Knowledge.* My NIV Life Application Study Bible defines knowledge as: "The state or fact of knowing; learning; awareness; sum of what has been learned or discovered." This is probably pretty straightforward for most of you. As I pointed out in Chapter 2, *spiritual knowledge* begins with our *fear* of God (Prov. 1:7). And, in Proverbs 9:10–11, it reads, "The fear of the Lord is the beginning of wisdom, and knowledge of the Holy One is understanding. For through me your days will be many, and years will be added to your life." Knowledge is one of the building blocks of wisdom. To summarize what the Bible says about knowledge, here are some key points to consider:

- Knowledge begins with the fear of God (Prov. 1:7; 9:10).
- God's Word (the Bible) is our source of spiritual knowledge (Prov. 2:6).
- Fools hate knowledge (Prov. 1:22).
- Discipline is a prerequisite to gaining knowledge (Prov. 12:1).
- An individual's spiritual knowledge is reflected in his speech (Prov. 12:23; 14:7; 15:2; 15:7; 17:27).
- Unless spiritual knowledge is combined with love for others, it is worthless (1 Cor. 8:1; 13:2; Col. 2:2).
- We must make an effort to continually grow in spiritual knowledge (2 Peter 3:18).

Closely related to Knowledge and another building block of wisdom is *Understanding.* Understanding is defined in my Bible as: "to comprehend, realize; discernment." Understanding must be combined with knowledge in order for knowledge to be useful. It is possible to know something and yet not have understanding to support that knowledge. For example, you may know that penicillin is used to treat infections and, yet, without understanding how penicillin is prescribed and how it works, you will not be very capable in terms of using it.

As you see from the definition of Understanding given above, *Discernment* is another building block of wisdom. Discernment is defined in my Bible as: "to discover; to recognize; the ability to discover or recognize." Discernment helps you to apply your knowledge and understanding in the right situations and at the right time.

To summarize how knowledge, understanding, and discernment are related, consider this example. As a physician, I have been exposed to a lot of information from books and classroom instruction. This has given me knowledge. My understanding of this knowledge is tested everyday in the clinical setting when I apply that knowledge correctly. I use discernment when I correctly determine what knowledge to apply and when. In the case that I described above, we were required to use our knowledge of ATLS, our understanding of the principles and theories of ATLS, and discernment—when and why to take each individual action—to develop a plan of care for the patient.

So, too, is the case with spiritual wisdom. The Bible is full of principles and sound teaching that give us knowledge. In order to use that knowledge, we must have an understanding of the principles that God teaches consistently throughout the Bible. Our ability to correctly apply that knowledge is evidence of our discernment.

The Bible uses another term closely related to discernment that you are probably familiar with: *Judgment.* Judgment has a couple of different definitions according to my Bible: "to pass sentence upon; to condemn; to act or decide as a judge; to form a negative opinion about; *good sense;* the final judgment by God." I have italicized good sense because that is the definition of judgment that is relevant here. To have discernment is to have good judgment or *good sense.* In medicine, we praise a doctor who has good "clinical judgment." Poor clinical judgment, obviously, is not such a good thing.

There are two other building blocks of wisdom that I want to discuss next: *Prudence* and *Discretion.* Prudence is defined in my Bible as: "sound judgment; discretion." Discretion is defined as: "good judgment; prudence in behavior, speech, and dress." These terms are somewhat interchangeable and both similar to Judgment. However, since all three terms are used in the Bible, I have included them here with their definitions.

Here are some key points to consider about Understanding, Discernment, Judgment, Prudence, and Discretion:

## UNDERSTANDING

- Spiritual understanding comes from God's Word and Holy Spirit (Ps. 119:130; Prov. 2:6; 4:5; Is. 11:2).
- The presence of spiritual understanding is evident in a man's speech (Prov. 11:12; 17:27).
- Discipline is a prerequisite to attaining spiritual understanding (Prov. 15:32).
- There is great value in attaining spiritual understanding (Prov. 3:13; 13:15; 16:16; 16:22; 19:8).
- Spiritual understanding leads to delight in wisdom (Prov. 10:23).
- Spiritual understanding leads to action (James 1:22–25).
- There are things about God that we cannot understand (Job 36:26; Ec. 11:5).
- Spiritual understanding resides in the heart (Matt. 13:15).

## DISCERNMENT

- Spiritual discernment is the ability to distinguish right from wrong, good from evil, important from unimportant, and valuable from valueless (1 Kings 3:9–12; Prov. 28:11; Phil. 1:9–10; Heb. 5:14).
- Discernment is evident in an individual's speech (Prov. 10:13; 17:28).
- Knowledge comes easily to one with discernment (Prov. 14:6).
- Discernment is a building block of wisdom (Prov. 14:33; 16:21).
- An individual with discernment appreciates discipline (Prov. 17:10; 19:25).
- An individual with discernment is always searching for wisdom and knowledge (Prov. 15:14; 17:24; 18:15).

## JUDGMENT

- God blesses those who have good judgment (1 Sam. 25:33; Prov. 3:21–26).
- Bad judgment brings adverse consequences (Prov. 6:23).
- The simple-minded (naïve and immature) lack judgment (Prov. 9:4, 16).
- Good judgment is evident in an individual's speech (Prov. 10:13; 10:21; 11:12).
- Poor judgment leads to poor financial decisions (Prov. 12:11; 17:18).
- Poor judgment leads to foolish behavior (Prov. 12:21).
- Poor judgment leads to laziness (Prov. 24:30–34).

- Good judgment is required for good leadership (Prov. 28:16).
- Good judgment is required to look past external appearances (John 7:24).

## PRUDENCE

- Prudence is evident in an individual's speech (Prov. 12:23).
- Knowledge precedes prudence (Prov. 13:16).
- Prudence involves thinking before acting, knowing when to do the right thing, and knowing the right thing to do (Prov. 12:16; 14:8; 14:15; 27:12; Amos 5:13).
- Exercising prudence leads to greater knowledge (Prov. 14:18).
- The prudent individual responds appropriately to correction (Prov. 15:5; 19:25).

## DISCRETION

- God will provide us with discretion if we ask him (1 Chron. 22:12).
- The Bible contains instruction to help us to develop discretion (Prov. 1:4; 2:11; 5:1–2).
- Lack of discretion in dress and behavior is unattractive and a waste of God's blessing of beauty (Prov. 11:22).
- Lack of discretion in speech makes others uncomfortable (Prov. 25:20; 26:18; 27:14).
- Discretion will help you to stay out of issues where you are unwelcome and may be injured (Prov. 26:17).

If you desire to be *Wise @ Heart*, then you must acquire these building blocks of wisdom. It is by seeking spiritual wisdom that you are exposed to opportunities to develop expertise in these areas. As you practice the principles that God teaches, you gain more experience and comfort in terms of when and how to use these building blocks to construct a life that reflects the majesty and grace of God—a life of wisdom.

**Appendix C** includes many verses that reference Knowledge, Understanding, Discernment, Judgment, Prudence, and Discretion. I have included a few of my favorites for you below. Please note that I have added the italics for my own emphasis.

Here are verses to consider for the Building Blocks of Wisdom:

- Proverbs 2:6—"For the Lord gives *wisdom*, and from his mouth come *knowledge* and *understanding*."
- Proverbs 3:19–20—"By *wisdom* the Lord laid the earth's foundations, by *understanding* he set the heavens in place; by his *knowledge* the deeps were divided, and the clouds let drop the dew."
- Proverbs 5:1–2—"My son, pay attention to my *wisdom*, listen well to my words of insight, that you may maintain *discretion* and your lips may preserve *knowledge*."
- Proverbs 12:23—"A *prudent* man keeps his *knowledge* to himself, but the heart of fools blurts out folly."
- Proverbs 13:16—"Every *prudent* man acts out of *knowledge*, but a fool exposes his folly."
- Proverbs 14:6—"The mocker seeks *wisdom* and finds none, but *knowledge* comes easily to the *discerning*."
- Proverbs 14:18—"The simple inherit folly, but the *prudent* are crowned with *knowledge*."

- Proverbs 15:14—"The *discerning* heart seeks *knowledge*, but the mouth of a fool feeds on folly."
- Proverbs 17:27—"A man of *knowledge* uses words with restraint, and a man of *understanding* is even-tempered."
- Proverbs 19:25—"Flog a mocker, and the simple will learn *prudence*; rebuke a *discerning* man, and he will gain *knowledge*."

# CHAPTER FOUR

# ALTERNATIVES
# TO WISDOM

I pulled the next chart out of the rack and headed into Room 4 to see the next patient. Room 4 is typically reserved for minor cases in our ER, so I was not anticipating anything too time-consuming. That was a good thing since the chart rack was overflowing and we had many patients waiting to be seen. The more serious patients are seen immediately, so the less serious patients may have to wait for several hours. I often joke that we should put a calendar, rather than a clock, in our waiting rooms.

Jason was waiting patiently (no pun intended) for me in Room 4. His complaint was "chest pain." Jason had experienced several episodes of mild pressure-like chest pain while walking up the four flights of stairs to his apartment. His last episode was just prior to coming to the ER and he still had mild pain in his mid-chest. Jason was twenty-five-years-old, not a smoker, and appeared to be fit. He really had no risk factors for heart disease except that his father had died in his thirties of a heart-attack and one of his brothers, age twenty-nine, had already had a coronary artery bypass surgery.

I immediately ordered an EKG, chest X-ray, and the typical lab work to check for a heart attack. The EKG showed worrisome signs of an impending heart attack. Jason was moved to a bed with a heart monitor. I called the medicine resident on-call to discuss admitting Jason and proceeding with a cardiac work-up. The resident looked at the EKG and immediately determined that the changes were "normal" and not indicative of a heart attack. I disagreed and called a cardiologist immediately.

The cardiologist asked the resident why he believed that this man had a normal EKG in light of the obvious abnormalities. The resident said, "Look, if this guy is having a heart attack, then I will quit medicine!" The cardiologist smiled at me and replied to the resident, "You had better start packing then. I'm taking this man to the cath lab right now to take a look at his coronary arteries." Sure enough, the coronary angiogram showed severe heart disease that required a bypass surgery. The resident did not actually resign, but he did learn a valuable lesson and was much more humble from that point forward.

The point of this story is that, in order to make wise decisions, each of us must make choices that require us to change our thinking and beliefs. This can be very hard to do. In the example above, the resident could not shake his belief that the young, fit patient in front of him was not having a heart attack. This kind of stubborn pride and rigid adherence to our beliefs can harm us spiritually as well as physically.

How does this apply to our discussion of wisdom? Here is how. Jesus said, "Enter through the narrow gate. For wide is the gate and broad is the road that leads to destruction, and many enter through it. But small is the gate and narrow is the road that leads to life and few will find it" (Matt. 7:13–14). Each of us has the opportunity to choose an eternal spiritual life in Christ or an eternal spiritual suffering apart from Christ. In this earthly life, we also have the choice to pursue wisdom—God's desire for all of us—or alternatives to wisdom. The writer of Proverbs describes four broad categories of individuals: the Wise, the Fools, the Mockers, and the Simple (or Immature). In this chapter, we will examine each of these alternatives to wisdom more closely. Let's start with the Fool.

You will see in the verses below that the Fool lives a life that starkly contrasts that of the Wise. King Solomon wrote much of the book of Proverbs and also wrote the book of Ecclesiastes. He often illustrates the contrast between the wise and the foolish as well as gives numerous examples for us to reflect upon. In Ecclesiastes 10:2, it says, "The heart of the wise inclines to the right, but the heart of the fool to the left." In other words, a Wise individual has very little in common with a Fool. While this may seem obvious, there are an astounding number of verses dedicated to the subject of Wisdom, Foolishness, Mockery, and Simple-mindedness. The implication is that this subject deserves considerable attention. Let's examine a few of the contrasts between wisdom and foolishness more closely. Here are some key points for your consideration:

- Unlike the Wise who make a habit of seeking wisdom and enjoy the pursuit of wisdom, Fools "delight" in their foolishness (Prov. 1:7; 10:23).
- Fools do not respond well to correction or rebuke (Prov. 17:10).
- Fools are trouble-makers (Prov. 20:3) and can often be found in the midst of conflicts that they are not eager to see resolved even when it is clear that they are the cause of the conflict (Prov. 14:19).
- Fools are often given away by their speech (Prov. 18:7), which is plentiful (Prov. 15:2; Ec. 5:3), slanderous (Prov. 10:18), opinionated (Prov. 12:23; 18:2), incites conflict

(Prov. 14:3; 18:6), and is frequently factually incorrect (Prov. 12:15; 14:7; 15:7; 18:2).

- Fools are never uncertain (Ec. 10:12–14).
- One simple way that a Fool might fly below the radar of the Wise and hide their foolishness is to keep their mouth shut. Proverbs 17:28 says, "Even a fool is thought wise if he keeps silent, and discerning if he holds his tongue."
- Fools are unreliable and undisciplined (Prov. 5:23; 9:13–18; 15:4; 22:15; 26:6; 26:10; Ec. 10:15).
- Fools do not control their anger (Prov. 12:16; 14:16–17; 29:11).
- Fools are often found in the company of other Fools (Prov. 13:19), which contributes to their persistent foolishness. It is often frustrating to leaders to observe that Fools are often easily led astray by a Mocker. We will discuss this later in the chapter.
- Fools often give poor advice (Prov. 10:21; 14:7) and will not accept wise advice (Prov. 12:15).
- When Fools give advice, according to Proverbs 26:9, their wisdom is "like a thornbush in a drunkard's hand."
- Fools are unrealistic in their expectations (Prov. 17:24) and unwilling to put forth the effort to achieve a worthy goal (Ec. 4:5).
- Fools are also unwilling to accept responsibility for the consequences of their foolishness (Prov. 19:3).
- If you are seeking wisdom, then you will find it very difficult to be around a Fool since it is nearly impossible to know what to say or do in their presence (Prov. 26:4–5).
- It is difficult to have a Fool for a boss, an employee, coworker, acquaintance, or family member, especially a child (Prov. 10:1; 11:29; 15:4; 15:20).

- In the case of a foolish child, we are instructed that strict discipline is the prescription (Prov. 22:15).
- The best course, whenever possible, is to avoid a Fool (Prov. 13:19; 14:7; 17:1).
- Your wisdom will be wasted on the Fool (Prov. 23:9).
- A Fool will often remain a Fool (Prov. 26:11).

Does the discussion above seem unreasonably harsh to you? It may help to consider that foolishness is a choice just as wisdom is a choice. Those who choose a path other than wisdom will suffer predictable consequences. We are not innocent victims in this instance. The path of wisdom leads to spiritual life. Every other path leads to spiritual disease and death: "For the wages of sin is death, but the gift of God is eternal life in Christ Jesus our Lord" (Rom. 6:23).

**Appendix D** contains many verses that deal with Fools, Mockers, and the Simple for your consideration and further study. Once again, you may be shocked by the sheer volume of verses that are devoted to these subjects. Now, let's take a look at another alternative to Wisdom: *Mockers*.

Have you ever had a Mocker in your midst? Have you ever been in a position of leadership or authority and had an employee or coworker make a difficult and thankless job even more difficult by challenging your authority or creating resistance to change? Or, perhaps you have an acquaintance or family member who habitually shoots down every idea that you voice and ridicules you in the process. Maybe you are the parent of a teenager who wants to dispute every rule or decision and insists that you just are not "smart enough" or "with it enough" to know what is best for them. Let's look at how the Bible defines a Mocker and how we are instructed to act in the presence of a Mocker.

My NIV Version of the Bible uses the word *Mocker* where other versions use the word *Scoffer* or *Scorner*. Regardless of the exact term, the characteristics are fairly apparent. Here are some key characteristics of a Mocker:

- A Mocker is an arrogant, prideful trouble-maker (Prov. 21:24) who seems to enjoy creating disruption in an organization (Prov. 1:22). The Mocker is contentious and contrary. He seems bent on creating instability.
- If you confront a mocker about his behavior, then he may become publicly hostile and accuse you of malicious intent (Prov. 9:7–9).

As a healthcare leader, executive, and consultant, I have had the unpleasant experience of confronting Mockers in organizations where I have worked. Virtually every organization struggles with change. Churches, private corporations, not-for-profit organizations, and even families will face change and the need to adapt to changing external circumstances. Invariably, this will lead to conflict. Those who have a responsibility to lead and manage change are confronted with those who intend to resist change.

The most troublesome of all of the resisters is the Mocker. The Mocker will often try to manipulate the emotions of the Fool and the Simple person and gain their support in resisting change or authority. The Fool and the Simple person are not able to see that they are being manipulated. The Mocker rarely offers anything but a self-serving solution to whatever issue is being discussed.

The Bible provides us with clear guidance for dealing effectively with a Mocker. There is a simple solution for a Mocker. However, it is not an easy solution. In short, we are advised to remove the Mocker from our midst. Look at Proverbs 22:10: "Drive out the mocker, and out goes strife; quarrels and insults are ended." Can you imagine that? Of course you can! We have all probably fantasized about this scenario but not had the courage or authority to act on it. Of course, your Human Resources department may not permit it; certainly not without months of documentation, counseling, performance improvement plans, and the expenditure of much energy, emotion, and effort.

If a church has a Mocker in its midst, it faces a significant challenge. What if the Mocker is a big financial donor to your organization or popular in the community or in the organization? These are all obstacles that get in the way of doing what God says is the most effective way of dealing with a Mocker. God's wisdom is not always trusted or embraced. As we discussed above, the consequences of rejecting God's wisdom has predictably adverse consequences.

In my experience, when the Mocker leaves, the whole organization improves. That is not to say that those left behind do not create a ruckus for a while. And, when the dust finally clears, the organization is better off for having eliminated the Mocker.

Here are benefits to removing the Mocker from your organization. First, the amount of time that you have spent dealing with the Mocker can now be used more productively. Second, the employees, volunteers, or staffers that have been adversely impacted by the Mocker suddenly become much more productive and the overall climate of the organization improves dramatically. In other words, getting rid of the Mocker helps you to keep the people you want to keep. Third, the Fools, Simple people, and other potential Mockers will take heed that there are consequences to mocking.

A friend of mine who owns a successful carpet cleaning business shared this experience. His number one producer was also his number one problem. In his words, "He was the south end of a horse headed north." When he finally fired this troublemaker, his shop was a better place to work, and the remaining employees were able to step up to fill the void in productivity. Learn to deal with a Mocker, according to God's wisdom, and you will be doing yourself, the Mocker, and all of those around you a great service.

Jesus had to deal with Mockers. There is one example in Matthew 15:1–20. I encourage you to read this passage for yourself. In briefly recounting the story, Jesus was confronted by the "Pharisees and teachers of the law" who wanted to know why Jesus' disciples did not wash their hands before eating. Now, for the record, I think that it is a good idea to wash your hands before you eat. But, Jesus knew—and I think you will agree—that this was not the Pharisees' concern at all. Jesus saw into their mocking hearts and identified that "their hearts are far from me." It was pointed out that these Mockers would be "pulled out by the roots" since they are "blind guides" leading other blind men into a pit. This is a great definition of what a Mocker does and how they should be dealt with. They should be removed by the roots so that they do not grow back. If this is not done—if the "garden is not weeded"—then the Mocker will gain traction in leading the Fool and the Simple person further astray. This should not be tolerated. Organizations would do well to adopt a "No Mockers" Rule.

The Simple person is an individual who is not wise, and yet not foolish, that we routinely encounter. The term "Simple" is not one that I feel comfortable using since, in our culture, it can sometimes have the connotation of a mental impairment or handicap. The writer of Proverbs is referring to an individual who is spiritually immature, naïve, or ignorant. So, when I read the word, "Simple," I transpose it in my mind to "Immature." The Immature person, by my thinking, deserves some special regard—some extra grace—from the more spiritually mature individuals. The spiritually mature have the responsibility of mentoring the spiritually immature or naïve. It is the same as a parent who has the responsibility for training their children "in the way they should go" so that they will become spiritually mature (Prov. 22:6). Children are, by definition, Immature. Likewise, a Christian who is not spiritually mature is Immature or Naïve in matters of spirituality.

Unlike a Fool or a Mocker, the Immature individual has, in most cases, not made an active choice to be Immature. They simply do not know any better. And, since they are Immature, they really do not even know that they are Immature! They lack knowledge and, therefore, they lack judgment (Prov. 7:7). A good example is the teenager who "knows what is best for them." This, of course, presents quite a challenge to the parent, teacher, youth minister, or any other authority that interacts with them. What the Immature individual needs most is the protection and guidance of the more spiritually mature and wise. They need the example of proper thought and action that a spiritually mature individual can provide. Given the proper example, the Immature person stands a better chance of growing to maturity and wisdom (Prov. 21:11). The cure for Immaturity is growth in the building blocks of wisdom that we discussed previously: Knowledge, Understanding, Discernment, Prudence, Judgment, and Discretion. All of us are Immature when we begin our physical and spiritual lives. We are expected to become mature and not *stay* Immature. Here are some key points about the Immature (Simple) person:

- The Immature are at a critical point where they need a safe environment in which to mature. Because they lack Judgment, they are at high risk for making decisions that may severely harm them (Prov. 1:32).
- The Immature are being tempted at every turn (Prov. 9:13–18).
- The Immature are likely to make poor decisions (Prov.

14:15) and may suffer serious consequences as a result (Prov. 27:12). Therefore, those who are more spiritually mature and wise have an obligation to protect them. This is often difficult to do since the Immature individual will often resent supervision. The Immature may exert significant pressure on the Wise to allow them more freedom and responsibility than they can safely handle. The Wise must be steadfast in their resolve to protect the Immature from their own immaturity and from the Fools and Mockers who often prey on them. This is a responsibility that all spiritually mature should take very seriously. God does. Proverbs 24:11–12 says, "Rescue those being led away to death; hold back those staggering toward slaughter. If you say, 'But we knew nothing about this,' does not he who weighs the heart perceive it? Does not he who guards your life know it? Will he not repay each person according to what he has done?"

The *Wise @ Heart* will seek to mentor and protect the spiritually Immature and help them to grow to maturity. Referring back to the clinical example that I described above, the resident was not malicious, just Immature, and perhaps a little prideful. However, his Immaturity and pride could have cost my patient his life. That is why it is important that those who are more mature be vigilant for the safety—physical and spiritual—of all.

Please see **Appendix D** for more verses that describe characteristics of the Immature, the Fool, and the Mocker. In the next four sections, we will take a close look at specific key principles that God teaches and how they relate to wisdom.

# WISE @ HEART IN HONORING GOD AND EARTHLY AUTHORITIES

*Submit yourselves for the Lord's sake to every authority instituted among men: whether to the king, as the supreme authority, or to governors, who are sent by him to punish those who do wrong and to commend those who do right. For it is God's will that by doing good you should silence the ignorant talk of foolish men. Live as free men, but do not use your freedom as a cover-up for evil; live as servants of God. Show proper respect to everyone: Love the brotherhood of believers, fear God, honor the king.*

—1 PETER 2:13–17

Submission is a loaded term in our culture today. To be submissive is often viewed as giving up "rights." That certainly is not attractive or desirable for many of us. Our confidence in our own opinions, abilities, beliefs, and intellect keep us from accepting the wisdom that is available to us. It is God's will that you be submissive—give honor, respect, and obedience—to him and to earthly authorities. God is the *ultimate* authority. There are also earthly authorities that we are to be submissive to, according to God's will. Consider carefully the wisdom of God and earthly authorities as you strive to become *Wise @ Heart*.

# CHAPTER FIVE

# Wise @ Heart in Honoring God and Earthly Authorities

Some ER shifts, particularly in the inner city environment, can be challenging when the local "knife and gun clubs" are having a jamboree. There must be a union hall where they all meet before getting drunk and/or high and then poking holes in each other with knives or bullets. I can picture them all standing at attention while they raise their right hands.

"Do you promise to do everything in your power to make this night a living hell for every police officer, paramedic, and emergency department?"

"I do!"

"Very well, you are dismissed." And then, the "fun" begins.

During one memorable ER shift, I was asked to evaluate a "gentleman" that was in police custody. I knew that a prisoner had been brought in since I could hear the jangling sound of ankle and wrist chains and the shuffling gait that usually signals their arrival. I made a mental note to get over to assess the patient next. I usually try to get the police officers out of the ER and back out on the street as quickly as possible. They have a very difficult job to do and, like most people, they do not relish hanging out in the ER. We are all better off when the police are out where they belong.

This patient had been brought in to have the Taser darts removed from his chest. My role was to remove the darts. Usually, they come out of the skin with a firm tug; sometimes, a small incision is required. Then, I was to determine whether or not the patient was fit to be taken to jail. It is generally considered poor form to have someone die in jail due to some unrecognized injury or illness. This patient was also creating a ruckus. From the minute the cops brought him in, he was yelling obscenities. Anyone who knows me well knows that I am not a big fan of yelling or loud noises in general. I never yell—honest, ask my wife and kids—and I really do not appreciate it when anyone else does.

It turned out that this individual had been arrested for creating a public disturbance in a bar. Witnesses had seen him drinking heavily. At some point in the evening, he became belligerent and began to threaten bar patrons. The cops were called. It took four cops to restrain him and the application of about fifty thousand volts delivered by a Taser gun. On my exam, I noticed that the Taser darts were still imbedded in the gentleman's chest and the wires were still connected to the Taser held by a police sergeant.

I wondered out loud if there was anything that could be done to quiet this man down. It would certainly facilitate my exam and eliminate his noise pollution. Almost as soon as the words left my mouth, the officer delivered a brief burst of fifty thousand volts to the prisoner. Sure enough, this former raging maniac became quiet, docile, and very eloquent. He actually apologized for creating a disturbance and politely requested that I remove the darts from his chest. I was happy to do so and send him on his way with the police.

The requirement to be obedient and give honor to someone in

authority is difficult for some people to accept. The Bible uses the term "submissive" to convey the honor that we give to someone in authority over us. Unfortunately, in our culture, the term "submissive" is somewhat of a loaded term. It raises the hair on the necks of people who feel that being submissive is the same as giving up rights. In reality, being submissive to authority simply means acknowledging the authority that is placed over us and being obedient to that authority.

Often, however, we want to feel like *we* are in control and not controlled by any authority. We want to be *the* authority over our lives. Some teenagers very irrationally and strenuously desire to have complete control over their lives. When they do not get their way, they throw a tantrum that just serves as proof that they are nowhere near mature enough to be unsupervised.

We want to be like God. That is the temptation that Adam fell for in the Garden of Eden (Gen. 3:4). The problem is that God is God and we are not. We will never be God. God did not create us to be clones of him. We were created *by God* to serve and obey God—period. We have been struggling against God's authority since the beginning of time. How futile is that? Like my prisoner/patient, we are just not going to win that battle.

As we have already discussed, wisdom begins with our "fear" of God. Submission is our expression of our "fear" for God—our acknowledgment of His supreme authority and sovereignty over us and all He created. Obeying God is *hard* and it is *good.* Voluntarily doing something that is hard and good is one marker of spiritual and emotional maturity. I tell my kids that I know that they are becoming mature when they *voluntarily accept responsibility* and do what is expected of them without being told. My fantasy is that they will do something that I know is distasteful to them without being told and with a cheerful attitude, out of obedience and gratitude for all that

I provide for them. But, is that any different than the expectations that God has for each of us?

In reading the verses included below, you will see that we need to be submissive and obedient in the following areas:

- Christians are to be submissive to God, the leaders of the church, non-church governing authorities, and "masters," which we refer to as employers these days.
- Children are to be submissive to their parents.
- Wives are to be submissive to their husbands.
- Young Christian men are to be submissive to older Christian men.

This is the hierarchy that God has established, so that there is *order* rather than *dis-order* in the church, our lives, and the world.

At the heart of our disobedience to God and to earthly authorities is our pride and self-interest. Pride is *the* major obstacle to submission. We may not agree with what we believe we are being asked or told to do. We may feel that we are being treated unfairly by those in authority over us. We may also think that those placed in authority over us are not fit to lead us. Regardless, we are expected to submit to authority as God commands us to do.

The prescription for our temptation to rebel against authority is a healthy dose of humility. As Peter advised, "All of you clothe yourselves with humility toward one another, because, 'God opposes the proud but gives grace to the humble.' Humble yourselves, therefore, under God's mighty hand, that he may lift you up in due time. Cast all your anxiety on Him because he cares for you" (1 Peter 5:5b–7).

We may not fully understand the "why" behind God's commands. Nonetheless, we are instructed in Isaiah 55:8–9: "'For my thoughts are not your thoughts, neither are your ways my ways,' declares the Lord. 'As the heavens are higher than the earth, so are my ways higher than your ways and my thoughts than your thoughts.'" And, in Romans 11:33, it says, "Oh, the depth of the riches of the wisdom and knowledge of God! How unsearchable his judgments, and his paths beyond tracing out!" Our minds are simply not capable of understanding "why" God requires our obedience in some cases. This is the equivalent of the "because I said so" rationale that I give to my kids when they want to know why they have to obey me. We should be obedient to God and other authorities if for no other reason than *because He says so.*

You may ask, "What if we are commanded by an earthly authority to do something that is in conflict with God's commands in the Bible?" This is a very good question and the answer is provided in the Bible. In Romans 13:1–7, the Apostle Paul instructs us to be submissive to the governing authorities. However, in Acts 4:18–20, Peter and John directly opposed the governing authority when they were commanded to cease speaking or teaching in the name of Jesus. Their response to this command was, "Judge for yourselves whether it is right in God's sight to obey you rather than God. For we cannot help speaking about what we have seen and heard."

The apparent conflict between these passages can be resolved by looking at the intent of those involved. In Romans, Paul was confronting what appears to be a desire to rebel against the government for personal gain (refusal to pay taxes) while Peter and John were acting on behalf of God's kingdom in preaching the gospel as they had been instructed to do by Jesus (Matt. 28:19–20). The Word of God is the ultimate authority and *always* trumps earthly authority.

God knows our heart and our motives: "For a man's ways are in full view of the Lord, and he examines all his paths" (Prov. 5:21). God demands that we be obedient to him and that we be submissive to earthly authorities as long their commands do not conflict with the commands of God. The verses below describe the importance of obedience to God and earthly authorities. The *Wise @ Heart* are obedient to God and earthly authorities as commanded by God. Here are a few verses for your consideration and there are many more included in **Appendix E.**

Here are verses to consider for giving honor to authorities:

- 2 Chronicles 31:21—"In everything that he undertook in the service of God's temple and in obedience to the law and the commands, he sought his God and worked wholeheartedly. And so he prospered."
- Proverbs 13:13—"He who scorns instruction will pay for it, but he who respects a command is rewarded."
- Proverbs 14:26—"He who fears the Lord has a secure fortress, and for his children it will be a refuge."
- Proverbs 19:16—"He who obeys instructions guards his life, but he who is contemptuous of his ways will die."
- Proverbs 19:20—"Listen to advice and accept instruction, and in the end you will be wise."
- Proverbs 19:23—"The fear of the Lord leads to life: Then one rests content, untouched by trouble."
- Proverbs 24:21–22—"Fear the Lord and the king, my son, and do not join with the rebellious, for those two will send sudden destruction upon them, and who knows what calamities they can bring?"
- Proverbs 29:25—"Fear of man will prove to be a snare, but whoever trusts in the Lord is kept safe."
- Proverbs 30:17—"The eye that mocks a father, that scorns obedience to a mother, will be pecked out by the ravens of the valley, will be eaten by the vultures."
- Ecclesiastes 8:2–6—"Obey the king's command, I say,

because you took an oath before God. Do not be in a hurry to leave the king's presence. Do not stand up for a bad cause, for he will do whatever he pleases. Since a king's word is supreme, who can say to him, 'What are you doing?' Whoever obeys his command will come to no harm, and the wise in heart will know the proper time and procedure. For there is a proper time and procedure for every matter, though a man's misery weighs heavily upon him."

- Romans 6:16—"Don't you know that when you offer yourselves to someone to obey him as slaves, you are slaves to the one whom you obey—whether you are slaves to sin, which leads to death, or to obedience, which leads to righteousness?"
- Romans 13:1–7:

Everyone must submit himself to the governing authorities, for there is no authority except that which God has established. Consequently he who rebels against the authority is rebelling against what God has instituted, and those who do so will bring judgment on themselves. For rulers hold no terror for those who do right, but for those who do wrong. Do you want to be free from fear from the one in authority? Then do what is right and he will commend you. For he is God's servant to do you good. But if you do wrong, be afraid, for he does not bear the sword for nothing. He is God's servant, an agent of wrath to bring punishment on the wrongdoer. Therefore, it is necessary to submit to the authorities, not only because of possible punishment but also because of conscience. This is also why you pay taxes, for the authorities are God's servants, who give their full time to governing. Give everyone what you owe him: if you owe taxes, pay taxes; if revenue, then revenue; if respect, then respect; if honor, then honor.

- Ephesians 5:21—"Submit to one another out of reverence for Christ."
- Ephesians 5:22–24—"Wives, submit to your husbands as to the Lord. For the husband is the head of the wife as Christ is the head of the church, his body, of which he is the Savior. Now as the church submits to Christ, so also wives should submit to their husbands in everything."
- Colossians 3:18—"Wives, submit to your husbands, as is fitting in the Lord."
- 1 Timothy 2:11–12—"A woman should learn in quietness and full submission. I do not permit a woman to teach or have authority over man; she must be silent."
- Titus 3:1–2—"Remind the people to be subject to rulers and authorities, to be obedient, to be ready to do whatever is good, to slander no one, to be peaceable and considerate and to show true humility toward all men."
- Hebrews 12:9—"Moreover, we have all had human fathers who disciplined us and we respected them for it. How much more should we submit to the Father of our spirits and live?"
- Hebrews 13:17—"Obey your leaders and submit to their authority. They keep watch over you as men who must give an account. Obey them so that their work may be a joy, not a burden, for that would be of no advantage to you."
- James 3:17—"But the wisdom that comes from heaven is first of all pure; then peace-loving, considerate, submissive, full of mercy and good fruit, impartial and sincere."

- James 4:7–8—"Submit yourselves, then, to God. Resist the Devil, and he will flee from you. Come near to God and he will come near to you."
- 1 Peter 2:13–17—"Submit yourselves for the Lord's sake to every authority instituted among men: whether to the king, as the supreme authority, or to governors, who are sent by him to punish those who do wrong and to commend those who do right. For it is God's will that by doing good you should silence the ignorant talk of foolish men. Live as free men, but do not use your freedom as a cover-up for evil; live as servants of God. Show proper respect to everyone: Love the brotherhood of believers, fear God, honor the king."
- 1 Peter 2:18–21—"Slaves, submit yourselves to your masters with all respect, not only to those who are good and considerate, but also to those who are harsh. For it is commendable if a man bears up under the pain of unjust suffering because he is conscious of God. But how is it to your credit if you receive a beating for doing wrong and endure it? But if you suffer for doing good and you endure it, this is commendable before God. To this you were called, because Christ suffered for you, leaving you an example, that you should follow in His steps."
- 1 Peter 3:1—"Wives, in the same way be submissive to your husbands so that, if any of them do not believe the word, they may be won over without words by the behavior of their wives."
- 1 Peter 5:5—"Young men, in the same way be submissive to those who are older."
- 2 John 6—"And this is love: that we walk in obedience to his commands. As you have heard from the beginning, his command is that you walk in love."

# CHAPTER SIX

# WISE @ HEART IN ACCEPTING ADVICE

"Indian Joe" was a "frequent flyer" in our ER. He was homeless, an alcoholic, and often found unconscious on the sidewalk near our ER. The paramedics would pick him up and bring him to us. We would clean him up, give him clean clothes, let him sleep it off, make sure he had not been injured in any way, and then lure him out of the ER with a donut and coffee in the morning. We would often put him on the "floor plan"—a mattress on the floor so that he would not fall out of bed and crack his head open.

The first time that I encountered Joe, I was about to examine him when a seasoned nurse warned me that Joe had a history of spitting on doctors. That is when I noticed that the paramedics had placed a surgical mask over his nose and mouth. He was sleeping soundly or, perhaps, was in an alcoholic coma. He seemed harmless enough. And then, just as I started to roll him over to examine his back for injuries, he reached up, pulled down his mask, and spit at me. His spit narrowly missed hitting me in the face. I ducked out of the way before he could summon up another mouthful of spit. The nurses were laughing like hyenas. I was more than a little embarrassed. Another lesson learned the hard way.

The willingness to accept advice from others is one of the key characteristics of the *Wise @ Heart*. In addition to the many important lessons that God wants to teach us, there are numerous valuable lessons that we can learn from those around us. It may seem like a paradox that those who are the wisest are also the most open to accepting advice and instruction. God's prescription for growing in wisdom is that we look to the counsel of others in order to add to our wisdom. Proverbs 19:20 says, "Listen to advice and accept instruction, and in the end you will be wise."

We read in Proverbs 19:27: "Stop listening to instruction, my son, and you will stray from the words of knowledge." The implication is that if we seek to become *Wise @ Heart*, then we must engage in a life-long process of learning from others and accepting wise advice from them. Becoming *Wise @ Heart* is a journey and not a destination. It is a journey that lasts a lifetime and even longer in the sense that others may learn from our wisdom long after we are gone. King Solomon's legacy of wisdom lives on in the book of Proverbs.

There is no lack of advice available to those who seek it. There is some good advice and some that is not so good. Most people are more than willing to share their opinion and advice on virtually any matter regardless of their knowledge or expertise. Imagine the improvement in the quality of your decisions if you relied on the wisdom of those who have been a little further down the road than you—people who have already seen the movie and could tell you how it is going to end.

In order to make wise decisions, we need *good* advice (Prov. 11:14; 15:22). The Bible provides us with guidance in determining who to look to for advice. The Bible is God's Word and the best source of wisdom. In 1 Kings 22, there is a story that is a great example of seeking advice from God. Ahab, King of Israel, was struggling to decide whether or not to engage an enemy in war. He sought the counsel of Jehoshaphat, King of Judah. Jehoshaphat advised Ahab to "first seek the counsel of the Lord" (1 Kings 22:5). Reflect on that for a moment. One King is asking another King for advice, and he has been advised to seek the counsel of the Lord first. Proverbs 8:14 tells us, in reference to God's wisdom that "counsel and sound judgment are mine. I have understanding and power."

It may seem like an overwhelming task to seek guidance from God's Word. My belief is that many people overcomplicate the process of reading and studying the Bible. For most of us lay people, finding a readable translation with a print size that is comfortable to read is more than half of the battle. It has been helpful to me to use a "study Bible," such as the NIV Life Application Study Bible published by Zondervan. I use the footnotes and dictionary/concordance extensively. I also take a very simplified approach to studying the Bible. When I read a passage, I ask myself four questions: What does this passage mean? How does this apply to my life? What action, if any, is required of me? What I am I going to do in response to this passage? It may seem tedious, but this process is actually very efficient.

Here is the most important thing to remember: You are responsible for your own learning. Take this responsibility seriously. One of the most valuable skills you can acquire is the ability to teach yourself. The second most valuable skill is to engage in the process of lifelong learning. It is important to take responsibility for your own study of the Bible so that you can test the advice that you are given from others to make sure that it is consistent with God's commands and teaching. It is also important to keep your pride in check when someone offers you advice. Unsolicited advice can sound and feel like criticism. The only proper response when someone gives advice is, "Thank you." I know it is hard, so you may need to practice saying this in front of a mirror before you go public with it. And, do not be surprised if your response shocks the advice giver, especially if you have a history of shooting the messenger.

Parents and other older family members can be a great source of advice. Unfortunately, many of us learn this too late to appreciate the wisdom that is available to us right in our own families. Read Proverbs 6:20–23: "My son, keep your father's commands and do not forsake your mother's teaching. Bind them on your heart forever; fasten them around your neck. When you walk, they will guide you; when you sleep, they will watch over you; when you awake, they will speak to you. For these commands are a lamp, this teaching is a light, and the corrections of discipline are the way to life." Even if your parents are not followers of Christ, they may have sage advice to share with you as a result of their life experiences. Regardless of our age, we are to honor our parents as we are commanded to by God: "'Honor your father and mother'—which is the first commandment with a promise—'that it may go well with you and that you may enjoy long life on the earth'" (Eph. 6:2, 3). My parents continue to amaze me with their wisdom and insight, and I often turn to them for advice on important matters.

Within the church, there are individuals serving in positions of leadership. Those individuals who meet the Biblical criteria for serving as an elder or deacon are a particularly valuable source of wise counsel. Let's review God's criteria for serving the church in these leadership roles found in 1 Timothy 3:2–12:

> Now the overseer must be above reproach, the husband of but one wife, temperate, self-controlled, respectable, hospitable, able to teach, not given to drunkenness, not violent but gentle, not quarrelsome, not a lover of money. He must manage his own family well and see that his children

obey him with proper respect. (If anyone does not know how to manage his own family, how can he take care of God's church?) He must not be a recent convert, or he may become conceited and fall under the same judgment as the devil. He must also have a good reputation with outsiders, so that he will not fall into disgrace and into the devil's trap. Deacons, likewise, are to be men worthy of respect, sincere, not indulging in much wine, and not pursuing dishonest gain. They must keep hold of the deep truths of the faith with a clear conscience. They must first be tested, and then if there is nothing against them, let them serve as deacons. In the same way, their wives are to be women worthy of respect, not malicious talkers but temperate and trustworthy in everything. A deacon must be the husband of but one wife and must manage his children and his household well.

I think you can see how valuable an individual who meets these standards for leadership would be to someone who is seeking wise advice. It is a tragedy when a church does not adhere to these standards when appointing leaders. True, these are lofty standards. Nonetheless, this is what God requires of those that are appointed to serve as elders or deacons in the church. When we compromise God's standards, we are standing on shaky ground. 1 Corinthians 3:10b–13 (see below) tells us that the quality of our work matters to God. Jesus laid a firm foundation for us to build upon. This foundation includes specific criteria for leadership. We are not to build on any other foundation than that which Jesus established for us.

Friends and associates are also a source of advice and counsel (Prov. 27:9). There is a caveat that we accept only that advice which is consistent with God's wisdom. The importance of choosing our friends wisely cannot be underestimated. The people we associate with will have a great impact on our spiritual maturity. This principle is taught in Proverbs 13:19: "He who walks with the wise grows wise, but a companion of fools suffers harm." Look closely at who you have chosen as your friends. If they are not the type of individuals that you can depend upon to give you wise advice, then you should seriously consider seeking new friendships.

On occasion, you may be called upon to give advice to others. This should be considered a very serious matter. Those who give advice to others have an obligation to give good advice. In James 3:1, it reads, "Not many of you should presume to be teachers, my brothers, because you know that we who teach will be judged more strictly." Because we will be judged "more strictly" when we give advice to others, it is important that we exercise caution. We must be very careful to give counsel that is consistent with God's wisdom. We should give advice that is honest, unbiased, and not self-serving. Be quick to refer the individual to someone with greater knowledge or experience if you do not feel that you have the expertise or wisdom to advise them. Be thoughtful. Take time to consider and pray about the matter. Answer thoughtfully after serious consideration. When someone comes to you for advice, their concerns become your concerns.

You will often find that God's wisdom is in conflict with the wisdom of the world. This is because man cannot think like God. God's ways will always be somewhat of a mystery to us. As we read in Proverbs 25:2, "It is the glory of God to conceal a matter; to search out a matter is the glory of kings." The culture of our world may try to convince you that asking for advice is a sign of weakness or incompetence. The verses below teach otherwise. The *Wise @ Heart* learn to seek and accept advice from others in order to better understand and be obedient to God's will.

Here are verses to consider about seeking and accepting advice:

- Proverbs 4:1–5—"Listen, my sons, to a father's instruction; pay attention and gain understanding. I give you sound learning, so do not forsake my teaching. When I was a boy in my father's house, still tender, and an only child of my mother, he taught me and said, 'Lay hold of my words with all your heart; keep my commands and you will live. Do not forsake wisdom, and she will protect you; love her, and she will watch over you.'"
- Proverbs 4:13—"Hold on to instruction, do not let it go; guard it well, for it is your life."
- Proverbs 5:11–14—"At the end of your life you will groan, when your flesh and body are spent. You will say, 'How I hated discipline! How my heart spurned correction! I would not obey my teachers or listen to my instructors. I have come to the brink of utter ruin in the midst of the whole assembly.'"
- Proverbs 8:14—"Counsel and sound judgment are mine; I have understanding and power."
- Proverbs 10:8—"The wise in heart accept commands, but a chattering fool comes to ruin."
- Proverbs 11:14—"For lack of guidance a nation falls, but many advisers make victory sure."
- Proverbs 12:5—"The plans of the righteous are just, but the advice of the wicked is deceitful."
- Proverbs 12:15—"The way of a fool seems right to him, but a wise man listens to advice."
- Proverbs 13:1—"A wise son heeds his father's instruction, but a mocker does not listen to rebuke."

- Proverbs 13:10—"Pride only breeds quarrels, but wisdom is found in those who take advice."
- Proverbs 15:12—"A mocker resents correction; he will not consult the wise."
- Proverbs 15:22—"Plans fail for lack of counsel, but with many advisers they succeed."
- Proverbs 16:23—"A wise man's heart guides his mouth, and his lips promote instruction."
- Proverbs 19:16—"He who obeys instructions guards his life, but he who is contemptuous of his ways will die."
- Proverbs 19:20—"Listen to advice and accept instruction, and in the end you will be wise."
- Proverbs 19:27—"Stop listening to instruction, my son, and you will stray from the words of knowledge."
- Proverbs 20:18—"Make plans by seeking advice; if you wage war, obtain guidance."
- Proverbs 23:12—"Apply your heart to instruction and your ears to words of knowledge."
- Proverbs 24:5–6—"A wise man has great power, and a man of knowledge increases strength; for waging war you need guidance, and for victory many advisers."
- Proverbs 27:9—"Perfume and incense bring joy to the heart, and the pleasantness of one's friend springs from his earnest counsel."
- Ecclesiastes 4:13—"Better a poor but wise youth than an old but foolish king who no longer knows how to take warning."
- Ecclesiastes 9:17—"The quiet words of the wise are more to be heeded than the shouts of a ruler of fools."
- 1 Corinthians 3:10b–13—"But each one should be careful how he builds. For no one can lay any foundation other

than the one already laid, which is Jesus Christ. If any man builds on this foundation using gold, silver, costly stones, wood, hay or straw, his work will be shown for what it is, because the Day will bring it to light. It will be revealed with fire, and the fire will test the quality of each man's work."

- James 3:1—"Not many of you should presume to be teachers, my brothers, because you know that we who teach will be judged more strictly."

# CHAPTER SEVEN

# WISE @ HEART IN
# LEADERSHIP

When I was just starting my practice as an emergency physician, I had the privilege of working with a doctor who
taught me some key lessons about leadership. He was serving as the
Medical Director of our emergency department. Basically, he was
the boss of the ER doctors. He worked as hard—if not harder—than
any of us. He practiced impeccable medicine. He was professional,
provided consistently great service, and was generous in sharing his
knowledge and wisdom. It was not unusual for me to come to work
and find an article from a recent medical journal, describing state-
of-the-art medical care, stapled to the chart of a patient that I had
seen. He would read every chart of every patient seen by every doctor in our ER. Then, he would take the time to do research and find
opportunities to teach us. He made us all practice better medicine.
He demanded more of us than we demanded of ourselves. That is
*leadership*.

If you listen carefully as you walk down the aisles of your local
bookstore or library, you can hear the shelves straining and groaning
under the weight of the multitude of books written on the subject
of leadership. As a student of leadership for over thirty years, I have

read many of the most popular books and innumerable articles, listened to countless live and recorded lectures, and spent many hours reflecting on the subject of leadership. Here is what I think: A lot of people have a lot to say about leadership. I have a lot to say about leadership that is probably enough to fill another book. God has a lot to say about leadership. Some of the contemporary writings and theories are consistent with God's teaching on leadership and some are not. As Christians, we have an obligation to lead by godly principles even if that means swimming against the tide of contemporary thought. Let me warn you that a godly style of leadership is not for the faint of heart.

There is no way that this chapter can do the subject of godly leadership justice. I hope that you will spend some time studying the principles of leadership that God presents in the scriptures. Pay particular attention to the characteristics that God requires of those who serve in formal positions of leadership in the church (deacons and elders) as described in 1 Timothy 3:1–13 and Titus 1:6–9. This is a matter of critical importance to all Christians. After all, it is difficult—perhaps impossible—for a church to be truly effective without sound godly leadership. There are also a great many examples of wise and unwise leadership in the Bible. There is great benefit to studying these examples.

Most of you will have an opportunity to serve in the capacity of a leader at some level. A leader is someone who *influences* someone else to move from a current way of thought, belief, or behavior to a different way of thought, belief, or behavior. *Leadership is influence.* In this sense, parents are leaders of their children while they have the ability to influence them. All of us are aware of various authority figures that have influence over us, such as family members, employers, governments, schools, and churches.

In the various positions of leadership that I have held—from grade school crossing guard to corporate CEO—I have enjoyed the guidance of some great mentors, such as the doctor mentioned above. I have learned many lessons and had the privilege of sharing many of these lessons with up-and-coming leaders. I have served under some very capable leaders and some not so capable leaders. Something has been learned from each and every experience. I have also had the privilege of teaching others to lead. Leadership involves not only continuous learning, but it also includes continuous teaching. You are not complete as a leader unless you engage in a process of continual learning and improvement as well as pass your experience and knowledge along for the benefit of others. Leaders learn, do, *and* teach.

Followers also need to know the godly principles of leadership. All Christians are to submit to the authority of God and to the authority of their church leadership. We are better followers—better able to submit—if we know the principles that our leaders are using for guidance. Leadership is improved when followers hold their leaders accountable and measure their effectiveness relative to God's standards of leadership. We are to submit to the authority of our leaders as God obligates us to do, keeping in mind that we are to follow God's laws rather than man's laws where there is a conflict. And, as we have already seen in previous chapters, God's standards are often different than the world's standards. This is just one more example of why knowledge of God's principles—as outlined in the Bible—is important to our lives as Christians.

All of us are accountable to God for our actions. The Bible tells us that leaders are held to an even higher level of accountability. Since they could potentially lead others astray, leaders are "judged more strictly" (James 3:1). Godly leadership is desirable in any setting and absolutely critical in our churches. One of the greatest tragedies that I have observed is the weakness in leadership in some churches that stems from not applying and adhering to godly principles in the selection and appointment of leaders. Any church that does not adhere to the principles of selecting leaders, as outlined in the Bible, is in grave danger.

Leadership is the foundation of any organization. Jesus and His teachings are the cornerstone (Eph. 2:20) upon which this foundation is laid. The members of the church—Christians—are the "living stones" that are used to build God's "spiritual house to be a holy priesthood, offering spiritual sacrifices acceptable to God through Jesus Christ" (1 Peter 3:4). Any church that does not wholeheartedly embrace the "trustworthy message" and "sound doctrine" (Titus 1:6) defined in the scriptures is building on a shaky foundation and runs the risk of leading others astray. It takes great courage and commitment to hold to God's standards when considering and selecting men and women for positions of leadership within the church or any other organization.

We are instructed to honor our leaders. Serving as a leader is a difficult and often thankless role. I tell leaders that I coach, "Rule Number One of leadership is: Do not expect any thanks for what you do. Rule Number Two is: Do not forget Rule Number One!" The same is true of parenting, which is also a key leadership role. Do you know what makes leadership much more difficult than it needs to be? Poor followers! Parenting is much more difficult if the children are not obedient and do not "honor" their parents.

Christian husbands have much more difficulty in their marriage when their wives are not submissive. The job of a church leader is made much more difficult when the members of the church do not submit to their authority when appropriate. That is probably why the Apostle Paul instructs that "the elders who direct the affairs of the church well are worthy of double honor, especially those whose work is preaching and teaching" (1 Tim. 5:17). It is easy to complain about leadership. We must remember to honor those who lead when appropriate and give double honor to "those who direct the affairs of the church well." Gifted godly leaders should not be taken for granted.

Godly leaders are in short supply. That is why it is so important for parents and churches to teach the principles of godly leadership. In order for the leaders of tomorrow to gain the skills that they need to be effective leaders, they need positive role models and examples that they can follow. Giving young people an opportunity to lead is important for their development. Giving support and mentoring to first-time or inexperienced leaders of any age is important for their spiritual development and their success as leaders. Developing leaders is a process much like learning to swim. If you push a dozen non-swimmers into a pool, then a few of them may show "natural" swimming ability. The rest may have to be rescued or they will drown. Those who have to be rescued may give up on swimming forever because they feel that they do not have "natural" ability. Wouldn't it be sad if some of those individuals who quit could have been trained to become Olympic-level swimmers if only they were provided with good coaching? Leaders are developed by giving them the opportunity—pushing them into the pool, if necessary—*and* by providing them with good coaching and encouragement.

If you are not currently serving in some leadership position, I encourage you to volunteer to serve or to accept the opportunity if it is offered. Even though leadership is difficult—and often thankless—it is also rewarding. As Mark Twain said, "If you hold a cat by the tail, you learn things that you cannot learn any other way." The same is true about leadership. There are things you learn as a leader that you can learn no other way.

Here are some key points about godly leadership for your consideration:

- God is the ultimate authority on matters of leadership (Exodus 3:11–12; Judges 6:14–16; 1 Sam. 15:22–23; Ps. 23:1–6; Prov. 29:26; 1 Tim. 3:1–13; Titus 1:6–9).
- Leadership ability is a spiritual gift. God confers leadership authority and responsibility on individuals as He sees fit (Exodus 3:11–12; Judges 6:14–16; 1 Sam. 9:20; Prov. 21:1; Ec. 10:5–7; Rom. 12:6–8; Eph. 4:11–12).
- God expects leaders to lead according to His commands, guidelines, and principles (1 Sam. 15:22–23; Prov. 29:18; Is. 40:11; Matt. 15:14; 1 Tim. 3:1–13; Titus 1:6–9).
- God provides guidance, support, and special honor to godly leaders (Ps. 23:1–6; 27:11; 143:10; Prov. 3:3–4; 8:14–16; Daniel 12:3; 1 Tim. 3:17–20).
- God gives guidance in resolving conflict (Prov. 9:7–9; 16:7; 18:17; 22:10).
- To be a leader, you must have followers (Prov. 14:28).
- Followers have a responsibility to guard against being led astray (1 John 3:7).
- Godly leaders promote justice and righteousness (Prov. 16:10; 16:12; 20:8; 20:26; 24:23–25; 28:3; 28:5; 28:15; 28:16; 28:28; 29:4; 29:14; 31:8–9).
- Godly leaders are honest (Prov. 16:13; 17:7; 17:26; 28:10; 28:16; 29:12).
- Godly leaders are loving and faithful (Prov. 3:3–4; 20:28).
- Godly leaders appreciate wisdom, honesty, skillful work, and faithfulness in the people they lead (Prov. 14:35; 16:13; 22:1; 22:29; 24:21–22; 25:4–5; 30:10).
- A Godly leader seeks wise advice (Prov. 24:5–6; Ec. 4:13–16; 7:19).
- A Godly leader avoids Fools and Mockers (Prov. 9:7–9; 26:10; 27:3).

- A Godly leader detects and protects against malice and disorder (Prov. 26:24–26; 28:2).
- Leaders leave a legacy for whoever follows (Ec. 2:18; 2:21).
- A wise leader has self-control and self-discipline (Prov. 31:4–7; Ec. 7:21–22; 8:8b; 10:16–17; 1 Tim. 3:1–13; Titus 1:3–9).
- A primary role of a leader is to build others up and help them to prepare for service (Eph. 4:11–12).

The *Wise @ Heart* practice godly leadership principles. **Appendix F** includes many verses pertaining to godly leadership for your further study. Here are a few of my favorites:

- Proverbs 8:14–16—"Counsel and sound judgment are mine; I have understanding and power. By me kings reign and rulers make laws that are just; by me princes govern, and all nobles who rule on earth." [Author's note: This verse is referring to *Wisdom* as the foundation of leadership.]
- Proverbs 10:17—"He who heeds discipline shows the way to life, but whoever ignores correction leads others astray."
- Proverbs 16:7—"When a man's ways are pleasing to the Lord, he makes even his enemies live at peace with him."
- Proverbs 16:10—"The lips of a king speak as an oracle, and his mouth should not betray justice."
- Proverbs 16:12—"Kings detest wrongdoing, for a throne is established through righteousness."
- Proverbs 16:13—"Kings take pleasure in honest lips; they value a man who speaks the truth."
- Proverbs 16:14—"A king's wrath is a messenger of death, but a wise man will appease it."

- Proverbs 16:15—"When a king's face brightens it means life; his favor is like a rain cloud in spring."
- Proverbs 17:7—"Arrogant lips are unsuited to a fool—how much worse lying lips to a ruler."
- Proverbs 19:6—"Many curry favor with a ruler, and everyone is the friend of a man who gives gifts."
- Proverbs 19:12—"A king's rage is like the roar of a lion, but his favor is like dew on the grass."
- Proverbs 20:2—"A king's wrath is like the roar of a lion; he who angers him forfeits his life."
- Proverbs 20:8—"When a king sits on his throne to judge, he winnows out all evil with his eyes."
- Proverbs 20:26—"A wise king winnows out the wicked; he drives the threshing wheel over them."
- Proverbs 20:28—"Love and faithfulness keep a king safe; through love his throne is made secure."
- Proverbs 21:1—"The king's heart is in the hand of the Lord; he directs it like a watercourse wherever he pleases."
- Proverbs 22:11—"He who loves a pure heart and whose speech is gracious will have the king for his friend."
- Proverbs 22:29—"Do you see a man skilled in his work? He will serve before kings; he will not serve before obscure men."
- Proverbs 24:5–6—"A wise man has great power, and a man of knowledge increases strength; for waging war you need guidance, and for victory many advisors."
- Proverbs 24:21–22—"Fear the Lord and the king, my son, and do not join with the rebellious, for those two will send sudden destruction upon them, and who knows what calamities they can bring?"
- Proverbs 24:23–25—"These are also sayings of the wise:

To show partiality in judging is not good: Whoever says to the guilty, 'You are innocent'—peoples will curse him and nations denounce him. But it will go well with those who convict the guilty, and rich blessing will come upon them."

- Proverbs 25:2—"It is the glory of God to conceal a matter; to search out a matter is the glory of kings."
- Proverbs 25:3—"As the heavens are high and the earth is deep, so the hearts of kings are unsearchable."
- Proverbs 25:4–5—"Remove the dross from the silver, and out comes material for the silversmith; remove the wicked from the king's presence, and his throne will be established through righteousness."
- Proverbs 28:2—"When a country is rebellious, it has many rulers, but a man of understanding and knowledge maintains order."
- Proverbs 28:3—"A ruler who oppresses the poor is like a driving rain that leaves no crops."
- Proverbs 28:10—"He who leads the upright along an evil path will fall into his own trap, but the blameless will receive a good inheritance."
- Proverbs 28:16—"A tyrannical ruler lacks judgment, but he who hates ill-gotten gain will enjoy long life."
- Proverbs 28:28—"When the wicked rise to power, people go into hiding; but when the wicked perish, the righteous thrive."
- Proverbs 29:4—"By justice a king gives a country stability, but one who is greedy tears it down."
- Proverbs 29:12—"If a ruler listens to lies, all his officials become wicked."
- Proverbs 29:14—"If a king judges the poor with fairness, his throne will always be secure."

- Proverbs 29:26—"Many seek an audience with a ruler, but it is from the Lord that a man gets justice."
- Proverbs 30:10—"Do not slander a servant to his master, or he will curse you, and you will pay for it."
- Proverbs 30:29–31—"There are three things that are stately in their stride, four that move with stately bearing: a lion, mighty among beasts, a strutting rooster, a he-goat, a king with his army around him."
- Proverbs 31:4–7—"It is not for kings...to drink wine, not for rulers to crave beer, lest they drink and forget what the law decrees, and deprive all the oppressed of their rights. Give beer to those who are perishing, wine to those who are in anguish; let them drink and forget their poverty and remember their misery no more."
- Ecclesiastes 4:13–16—"Better a poor but wise youth than an old but foolish king who no longer knows how to take warning. The youth may have come from prison to the kingship, or he may have been born in poverty within his kingdom. I saw that all who lived and walked under the sun followed the youth, the king's successor. There was no end to all the people who were before them. But those who came later were not pleased with the successor. This too is meaningless, a chasing after the wind."
- Ecclesiastes 7:19—"Wisdom makes one wise man more powerful than ten rulers in a city."
- Ecclesiastes 7:21–22—"Do not pay attention to every word people say, or you may hear your servant cursing you—for you know in your heart that many times you have cursed others."
- Ecclesiastes 8:9b—"There is a time when a man lords it over others to his own hurt."

- Ecclesiastes 10:5–7—"There is an evil I have seen under the sun, the sort of error that arises from a ruler: Fools are put in many high positions, while the rich occupy the low ones. I have seen slaves on horseback, while princes go on foot like slaves."
- Ecclesiastes 10:16–17—"Woe to you, O land whose king was a servant and whose princes feast in the morning. Blessed are you, O land whose king is of noble birth and whose princes eat at a proper time—for strength and not for drunkenness."
- Matthew 15:14—"Leave them; they are blind guides. If a blind man leads a blind man, both will fall into a pit."
- Romans 12:6–8—"We have different gifts according to the grace given us. If a man's gift is...leadership, let him govern diligently."
- Ephesians 4:11–12—"It was he who gave some to be apostles, some to be prophets, some to be evangelists, and some to be pastors and teachers, to prepare God's people for works of service, so that the body of Christ may be built up."
- 1 Timothy 3:1–13:

Here is a trustworthy saying: If anyone sets his heart on being an overseer, he desires a noble task. Now the overseer must be above reproach, the husband of one wife, temperate, self-controlled, respectable, hospitable, able to teach, not given to drunkenness, not violent but gentle, not quarrelsome, not a lover of money. He must manage his own family well and see that his children obey him with proper respect. (If anyone does not know how to manage his own family how can he take care of God's church?) He must not be a recent convert, or he may become conceited and fall under the same judgment as the devil. He must also have a good reputation with outsiders, so that he will not fall into disgrace and into the devil's trap. Deacons, likewise, are to be men of worthy of respect, sincere, not indulging in much wine, and not pursuing dishonest gain. They must keep hold of the deep truths of the faith with a clear conscience. They must first be tested and then if there is nothing against them, let them serve as deacons. In the same way, their wives are to be women worthy of respect, not malicious talkers but temperate and trustworthy in everything. A deacon must be the husband of but one wife and must manage his children and his household well. Those who have served well gain an excellent standing and great assurance in their faith in Christ Jesus.

- 1 Timothy 5:17–19—"The elders who direct the affairs of the church well are worthy of double honor, especially those whose work is preaching and teaching. For the Scripture says, 'Do not muzzle the ox while it is treading out the grain,' and 'The worker deserves his wages.' Do not entertain an accusation against an elder unless it is brought by two or three witnesses."
- Titus 1:6–9:

An elder must be blameless, the husband of but one wife, a man whose children believe and are not open to the charge of being wild and disobedient. Since an overseer is entrusted with God's work, he must be blameless—not overbearing, not quick-tempered, not given to drunkenness, not violent, not pursuing dishonest gain. Rather he must be hospitable, one who loves what is good, who is self-controlled, upright, holy and disciplined. He must hold firmly to the trustworthy message as it has been taught, so that he can encourage others by sound doctrine and refute those who oppose it.

- James 3:1—"Not many of you should presume to be teachers, my brothers, because you know that we who teach will be judged more strictly."
- 1 John 3:7—"Dear children, do not let anyone lead you astray."

# WISE @ HEART
# IN SERVICE

*It was he who gave some to be apostles, some to be prophets, some to be evangelists, some to be pastors and teachers, to prepare God's people for works of service so that the body of Christ may be built up until we all reach unity in the faith and in the knowledge of the Son of God and become mature, attaining to the whole measure of the fullness of Christ.*

—EPHESIANS 4:11–13

*Each one should use whatever gift he has received to serve others, faithfully administering God's grace in its various forms.*

—1 PETER 4:10

*Serve wholeheartedly, as if you were serving the Lord, not men, because you know that the Lord will reward everyone for whatever good he does.*

—EPHESIANS 6:7–8

*As the body without the spirit is dead, so faith without deeds is dead.*

—JAMES 2:26

Each of us, from the moment we accept Christ as our Savior, have enlisted in God's army. God is counting on each of us to do what only we can do. Each of us brings unique skills, passions, experiences, and knowledge into our relationship with Christ. As we mature and grow in spiritual wisdom, we gain insight into how we can use our gifts to serve God and serve others. Not only are we able to serve, but we are also *required* to serve. In our acts of service to others, we both honor God and expose others to God's grace. Our acts of service are unmerited favor bestowed on others—the very definition of grace—in the name of Christ our Lord. The *Wise @ Heart* serve others "wholeheartedly."

# CHAPTER EIGHT

# WISE @ HEART IN SERVING YOUR NEIGHBORS

For a few years, I would travel from Hawaii to Dallas, Texas every other month to attend classes while I was completing a master's degree in management. My typical routine was to work a shift in the ER and get off work at about 7 p.m. Then, I would head to the airport and catch a red-eye flight, leaving for Dallas at about 10 p.m. After flying all night, I would arrive in Dallas, catch a cab, and arrive in time to attend class for eight hours a day for five days and then fly home.

On one occasion, I boarded the plane headed for Dallas at 10 p.m. wearing jeans, a hooded sweatshirt, and dark sunglasses, which I used as eyeshades during the flight. I looked pretty unshaven by that time of night after being up since about 4:30 a.m. My goal was to get to my seat, put in my earplugs, pull the hood over my head and fall asleep, and awaken in Dallas eight hours later. Sleep was very important since I would be up all the next day and feeling the effects of jet lag for several days.

All was going according to plan when, through the fog of semi-sleep and my foam earplugs, I heard an urgent voice on the PA system asking if there was a doctor or a nurse on the plane. My immediate response was, "You've got to be kidding me!" But, as has happened many times in the past, my sense of duty was stronger than my desire to get some much-needed rest. I activated my call light to summon the flight attendant. I was hoping that someone else had already responded and that I would look good for having volunteered without having to actually do anything.

The female flight attendant walked down the aisle towards me, saw my call light, looked at me, looked at every passenger around me, looked at me again, and then asked me, "Can I help you, sir?" I lifted my sunglasses up and replied that I was responding to her request for a physician. She looked at me suspiciously and asked, "Are you a doctor?" I nodded yes. "What kind of doctor?" she asked, even more suspiciously. "An ER doctor," I replied taking my sunglasses off and lowering my hood while trying to appear and sound like a member of my honorable profession. Her continued questions were proof that I was failing miserably. In defense of the flight attendant, I admit that I probably looked more like an unemployed surfing construction worker than a physician. "Do you have any ID?" she asked, clearly not buying it. "Yes," I said with a slight grin. "May I see your ID please?" she asked. Everybody around us was paying very close attention to our conversation. "Will you tell me why you need a doctor?" I asked. "There is a lady having chest pain and trouble breathing," she replied with arms folded across her chest as she looked down her nose at me.

At this point, I became wide-awake, pulled out my wallet, flipped it open, and showed her my medical license. I then extracted a business card and handed it to her while heading toward the front of the plane where the emergency was taking place. Duty called. Just like that, I became a physician who was ready to drag some unfortunate individual back from the brink of death. My only hope was that she was only on the brink and not in the abyss. It is really difficult to bring someone back to life that is actually dead. It can happen, but I would much rather try to keep someone alive than try to bring them back from the dead. I am pretty confident in my medical skills but not so confident in my ability to perform a miracle.

The short version of this story is that the woman was having significant trouble breathing and chest pain most likely due to an impending heart attack. While I was evaluating the patient, the pilot came back and asked me if I thought that he should turn the plane around and head back to Honolulu. "Well, I don't know where we are," I said, "but this lady should be taken to the nearest ER." The plane did a U-turn and headed back to Hawaii—we were about an hour away—while I initiated care using the very well-stocked medical kit supplied by the flight attendant. The woman made it to the ground and off the plane alive and in an improved condition. The plane re-fueled and took off again. A few weeks later, I received a very nice letter from the patient and her husband, telling me that they had made it safely home to Alabama. I also received some frequent-flyer miles from the airline as a token of their thanks. I used them for my next trip to Dallas.

It seems as though I am a magnet for these events; they happen fairly frequently. As one of my friends says, "If you travel with Pierce, get used to people trying to drop dead around you. Pierce attracts them!" I am not sure that is really the case, but there is a lot of evidence to support his statement. Even though I was reluctant to respond in the example above, I do consider it a privilege to be able to help someone in an emergency. And, as inconvenient as it can be sometimes, I know that it is absolutely the right thing to respond to an emergency when needed or requested. This philosophy is consistent with what Jesus teaches us to do. God has given me the "gift" of a medical education. It is my responsibility to use that gift whenever and wherever there is a need.

Most of you, unless you are a total recluse, interact with other people to some extent. Some of these individuals you may know very well and consider friends. Some are family. Some are co-workers. Others are merely members of your community and you may or may not know them very well at all. Those individuals—who are members of your community rather than your family, who you may not even know, and who exist in this world with you—are your neighbors. As you will see, a neighbor is not just someone who lives near you.

You may be familiar with the Parable of the Good Samaritan. It can be found in Luke 10:25–37. Jesus taught this parable in response to a question posed by an expert in Jewish law. This Jewish lawyer asked Jesus, "What must I do to inherit eternal life?" Jesus turned the question back on the "lawyer" by asking him how he interpreted the law in this matter. The lawyer replied, "'Love the Lord your God with all your heart and with all your soul and with all your strength and with all your mind,' and 'Love your neighbor as yourself.'" When Jesus confirmed that the lawyer was correct, the lawyer—probably with less than honorable intentions—then asked of Jesus, "And who is my neighbor?"

In response to the lawyer's question, Jesus proceeded to tell a story about a Jewish man who had been beaten by robbers and left for dead. Jewish religious leaders, who happened upon the victim, did not stop to help the injured man. However, a Samaritan, who in those times was considered to be of lower social class than the Jews, stopped to give the man assistance and even paid for his care at a local inn. The message of this parable is that we have an inherent moral obligation to help those in need. This obligation supersedes any social or legal requirement to do so.

It is this important teaching from Jesus and the inherent moral goodness of it that inspired the enactment of Good Samaritan laws in the United States and Canada. These laws are meant to reduce the legal risk to a bystander who unintentionally harms an ill or injured individual while attempting to help that individual. The purpose of the Good Samaritan Law is to encourage us, by reducing our fear of litigation, to help out those who need help—our neighbors. It is apparent that not much has changed since the time of Jesus in regards to our willingness to help out others who are in need. How ironic that just as this parable was presented in response to a lawyer, our own Good Samaritan laws are the result of the climate of fear that exists in our culture—a fear bred by litigation brought on by lawyers against well-intentioned bystanders who are engaged in doing the very thing that Jesus said we are to do in order to live in fulfillment of God's law, which is to help our neighbor.

Here are some key points about our relationship with our neighbors to consider:

- Do not let your neighbor influence you to do wrong (Ex. 23:24–25).
- Do not influence your neighbor to do wrong (Prov. 16:29).
- Deal with your neighbor justly (Deut. 2:4–6; 19:14; Prov. 21:10).
- Do not tell lies about your neighbor (Ex. 20:16; Ps. 15:3; Prov. 11:9;11:12; 24:28–29; 25:8; 25:18).
- Do not envy or covet what belongs to your neighbor (Ex. 20:17; Deut. 5:21; Ec. 4:4).
- Do not defraud your neighbor or steal from him (Lev. 19:13).
- Love your neighbor as yourself (Lev. 19:18; Matt. 19:19; James 2:8; Rom. 13:10).
- Do not plan to harm your neighbor (Prov. 3:29–30; 29:5).

- Do not seek revenge against your neighbor (Prov. 24:28–29).
- Do not wear out your welcome with your neighbor (Prov. 25:16–17).
- Go to your neighbor when you need help (Prov. 27:10).
- Be considerate towards your neighbor (Prov. 27:14).
- Encourage and build up your neighbor (Rom. 15:2).
- Be generous with your neighbor when he is in need (Prov. 3:27–28; 14:20–21; 17:18).
- Do not betray a confidence to your neighbor (Prov. 25:9–10).
- Do not judge your neighbor (James 4:12).

The *Wise @ Heart* will seek to serve his neighbor as Jesus instructed. Here are some verses to consider:

- Proverbs 3:27–28—"Do not withhold good from those who deserve it, when it is in your power to act. Do not say to your neighbor, 'Come back later; I'll give it tomorrow'—when you now have it with you."
- Proverbs 3:29–30—"Do not plot harm against your neighbor, who lives trustfully near you. Do not accuse a man for no reason—when he has done you no harm."
- Proverbs 11:9—"With his mouth the godless destroys his neighbor, but through knowledge the righteous escape."
- Proverbs 11:12—"A man who lacks judgment derides his neighbor, but a man of understanding holds his tongue."
- Proverbs 14:20–21—"The poor are shunned even by their neighbors, but the rich have many friends. He who despises his neighbor sins, but blessed is he who is kind to the needy."

- Proverbs 16:29—"A violent man entices his neighbor and leads him down a path that is not good."
- Proverbs 17:18—"A man lacking in judgment strikes hands in pledge and puts up security for his neighbor."
- Proverbs 21:10—"The wicked man craves evil; his neighbor gets no mercy from him."
- Proverbs 24:28–29—"Do not testify against your neighbor without cause, or use your lips to deceive. Do not say, 'I'll do to him as he has done to me; I'll pay that man back for what he did.'"
- Proverbs 25:8—"What you have seen with your eyes do not bring hastily to court, for what will you do in the end if your neighbor puts you to shame?"
- Proverbs 25:9–10—"If you argue your case with a neighbor, do not betray another man's confidence, or he who hears it may shame you and you will never lose your bad reputation."
- Proverbs 25:16–17—"If you find honey, eat just enough—too much of it and you will vomit. Seldom set foot in your neighbor's house—too much of you, and he will hate you."
- Proverbs 25:18—"Like a club or a sword or a sharp arrow is the man who gives false testimony against his neighbor."
- Proverbs 27:10—"Do not forsake your friend and the friend of your father, and do not go to your brother's house when disaster strikes you—better a neighbor nearby than a brother far away."
- Proverbs 27:14—"If a man loudly blesses his neighbor early in the morning, it will be taken as a curse."
- Proverbs 29:5—"Whoever flatters his neighbor is spreading a net for his feet."

- Ecclesiastes 4:4—"And I saw that all labor and all achievement spring from man's envy of his neighbor. This too is meaningless, a chasing after the wind."
- Matthew 19:19—"...and love your neighbor as yourself."
- Luke 10:36–37—"'Which of these three do you think was a neighbor to the man who fell into the hands of robbers?' The expert in the law replied, 'The one who had mercy on him.' Jesus told him, 'Go and do likewise.'"
- Romans 13:10—"Love does no harm to its neighbor. Therefore love is the fulfillment of the law."
- Romans 15:2—"Each of us should please his neighbor for his good, to build him up."
- Ephesians 4:25—"Therefore each of you must put off falsehood and speak truthfully to his neighbor, for we are all members of one body."
- James 2:8—"If you really keep the royal law found in Scripture, 'Love your neighbor as yourself,' you are doing right."
- James 4:12—"There is only one Lawgiver and Judge, the one who is able to save and destroy. But you—who are you to judge your neighbor?"

# CHAPTER NINE

# WISE @ HEART IN SERVING YOUR SPOUSE

Mary was one of our "frequent flyers" in the ER. She was an elderly lady who suffered from severe heart disease and diabetes, so she would often turn up with what appeared to be heart failure. Mary also struggled with severe anxiety that was made worse by her chronic breathing problems. We saw her often, usually after 10 p.m. We would keep her in the ER and "tune her up" and then discharge her home in the morning. What was remarkable about Mary was that her husband was always at her side in the ER. He would sit in a chair by her bed and was always frantically concerned. He doted on her every need.

When Mary would start to feel better, breath easier, and feel less anxious, she would drift off to sleep. Her husband would sit by her bedside in a chair, refusing our offer to let him lie down in an adjacent bed, and watch his wife sleep. He would often return in a couple of days with some fruit or a baked treat for the ER staff to thank us for caring for his wife. It was impossible to not be touched by the love and devotion he had for his wife.

When Mary eventually died, her husband followed her in death within a few weeks. Yet, none of us could ever recall having treated her husband for a medical problem in all the years that we took care of Mary. I think he died of a broken heart. He could not go on living after having lost such an important part of him. He and his wife were one flesh. Wherever one went, the other went, even in death.

One of my psychology professors in college once said, "There is nothing more satisfying than a healthy marriage." Proverbs 18:22 says, "He who finds a wife finds what is good and receives favor from the Lord." Why, then, does Jesus (Matt. 19:9) and later the Apostle Paul (1 Corinthians 7:1) discourage marriage?

It could be because maintaining a healthy marriage is hard work! In 1 Corinthians 7:28, Paul says that "those who marry will face many troubles in this life." And, if the rate of divorce in America is any indication, it would appear that most marriages are not terribly satisfying. My father, who recently celebrated fifty years of marriage to my mother, quipped to me that he had been happily married for twenty-five years! According to my dad, being happy with your marriage half of the time is a pretty good track record. My wife and I recently celebrated our twenty-fifth anniversary and we both agree that we have been happy well over half of the time. I hope the next twenty-five years go as well as the first half did.

In speaking about marriage, it is important to understand what defines a "Christian" marriage. In my opinion, the biggest obstacle to achieving a godly marriage is our own bias about what defines a Christian marriage. It should come as no surprise that a Christian marriage is focused on Christ. My suspicion is that most of us do not suffer from an absence of knowledge about this subject but rather an absence of obedience to the commands of God as they relate to marriage. Once again, the difficulty we face is that what our culture teaches often conflicts with what God teaches. Or, perhaps, we "feel" that God would agree with us since we "feel" so strongly that what we believe is true even if it conflicts with what the scriptures teach. Our emotions notwithstanding, if we choose to oppose God's teaching, then we are skating on thin ice and there are predictable consequences for that.

The Bible provides us with a great example of a Christian marriage. In the book of Acts 18, there is the story of Aquila and his wife, Pricilla. This couple (also mentioned in Rom. 16:3–5; 1 Cor. 16:19; and 2 Tim. 4:19) opened their home in Corinth to the apostle Paul. They traveled with Paul and risked their lives (Rom. 16:4) to spread the gospel. They worked as tentmakers with Paul to support themselves. The church met in their home (Rom. 16:5; 1 Cor. 16:19). They undertook missionary efforts in Ephesus (Acts 18:19). In short, they were devoted to God and to each other.

The verses that I have included below deal with broad principles applicable to marriage. You may not necessarily find the answers to the *specific* questions that you may have about marriage. However, these principles will provide a guideline for you to use in discovering God's will in your marriage. As is frequently the case, God provides us principles rather than specific rules. It is similar to me telling my children to "be careful" instead of advising them with "don't run with scissors."

Here are some key principles that are taught in the verses below:

- If you can avoid marriage, avoid it. Marriage is hard! Marriage can be a distraction to your service to God (Matt. 19:8–12; 1 Cor. 7:1–7; 27–28).
- God comes first. It is not possible to have a healthy Christian marriage unless both partners put God as their first priority and as if they are "one flesh" (Gen. 2:24; Matt. 19:4–6).

- Christians, if you feel that you must marry, then marry a Christian (1 Cor. 7:39; 2 Cor. 6:14).
- Stay married unless your spouse is unfaithful to you or they are an unbeliever who voluntarily leaves you (Matt. 5:32; 19:4–6; 19:8–9; Luke 16:18; Rom. 7:2–3; 1 Cor. 7:10–16; 27–28; 32–34; 39).
- If you are married to a non-Christian, then stay married to your unbelieving spouse unless they voluntarily leave you (1 Cor. 7:12–16).
- Husbands, love your wife more than you love yourself. Your obligation is to foster the spiritual and physical well-being of your wife. That is God's will (Prov. 5:18–19; 30:21–23; Ec. 9:9; Eph. 5:25–33; 1 Pet. 3:7; Col. 3:19).
- Remain faithful to your spouse. Regardless of how glamorous an illicit affair may seem on television or in a movie, it will destroy your marriage, your family, and you. (Gen. 20:14; Lev. 18:20; Matt. 5:27–28; Heb. 13:4).
- Wives, submit to your husband in everything. He has a very difficult job to do. His job is to put God first and then you before himself. Do not make your husband's job harder by trying to put yourself (your desires, biases, ideas, and personal preferences) before God. And, do not be quarrelsome. Be a "wife of noble character." That is God's will (Prov. 12:4; 14:1; 19:13; 19:14; 21:9; 21:19; 27:15–16; 31:10–31; Eph. 5:22–24; Titus 2:4; 1 Pet. 3:1–2; Col. 3:18).
- A healthy marriage includes sex (1 Cor. 7:1–7).
- Stay faithful to each other until death. If you are a widow or a widower, then you are free to remarry to a Christian (Rom. 7:2–3; 1 Cor.7:39; 1 Tim. 5:14).

The *Wise @ Heart* follow God's commands for marriage.
Here are some verses to consider concerning marriage:

- Genesis 2:24—"For this reason a man will leave his father and mother and be united to his wife and they will become one flesh."
- Exodus 20:14—"You shall not commit adultery."
- Leviticus 18:20—"Do not have sexual relations with your neighbor's wife and defile yourself with her."
- Proverbs 5:3–5—"For the lips of an adulteress drip honey, and her speech is smoother than oil; but in the end she is bitter as gall, sharp as a double-edged sword. Her feet go down to death; her steps lead straight to the grave."
- Proverbs 5:18–19—"May your fountain be blessed, and may you rejoice in the wife of your youth. A loving doe, a graceful deer—may her breasts satisfy you always, may you ever be captivated by her love."
- Proverbs 12:4—"A wife of noble character is her husband's crown, but a disgraceful wife is like decay in his bones."
- Proverbs 14:1—"The wise woman builds her house, but with her own hands the foolish one tears hers down."
- Proverbs 18:22—"He who finds a wife finds what is good and receives favor from the Lord."
- Proverbs 19:13—"A foolish son is his father's ruin, and a quarrelsome wife is like a constant dripping."
- Proverbs 19:14—"Houses and wealth are inherited from parents, but a prudent wife is from the Lord."
- Proverbs 21:9—"Better to live on a corner of the roof than share a house with a quarrelsome wife."
- Proverbs 21:19—"Better to live in a desert than with a quarrelsome and ill-tempered wife."

- Proverbs 25:24—"Better to live on a corner of the roof than share a house with a quarrelsome wife."
- Proverbs 27:15–16—"A quarrelsome wife is like a constant dripping on a rainy day; restraining her is like restraining the wind or grasping oil with the hand."
- Proverbs 30:21–23—"Under three things the earth trembles, under four it cannot bear up: a servant who becomes king, a fool who is full of food, an unloved woman who is married, and a maidservant who displaces her mistress."
- Proverbs 31:10–31—(summarized) A Wife of Noble Character:
  - She is worth far more than rubies.
  - Her husband has confidence in her and lacks nothing of value.
  - She brings her husband good, not harm.
  - She works eagerly, diligently, and vigorously to provide for her family; she is not idle.
  - She is generous to the poor and needy.
  - She prepares for her family's needs against adversity.
  - She is a good housekeeper and keeps herself clothed attractively.
  - Because of her, her husband has respect in the community.
  - She is wise and faithful in speech.
  - She is strong and dignified and does not fear the future.
  - Her children bless her and treat her respectfully.
  - Her husband praises her.
  - She fears the Lord.
  - She is praised by all because of her actions.

- Ecclesiastes 9:9—"Enjoy life with your wife, whom you love, all the days of this meaningless life that God has given you under the sun—all your meaningless days."
- Matthew 5:27–28—"You have heard it was said, 'Do not commit adultery.' But I tell you that anyone who looks at a woman lustfully has already committed adultery with her in his heart."
- Matthew 5:32—"But I tell you that anyone who divorces his wife, except for marital unfaithfulness, causes her to become an adulteress, and anyone who marries the divorced woman commits adultery."
- Matthew 19:4–6—" 'Haven't you read,' he replied, 'that at the beginning the Creator 'made them male and female,' and said, 'For this reason a man will leave his father and mother and be united to his wife, and the two will become one flesh?' So they are no longer two, but one. Therefore what God has joined together, let man not separate."
- Matthew 19:8–12:

Jesus replied, "Moses permitted you to divorce your wives because your hearts were hard. But it was not this way from the beginning. I tell you that anyone who divorces his wife, except for marital unfaithfulness, and marries another woman commits adultery." The disciples said to him, "If this is the situation between husband and wife, it is better not to marry." Jesus replied, "Not everyone can accept this word, but only those to whom it has been given. For some are eunuchs because they were born that way; others were made that way by men; and others have renounced marriage because of the kingdom of heaven. The one who can accept this should accept it."

- Matthew 22:30—"At the resurrection people will neither marry nor be given in marriage; they will be like the angels in heaven."
- Luke 16:18—"Anyone who divorces his wife and marries another woman commits adultery, and the man who marries a divorced woman commits adultery."
- Romans 7:2–3—"For example, by law a married woman is bound to her husband as long as he is alive, but if her husband dies, she is released from the law of marriage. So then, if she marries another man while her husband is still alive, she is called an adulteress. But if her husband dies, she is released from that law and is not an adulteress, even though she marries another man."
- 1 Corinthians 7:1–7:

It is good for a man not to marry. But since there is so much immorality, each man should have his own wife, and each woman her own husband. The husband should fulfill his marital duty to his wife, and likewise the wife to her husband. The wife's body does not belong to her alone but also to her husband. In the same way, the husband's body does not belong to him alone but also to his wife. Do not deprive each other except by mutual consent and for a time, so that you may devote yourselves to prayer. Then come together again so that Satan will not tempt you because of your lack of self-control. I say this as a concession, not as a command.

- 1 Corinthians 7:8–9—"Now to the unmarried and the widows I say: It is good for them to stay unmarried, as I am. But if they cannot control themselves, they should marry, for it is better to marry than to burn with passion."

- 1 Corinthians 7:10–11—"A wife must not separate from her husband. But if she does, she must remain unmarried or else be reconciled to her husband. And a husband must not divorce his wife."
- 1 Corinthians 7:12–16:

If any brother has a wife who is not a believer and she is willing to live with him, he must not divorce her. And if a woman has a husband who is not a believer and he is willing to live with her, she must not divorce him. For the unbelieving husband has been sanctified through his wife, and the unbelieving wife has been sanctified through her believing husband. Otherwise your children would be unclean, but as it is, they are holy. But if the unbeliever leaves let him do so. A believing man or woman is not bound in such circumstances. God has called us to live in peace. How do you know, wife, whether you will save your husband? Or, how do you know husband, whether you will save your wife?

- 1 Corinthians 7:27–28—"Are you married? Do not seek a divorce. Are you unmarried? Do not look for a wife. But if you do marry, you have not sinned; and if a virgin marries, she has not sinned. But those who marry will face many troubles in this life, and I want to spare you this."
- 1 Corinthians 7:32–34—"I would like for you to be free from concern. An unmarried man is concerned about the Lord's affairs—how he can please the Lord. But a married man is concerned about the affairs of this world—how he can please his wife—and his interests are divided. An unmarried woman or virgin is concerned about the Lord's affairs: Her aim is to be devoted to the Lord in both body

and spirit. But a married woman is concerned about the affairs of this world—how she can please her husband."

- 1 Corinthians 7:39—"A woman is bound to her husband as long as he lives. But if her husband dies, she is free to marry anyone else she wishes, but he must belong to the Lord."

- 2 Corinthians 6:14—"Do not be yoked together with unbelievers."

- Ephesians 5:22–24—"Wives, submit to your husbands as to the Lord. For the husband is the head of the wife as Christ is the head of the church, his body, of which he is the Savior. Now as the church submits to Christ, so also wives should submit to their husbands in everything."

- Ephesians 5:25–33:

Husbands love your wives just as Christ loved the church and gave himself up for her to make her holy, cleansing her by the washing with water through the word, and to present her to himself as a radiant church, without stain or wrinkle or any other blemish, but holy and blameless. In this same way, husbands ought to love their wives as their own bodies. He who loves his wife loves himself. After all, no one ever hated his own body, but he feeds it and cares for it, just as Christ does the church—for we are members of his body. For this reason a man will leave his father and mother and be united to his wife, and the two will become one flesh …each one of you also must love his wife as he loves himself, and the wife must respect her husband.

- 1 Timothy 3:2,11—"Now the overseer must be…the husband of but one wife…In the same way, their wives are to be women worthy of respect, not malicious talkers but temperate and trustworthy in everything."

- 1 Timothy 5:14—"So I counsel younger widows to marry, to have children, to manage their homes and to give the enemy no opportunity for slander."
- Titus 2:4—"Train the younger women to love their husbands and children, to be self-controlled and pure, to be busy at home, to be kind, and to be subject to their husbands, so that no one will malign the word of God."
- Hebrews 13:4—"Marriage should be honored by all, and the marriage bed kept pure, for God will judge the adulterer and all the sexually immoral."
- 1 Peter 3:1–2—"Wives, in the same way be submissive to your husbands so that, if any of them do not believe the word, they may be won over without words by the behavior of their wives, when they see the purity and reverence of your lives."
- 1 Peter 3:7—"Husbands, in the same way be considerate as you live with your wives, and treat them with respect as the weaker partner and as heirs with you of the gracious gift of life, so that nothing will hinder your prayers."
- Colossians 3:18—"Wives, submit to your husbands, as is fitting in the Lord."
- Colossians 3:19—"Husbands, love your wives and do not be harsh with them."

# CHAPTER TEN

# Wise @ Heart in Honoring Parents and Raising Children

While standing at the counter in front of the nurse's station writing on a medical chart, I observed the triage nurse bringing back a couple and their young son. I recognized them from having seen them a couple of days prior. Their four-year-old son, Jimmy, was diagnosed with an ear infection and I had prescribed amoxicillin for the child. After completing my chart, I headed over to see why they had returned.

The mom did all of the talking at first. She seemed somewhat hostile. The dad was silent and looked somewhat embarrassed. Dad was sitting on the gurney with the child in his lap. Mom was standing with arms crossed. "Jimmy is still running a fever. He isn't getting any better. I've had to miss three days of work because he isn't allowed to go to preschool with a fever," she said. The dad was looking at the floor. I responded, "Well, let me examine Jimmy and then let's see what we can do to get him better."

After examining the child, which revealed a persistent middle ear infection, I indicated that I recommended switching him to a different antibiotic since the amoxicillin did not appear to be working. "This happens sometimes," I explained. "He will probably improve within twenty-four hours on the new antibiotic." I reassured her. It was at this point that dad joined the conversation.

The father told me that the child had actually not received any of the antibiotics that I had prescribed three days earlier. I'm thinking, "Como?" What I said was, "Excuse me?" Dad continued, "Well, we picked up the medicine like you recommended. But, Jimmy didn't want to take it. He doesn't like to take medicine. My wife wanted me to force him to take it since he won't take it from her. I don't agree with her. I think that is a little extreme. What do you think, doc?"

Well, I have taken a lap around that desert before. This was a textbook case of "kid in charge." I was not about to get in the middle of their parenting conflict. That is the domain of a mother-in-law. I have developed a standard approach to dealing with this issue. The child was glaring at me throughout this whole conversation. I think he suspected that I was going to be the perpetrator of something unpleasant that would happen to him soon.

"I understand," I told the father, completely ignoring his question. "These things happen. Let's try another approach." I then looked straight at the boy and very calmly and slowly said, "Jimmy, in order to get better, you need medicine. I want you to take the medicine that your mother has been trying to give you. Will you do that?"

"No," he said defiantly.

"Okay," I said. "The nurse will be in to give you a shot in a minute." As his eyes began to fill with tears, I said, "Unless you would like to take the medicine instead of getting a shot."

The boy exclaimed, "No! I don't like the medicine and I don't want a shot!"

I replied, "I understand how you feel" and then turned to walk out of the exam room.

Just as I was leaving the room, a nurse entered with a syringe full of Ceftriaxone, a powerful antibiotic that can be given in a single dose to treat ear infections. The screaming commenced five seconds later and the nurse emerged twenty-five seconds later. Mission accomplished.

Parenting is one of the greatest tests of wisdom and patience many of us will face. Among the myriad books and articles written about parenting, one can find support for just about any strategy or philosophy imaginable. There also seems to be an endless supply of advice and information about parenting that is readily available from family, friends, neighbors, talk-show psychologists, parachurch organizations, and even complete strangers who are standing behind you in the check-out line at the grocery store. To complicate matters further, moms and dads often disagree on parenting philosophies. This is primarily due to the different parenting styles that the parents themselves experienced as children—probably by parents who did not see eye to eye about parenting either.

My wife, Diane, and I grew up in the same community and went to the same schools. Our dads worked for the same US government agency. Despite similar values, our parents differed significantly in parenting style and in what they emphasized as priorities. This leads to the *occasional* disagreement between us about how to approach a particular parenting challenge. While infrequent, some of these disagreements have been significant.

Diane and I both believe that we turned out okay and, of course, our bias is to raise our kids essentially "the way we were raised." These differences lead to conflict. Since there are readily available sources to support each of our opinions, we will have to find some authority that we agree on to settle our differences should these conflicts escalate. To what authority do you ultimately appeal in these cases?

Fortunately, as you will see below, God has much to say about parenting. It is clear that God places great importance on the roles of parents and children. In fact, God uses the analogy of parenting in reference to His relationship to us. For example, in Proverbs 3:12, it says, "...the Lord disciplines those he loves, as a father the son he delights in." Therefore, it is possible to appeal to His authority, through His written word, on these matters.

Unfortunately, as in other areas of your life, you may find His instructions difficult to accept and even more difficult to apply. This is especially true if your opinion about parenting differs from God's opinion. It is very difficult to overcome the biases and values imprinted in our minds as children. At times, God's wisdom is in conflict with cultural wisdom and our opinions.

The instructions on parenting in the Bible focuses not on specific issues but on the broad overarching values that serve as the framework, or guidelines, within which we are able to make wise decisions. Our children will carry these values forward into adulthood. If we are successful in teaching these values to our children, then they will, in turn, teach them to their children.

The importance of raising children properly cannot be overemphasized. The home is where children learn the most basic and important values that they will carry forward into adulthood. The home is where children learn respect for authority, selfless service, the importance of their role in society, and important social skills. The home is where children learn to accept responsibility and accountability for their actions. The home is where children learn discipline and obedience. God holds parents accountable for teaching and modeling these important values: "These commandments that I give you today are to be upon your hearts. Impress them on your children. Talk about them when you sit at home and when you walk along the road, when you lie down and when you get up" (Deut. 6:6–7).

The ultimate responsibility for parenting remains with the parents. We cannot shift responsibility for parenting to the schools, the church, or any other organization. Many schools and public organizations have policies that prohibit prayer or any religious discussion or teaching. It is up to parents to sift through the often-conflicting advice that they may encounter. The ultimate authority on parenting is the Word of God.

When Paul instructed Timothy about the criteria for selection of church leaders, he emphasized the importance of choosing men who had demonstrated the ability to raise children properly. In 1 Timothy 3:4–5, he states, "He must manage his own family well and see that his children obey him with proper respect. If anyone does not know how to manage his own family, how can he take care of God's church?"

With this statement, Paul implies that the family is where men have the opportunity to develop the skills that translate into superior church leadership. This is so important that Paul effectively disqualifies an individual from serving as an overseer (elder) in the church if they have not demonstrated the ability to manage their children well. This should be a sobering thought for all of us, especially to anyone who aspires to a position of leadership in the church or is in a position to select leaders for the church. It should be encouraging to parents to know that a properly qualified leader in the church can be a valuable source of assistance on parenting issues as well as other spiritual issues.

If you are tempted to minimize the importance of child discipline, be aware that Paul includes disobedience to parents in a list of other heinous behaviors. In Romans 1:29–31, Paul writes, "They have become filled with every kind of wickedness, evil, greed and depravity. They are full of envy, murder, strife, deceit and malice. They are gossips, slanderers, God-haters, insolent, arrogant and boastful; they invent ways of doing evil; they disobey their parents; they are senseless, faithless, heartless, ruthless."

In 2 Timothy 3:1–5, Paul writes, "But mark this: There will be terrible times in the last days. People will be lovers of themselves, lovers of money, boastful, proud, abusive, disobedient to their parents, ungrateful, unholy, without love, unforgiving, slanderous, without self-control, brutal, not lovers of the good, treacherous, rash, conceited, lovers of pleasure rather than lovers of God—having a form of godliness but denying its power. Have nothing to do with them." Clearly, Paul places great importance on obedience to parents! And, as you may recall, God includes this as one of His commandments to Israel, "Honor your father and mother as the Lord your God has commanded you, so that you may live long and that it may go well with you"(Deut. 5:16).

As you will see in the verses below, parents have a clear responsibility to teach their children discipline. It is very hard to teach something that you do not demonstrate in your own life. Parents have a responsibility to practice what they preach. Most people—children included—learn better with their eyes than with their ears. It takes discipline to teach discipline! A child's physical health, as demonstrated in my story above—and, more importantly, the spiritual health—is endangered by a parent's unwillingness to discipline them. The stakes are higher and the challenge becomes more difficult as the child reaches the teen years.

An undisciplined adult is at a disadvantage for the duration of their life. Discipline is a prerequisite to developing spiritual knowledge and wisdom: "Whoever loves discipline loves knowledge, but he who hates correction is stupid" (Prov. 12:1), and, "The fear of the Lord is the beginning of knowledge, but fools despise wisdom and discipline" (Prov. 1:7). If we do not have the commitment and courage to discipline our children, then we place their spiritual and physical lives at risk.

King Solomon says in the book of Ecclesiastes 1:9 that "…there is nothing new under the sun." God is the ultimate authority on parenting. The fundamental values that God has established for parenting are unchanging, transcend all generations, and are relevant for all times. These values center on the role of the parents in teaching their children what God demands of all His children. This requires that parents be role models for this teaching. The parent who is *Wise @ Heart* will "train a child in the way he should go" (Prov. 22:6), so that the child will, in turn, become *Wise @ Heart*.

This chapter would not be complete without some mention of the obligation of children. Kids, regardless of how old you are, you are to honor your parents. This is true even if your parents are not honorable. Keep in mind the words of God in Deuteronomy 5:16: "Honor your father and your mother as the Lord your God has commanded you, so that you may live long and that it may go well with you." Paul repeated these words in Ephesians 6:1–3: "Children, obey your parents in the Lord, for this is right. Honor your father and mother—which is the first commandment with a promise—that it may go well with you and that you may enjoy long life on earth."

Here are some verses for parents and children to consider:

- Deuteronomy 5:16—"Honor your father and your mother as the Lord your God has commanded you, so that you may live long and that it may go well with you."
- Deuteronomy 6:6–7—"These commandments that I give you today are to be upon your hearts. Impress them on

your children. Talk about them when you sit at home and when you walk along the road, when you lie down and when you get up."

- Proverbs 1:8–9—"Listen, my son, to your father's instruction and do not forsake your mother's teaching. They will be a garland to grace your head and a chain to adorn your neck."
- Proverbs 3:11–12—"My son do not despise the Lord's discipline and do not resent his rebuke, because the Lord disciplines those he loves, as a father the son he delights in."
- Proverbs 10:1—"A wise son brings joy to his father, but a foolish son grief to his mother."
- Proverbs 10:5—"He who gathers crops in summer is a wise son, but he who sleeps during harvest is a disgraceful son."
- Proverbs 11:29—"He who brings trouble on his family will inherit only the wind and the fool will be servant to the wise."
- Proverbs 13:1—"A wise son heeds his father's instruction, but a mocker does not listen to rebuke."
- Proverbs 13:20—"He who walks with the wise grows wise, but a companion of fools suffers harm."
- Proverbs 13:24—"He who spares the rod hates his son, but he who loves him is careful to discipline him."
- Proverbs 15:20—"A wise son brings joy to his father, but a foolish man despises his mother."
- Proverbs 17:6—"Children's children are a crown to the aged, and parents are the pride of their children."
- Proverbs 17:21—"To have a fool for a son brings grief; there is no joy for the father of a fool."

- Proverbs 17:25—"A foolish son brings grief to his father and bitterness to the one who bore him."
- Proverbs 19:13—"A foolish son is his father's ruin, and a quarrelsome wife is like a constant dripping."
- Proverbs 19:18—"Discipline your son, for in that there is hope; do not be a willing party to his death."
- Proverbs 19:26—"He who robs his father and drives out his mother is a son who brings shame and disgrace."
- Proverbs 19:27—"Stop listening to instruction, my son, and you will stray from the words of knowledge."
- Proverbs 20:7—"The righteous man leads a blameless life; blessed are his children after him."
- Proverbs 20:11—"Even a child is known by his actions, by whether his conduct is pure and right."
- Proverbs 20:20—"If a man curses his father or mother, his lamp will be snuffed out in pitch darkness."
- Proverbs 22:6—"Train a child in the way he should go, and when he is old he will not turn from it."
- Proverbs 22:15—"Folly is bound up in the heart of a child, but the rod of discipline will drive it far from him."
- Proverbs 23:13–14—"Do not withhold discipline from a child; if you punish him with the rod, he will not die. Punish him with the rod and save his soul from death."
- Proverbs 23:15–16—"My son, if your heart is wise, then my heart will be glad; my inmost being will rejoice when your lips speak what is right."
- Proverbs 23:19–21—"Listen, my son, and be wise, and keep your heart on the right path. Do not join those who drink too much wine or gorge themselves on meat, for drunkards and gluttons become poor, and drowsiness clothes them in rags."

- Proverbs 23:22–25—"Listen to your father, who gave you life, and do not despise your mother when she is old. Buy the truth and do not sell it; get wisdom, discipline and understanding. The father of a righteous man has great joy; he who has a wise son delights in him. May your father and mother be glad; may she who gave you birth rejoice."
- Proverbs 24:13–14—"Eat honey, my son, for it is good; honey from the comb is sweet to your taste. Know also that wisdom is sweet to your soul; if you find it, there is a future hope for you, and your hope will not be cut off."
- Proverbs 24:21–22—"Fear the Lord and the king, my son, and do not join with the rebellious, for those two will send sudden destruction upon them, and who knows what calamities they can bring?"
- Proverbs 27:11—"Be wise, my son, and bring joy to my heart; then I can answer anyone who treats me with contempt."
- Proverbs 28:7—"He who keeps the law is a discerning son, but a companion of gluttons disgraces his father."
- Proverbs 29:3—"A man who loves wisdom brings joy to his father, but a companion of prostitutes squanders his wealth."
- Proverbs 29:15—"The rod of correction imparts wisdom, but a child left to himself disgraces his mother."
- Proverbs 29:17—"Discipline your son, and he will give you peace; he will bring delight to your soul."
- Proverbs 30:17—"The eye that mocks a father, that scorns obedience to a mother, will be pecked out by the ravens of the valley, will be eaten by the vultures."
- Ephesians 6:1–3—"Children, obey your parents in the Lord, for this is right. Honor your father and mother—

which is the first commandment with a promise—that it may go well with you and that you may enjoy long life on earth."

- Ephesians 6:4—"Fathers, do not exasperate your children; instead, bring them up in the training and instruction of the Lord."
- Colossians 3:20—"Children, obey your parents in everything, for this pleases the Lord."
- Colossians 3:21—"Fathers, do not embitter your children, or they will become discouraged."
- 1 Timothy 3:4—"He must manage his own family well and see that his children obey him with proper respect. If anyone does not know how to manage his own family, how can he take care of God's church?"

# CHAPTER ELEVEN

# Wise @ Heart in Serving Your Brother's and Sisters

We moved to Hawaii in September 1995. Our lives were already hectic and made even more complicated by the logistically difficult move to Hawaii. Diane was just emerging from a serious bout of clinical depression. We had an eight-year-old son, a four-year-old daughter, and a two-year-old daughter. I reported to work in the ER within a few days of our arrival. We were living in a motel while trying to find a house to rent. At the time, rentals were in very short supply.

We were lucky to find a rental house in a neighborhood with a good school and lots of kids. When our container of furniture arrived, we were alarmed to see many of the neighbors coming over. I was not sure if they were coming to help us move or were trying to case out our stuff for a future theft. After all, we had just moved from Southern California where neighbors are not always neighborly and crime is in great supply.

One of the first individuals to introduce themselves was our next-door neighbor. He offered to watch our kids while we unpacked. I am thinking, "Great we just arrived and already the neighborhood pedophile has appeared!" It turns out that he was the pastor of a local church with a booming youth ministry. It was a church that we soon joined. My kids have also become life-long friends with his kids. The other neighbors had equally pure intentions. We moved in and unpacked within a couple of hours thanks to the many volunteers. This event assured us that we had made the right decision in moving to Hawaii. Then, something else happened that topped even that.

On Christmas Eve of 1995—after we had been in Hawaii only a couple of months—we were home having a quiet evening, eating dinner and hoping that the kids would go to bed early. There was a knock on our door at about 6 p.m. One of our neighbors and members of our church had come over to deliver presents for each of our kids. She said, "I know that this is your first Christmas here and you are probably missing your family. I just want to make sure you all have a great Christmas." Stunned and speechless, barely able to croak out a "thank you," I took the packages from her. When I explained to Diane, who was at the dinner table with the kids, what had happened, she was equally shocked. Then the doorbell rang again, and again, and again.

Throughout the evening, over a dozen church members arrived bearing gifts for our kids. It was our best Christmas ever. There was not enough room under the tree for all of the gifts. Diane and I were both in tears, and I still cannot tell this story—over a dozen years later—without choking up. It is the best demonstration of Christian love that I had ever experienced. 1 Thessalonians 4:9 reads, "Now about brotherly love we do not need to write you, for you yourselves have been taught by God to love each other." In this verse, Paul is speaking about love for spiritual brothers and sisters. There is a bond between biological siblings that is different from friendship. Likewise, there is a bond between spiritual siblings that is different from biological siblings. Throughout the Bible, we see that Christians are obligated to show a special concern and regard for their spiritual family. Jesus seems to indicate that our spiritual family may even need to come before our biological family when we are engaged in the important work of spreading the gospel.

For example, in Matthew 12:46, there is an account of Jesus' response when he was informed that his mother and brothers wanted to speak to him. Jesus was in the process of speaking to a crowd of people. Jesus replied to the person who interrupted him, "'Who is my mother, and who are my brothers?' Pointing to his disciples, he said, 'Here are my mother and my brothers. For whoever does the will of my Father in heaven is my brother and sister and mother.'" It appears that Jesus placed a higher value on his ministry than his relationship with his family. He also defines his family as those who do the will of God.

Jesus had taught another lesson about family earlier in the book of Matthew 10:37–39: "Anyone who loves his father or mother more than me is not worthy of me; anyone who loves his son or daughter more than me is not worthy of me; and anyone who does not take his cross and follow me is not worthy of me. Whoever finds his life will lose it, and whoever loses his life for my sake will find it." I know that this is a hard concept to wrap your mind around.

Here is another interesting bit of information. Jesus experienced conflict with his siblings! In the gospel of John 7:1–9, there is an account of such a conflict. I encourage you to read the text for yourself. I will paraphrase it here. What happened was that Jesus' brothers approached him after Jesus had already performed a few miracles in their hometown—like walking on water, changing water into wine, and healing the sick, to name a few—and suggested to Jesus that he should consider taking his show on the road. "Show yourself to the world," they said. Now, maybe I am just cynical, but I believe that they might have been just a little bit jealous of Jesus and would have been quite happy for Jesus to leave their town. As it says in verse 5 of this passage, "For even his brothers did not believe in him."

The Bible is replete with many other examples of sibling rivalry, including that of Cain and Abel (Gen. 4), Isaac and Ishmael (Gen. 21), Jacob and Esau (Gen. 25–28), and Joseph and his brothers (Gen. 37). The underlying theme here is that of conflict incited by some sin—often jealousy. God has high expectations for our relationships with our siblings—physical and spiritual—and provides clear guidelines.

I have several memories from my childhood that are examples of Proverbs 17:17: "A friend loves at all times, and a brother is born for adversity." I have half a dozen close friendships that I have developed during various periods of my life: grade school, junior high school, high school, college, medical school, work environments, and various churches where we have worshipped. I believe that I can count on the assistance of any of these friends when and if I face adversity. Likewise, I believe that they know they can count on me to help them in their time of need. And, as much as my friends and I are loyal to each other, it still does not compare to the intense sense of duty that I feel toward my physical brothers. And, I have ample evidence that they feel the same way.

During our school years, my brothers and everyone else knew that we would always be there to back each other up when needed. If someone picked a fight with one Pierce, they picked a fight with all three of us. I never had to think twice about defending either of my brothers even if they were in the wrong. This is how our parents raised us.

One summer, when my older brother and I were working

together in a manual labor job, we earned the nickname, "The Rat Brothers," because we would engage in fairly sneaky and malicious behavior. We would go to great lengths to get someone back for some perceived wrongdoing. Sometimes, our adversary was bigger, stronger, and meaner than us. But, they were never more devious or more persistent than us. To be fair, I have to admit that, sometimes, we were the instigators in some of these conflicts. The point is that brothers, whether biological or spiritual, must stick together in times of adversity. And, sometimes, it is the adversity that allows them to identify their true "brothers" and friends.

If you desire to be *Wise @ Heart*, then there are some important points for you to consider regarding your relationship with siblings:

- We are commanded to love and serve our brothers and sisters (1 Thess. 4:9; 1 Peter 2:17; 2 Peter 1:5–7; 1 John 2:9; 3:15–17).
- We are to provide for the needs of our brothers and sisters (James 2:15–16).
- Our friends and our siblings each have a role to play when we face adversity (Prov. 17:17; 27:10).
- It is hard to reconcile with a sibling that we have offended (Prov. 18:19).
- We must reconcile with our siblings before we can offer worship to God (Matt. 5:23–24; Matt. 18:15).
- Our spiritual siblings are all of the individuals who do God's will (Mark 3:35).
- We are to intervene if our sibling is involved in sin (Luke 17:3; 1 John 5:16).
- We are not to judge or place spiritual obstacles in our sibling's path (Matt. 7:5; Rom. 14:13, 15, 21; 1Cor. 8:13; James 4:11).

Some further reference verses to consider include:

- Proverbs 17:17—"A friend loves at all times, and a brother is born for adversity."
- Proverbs 18:19—"An offended brother is more unyielding than a fortified city, and disputes are like the barred gates of a citadel."
- Proverbs 27:10—"Do not forsake your friend and the friend of your father, and do not go to your brother's house when disaster strikes you—better a neighbor nearby than a brother far away."
- Matthew 5:23–24—"Therefore, if you are offering your gift at the alter and then remember that your brother has something against you, leave your gift there in front of the alter. First go and be reconciled to your brother; then come and offer your gift."
- Matthew 7:5—"You hypocrite, first take the plank out of your own eye, and then you will see clearly to remove the speck from your brother's eye."
- John 7:5—"For even his own brothers did not believe in him."
- Matthew 18:15—"If your brother sins against you, go and show him his fault, just between the two of you. If he listens to you, you have won your brother over."
- Mark 3:35—"Whoever does God's will is my brother and sister and mother."
- Luke 17:3—"If your brother sins, rebuke him, and if he repents, forgive him."
- Romans 14:13—"Therefore let us stop passing judgment on one another. Instead make up your mind not to put any stumbling block or obstacle in your brother's way."

- Romans 14:15—"If your brother is distressed because of what you eat, you are no longer acting in love. Do not by your eating destroy your brother for whom Christ died."
- Romans 14:21—"It is better not to eat meat or drink wine or to do anything else that will cause your brother to fall."
- 1 Corinthians 8:13—"Therefore, if what I eat causes my brother to sin, I will never eat meat again, so that I will not cause him to fall."
- 1 Thessalonians 4:9—"Now about brotherly love we do not need to write to you, for you yourselves have been taught by God to love each other."
- 2 Thessalonians 3:14–15—"If anyone does not obey our instruction in this letter, take special note of him. Do not associate with him, in order that he may feel ashamed. Yet do not regard him as an enemy, but warn him as a brother."
- James 2:15–16—"Suppose a brother or sister is without clothes and daily food. If one of you says to him, 'Go, I wish you well; keep warm and well fed,' but does nothing about his physical needs, what good is it?"
- James 4:11—"Brothers, do not slander one another. Anyone who speaks against his brother or judges him speaks against the law and judges it. When you judge the law, you are not keeping it, but sitting in judgment on it."
- 1 Peter 2:17—"Show proper respect to everyone: Love the brotherhood of believers, fear God, honor the King."
- 2 Peter 1:5–7—"For this reason, make every effort to add to your faith goodness, and to goodness knowledge, and to knowledge, self-control, and to self-control, perseverance; and to perseverance, godliness; and to godliness, brotherly kindness; and to brotherly kindness, love."

- 1 John 2:9—"Anyone who claims to be in the light but hates his brother is still in the darkness."
- 1 John 3:10—"This is how we know who the children of God are and who the children of the devil are: Anyone who does not do what is right is not a child of God; nor is anyone who does not love his brother."
- 1 John 3:15—"Anyone who hates his brother is a murderer, and you know that no murderer has eternal life in him."
- 1 John 3:16–17—"This is how we know what love is: Jesus Christ laid down his life for us. And we ought to lay down our lives for our brothers. If anyone has material possessions and sees his brother in need but has no pity on him, how can the love of God be in him?"
- 1 John 4:20–21—"If anyone says, 'I love God,' yet hates his brother, he is a liar. For anyone who does not love his brother, whom he has seen, cannot love God, whom he has not seen. And he has given us this command: Whoever loves God must also love his brother."
- 1 John 5:16—"If anyone sees his brother commit a sin that does not lead to death, he should pray and God will give him life."

# WISE @ HEART IN THOUGHT AND BEHAVIOR

*In everything set them an example by doing what is good. In your teaching show integrity, seriousness and soundness of speech that cannot be condemned, so that those who oppose you may be ashamed because they have nothing bad to say about us.*

—TITUS 2:7–8

As Christians, we are to set an example that reflects the work of Christ in our lives. Our outward behavior reflects our inner beliefs and values. The world around us judges us by our behavior. Those that oppose Christianity judge Christianity by how Christians behave. All Christians have a responsibility to reflect the virtues of Christ in their lives. The *Wise @ Heart* will strive to represent Christ in their thoughts and behavior.

# CHAPTER TWELVE

# WISE @ HEART
# IN CHARACTER

All nurses go to heaven. You can take that to the bank. If you know what a nurse does, then you know why. Nursing is a very difficult job. And, to do it well, it must be a *calling*, not just a career. Regardless of whether nursing is a calling or a career, it is a very difficult job. It is not a glamorous job. The hours are difficult because hospitals are open twenty-four hours per day, every day. It is a very stressful job with exposure to significant personal risk, including disease, violence, and burnout. A nurse witnesses the dark underbelly of humanity close up. It is no surprise that there has been a shortage of nurses in the United States for many years. In my opinion, any individual who pursues a career in nursing automatically qualifies for sainthood.

One nurse who I worked with for several years is a great example of the characteristics of a first-rate nurse. Mary (not her real name) was fairly "experienced" at the time I met her. I never found out her actual age, but she had been nursing for over forty years when I met her in an urban emergency room where I was working. It was one of my first jobs as an emergency physician.

Within seconds of meeting her, I knew that Mary was special. Mary took it upon herself to make sure that I felt welcome in the ER. She gave me a very detailed tour of the ER and the hospital as well as introduced me to everyone that we encountered. She knew everybody and everybody knew her. She said something kind about everyone that she introduced me to. For example, she said, "This is John. He is one of our security guards. John used to play football in college and we all feel safe with John around." Within an hour, Mary had coaxed my life story out of me and was sharing it with people that we met. She would say, "This is Dr. Pierce. He grew up in Panama and speaks Spanish. His wife is a nurse. He loves to surf."

What really impressed me about Mary was the care that she gave to every person with whom she came in contact. She seemed to take an immediate deep interest in everybody—patients or staff. And, she really *cared*. She would dig deep into the lives of the people that she encountered. All individuals who crossed her path were her patients. Here is just one example of how she would go above and beyond the call of duty.

One day, a twenty-something year old man came to the ER with an injured hand. The patient had been in a fight the evening before and his closed fist had come into forceful contact with another individual's head. His hand was swollen, painful, and deformed. Mary brought him back to the exam room. After I examined the patient and looked at his X-rays—which revealed a classic "boxer's" fracture—I asked Mary to put a splint on his hand. When I returned to give the patient some pain medication and his discharge instructions, I saw that Mary had applied the splint expertly as usual. She was still at his bedside and was holding the classified ads from the local newspaper in one hand. In her other hand, she was holding a tri-color pen that nurses used in those days—a different color was used for each shift—and she was circling ads with red ink.

After the patient left, I asked Mary what she had been doing with the classified ads. "Oh, Michael (that was the patient's name) needs to find a job. He has too much time on his hands and he hangs out all day with people that are a bad influence on him. That's why he was out drinking late last night and got into a fight. He doesn't have a phone where he lives, so I'm going to call some of these jobs for him. He's going to come back tomorrow morning and I'm going to set him up with some job interviews. I may have to drive him to some of the interviews later this week when I have a day off." My thoughts were, "First of all, you are probably the only person besides his mother that calls him 'Michael.' He probably has a gang nickname line 'M-Daddy Dread.' Second, you have just wasted a lot of time and energy." Really, what were the odds that "Michael" would even show up tomorrow? Not likely. Most of our patients were unemployed and on public assistance. Many were homeless. And, a significant number were alcoholic, drug addicted, mentally ill, or all of the above. Mary had said all of this matter-of-factly as if it is the most normal thing in the world for her to help a patient find a job.

"Are you related to this guy?" I asked.

"No, I just met him today." She went on, "He's a nice boy. He just needs a job so that he is not out on the streets causing trouble. He'll do fine. A little help is all he needs."

For the record, I'm pretty sure that this "nice boy" had done some jail time since I observed what I am pretty sure were "prison" tattoos on his arms. He also had a very high tattoo-to-teeth ratio— way more tattoos than teeth. I have found that the tattoo-to-teeth ratio is a fairly reliable indicator of the likelihood that the individual has been involved in a violent activity that landed them in the ER. It is also a pretty good sign that their violence may be extended to me. Sometimes, the life you save in the ER may one day take yours.

Much to my surprise, Michael showed up the next day. Mary was ready with a list of possible employers. She also had a clean shirt for him. She took the dirty "wife-beater" t-shirt that he was wearing and tossed it in the trash. She sent him to the bathroom to shave with a hospital-issue disposable razor. She also gave him a bus token to get where he needed to go. Michael was somewhat surly, "Aw man, tha's wacked! You done tho'd my shirt in the trash, woman! Why you done that?" he demanded.

"You don't need that nasty shirt, Michael," replied Mary. "And you are never going to get a job looking like that. I want you to come right back here tonight and tell me how your day went. If you don't, I'm going to send the police to your house to get you." I could tell that Michael did not doubt her. I know I did not. Then, as Michael started to walk out of the ER, Mary said, "Wait, wait!" She motioned for Michael to come back to her. When he did, she gave him a huge bear hug. Michael had the expression of a ten-year old being hugged by his mom in front of his baseball teammates. She then shooed him out of the ER. It turned out that he actually did get a job cleaning up a construction site. I was wrong. Generally, I hate it when I am not perfect, but not so much in this case.

This was not an isolated incident. Over the next six years that I worked with Mary, I saw many scenarios like "Michael" play out. Not all of these rescue attempts had a happy ending. It did not seem to faze her, however, and she never became jaded and cynical like the rest of us. Her care for patients and their families always exceeded expectations. She gave every patient a hug before they left the ER. "Everybody needs a hug," she would say. I know from personal experience that she gave good hugs, too.

One time, I saw Mary hand a pair of scissors to the grieving mother of a seven-year old child that had been killed by a stray bullet in a drive-by shooting. Mary encouraged the mother to cut a lock of hair from the dead child's head. Mary then carefully placed the lock of hair in a clear plastic envelope for the mother. The mother clutched this envelope to her chest as she grieved for her child. Later, Mary encouraged the mother to bathe her child with warm water and then Mary lovingly and gently helped the mother dress the child in clean warm clothes. It was so amazing to watch how Mary knew just what to do to comfort somebody.

Mary was a nurse through and through. You could not separate the "nurse" from Mary. Her character defined the values, principles, and beliefs of nursing. For Mary, nursing was not just a career; it was her calling. She was a gifted caregiver. And, she honored everybody, and herself, with the gift that she had been given. Every part of her character reflected the ideals of nursing. There was never a moment of her life in which she was not a nurse. Likewise, our calling as Christians is to develop our character to reflect the values, principles, and beliefs of Christianity (see 2 Peter 1:3–11 below).

Our character is that part of us that resides in our heart. It is who we really are at our very core. Our character is defined by our values and beliefs. Our behavior is the outward display of those beliefs. Just as Mary was defined by her "nurse-ness," Christians are defined by the behaviors that reflect the values, beliefs, and principles—the characteristics—of Christianity. The Bible provides us with many examples of the characteristics of the Christian life—those elements that make up the character of the ideal Christian. These will be discussed in more detail later in this chapter.

In order to develop a *godly* character, we must have knowledge and understanding of the principles of godliness that are taught in the Bible. That is one reason why the study of God's Word—the Bible—is so important to our spiritual development as Christians. Becoming *Wise @ Heart* requires a commitment to searching the scriptures to find those principles and apply them to our lives. This can be accomplished by regular Bible reading, prayer, and reflection on the scriptures.

Character is different from *personality*. The two are often confused. This is a common pitfall. If someone is charming, eloquent, or charismatic, then we may make the mistake of viewing these personality traits as evidence of a sound character. We have seen this many times when religious leaders—who may be eloquent, well-published, and charismatic—fall from grace. All of us—not just the famous— are at risk of being found guilty of the same hypocrisy that Jesus pointed out in some of the religious leaders of His day when He said, "You hypocrites! Isaiah was right when he prophesied about you: 'These people honor me with their lips, but their hearts are far from me. They worship me in vain; their teachings are but rules taught by men.'" God knows the true nature of our hearts and our character.

The *Wise @ Heart* are able to see beneath the veneer of personality to discern the true character of an individual. We are told in Proverbs 20:5: "The purposes of a man's heart are deep waters, but a man of understanding draws them out." If we are not careful, then we might be deceived by the pleasant outward personality characteristics of an individual who may have a corrupt character. We must also be careful that we do the hard work of developing our own character and not just focus on improving our personality or charisma. Otherwise, we may run the risk of becoming a "white-washed wall" (Acts 23:3) that has an attractive exterior and a rotten interior.

What are the character traits that we ought to strive for as Christians? In my opinion, the best examples given in the New Testament of the character traits that God holds out as the ideal are found in the passages that describe the criteria for the selection of leaders in the Church. When you read the following verses, I think you will agree that God's standards for leaders are all admirable characteristics that we should all strive to emulate. Look at 1 Timothy 3:1–13:

Here is a trustworthy saying: If anyone sets his heart on being an overseer, he desires a noble task. Now the overseer must be above reproach, the husband of but one wife, temperate, self-controlled, respectable, hospitable, able to teach, not given to drunkenness, not violent but gentle, not quarrelsome, not a lover of money. He must manage his own family well and see that his children obey him with proper respect. (If anyone does not know how to manage his own family, how can he take care of God's church?) He must not be a recent convert, or he may become conceited and fall under the same judgment as the devil. He must also have a good reputation with outsiders, so that he will not fall into disgrace and into the devil's trap. Deacons, likewise, are to be men worthy of respect, sincere, not indulging in much wine, and not pursuing dishonest gain. They must keep hold of the deep truths of the faith with a clear conscience. They must first be tested; and then if there is nothing against them, let them serve as deacons. In the same way, their wives are to be women worthy of respect, not malicious talkers, but temperate and trustworthy in everything. A deacon must be the husband of but one wife, and must manage his children and his household well. Those who have served well gain an excellent standing and great assurance in their faith in Christ Jesus.

And, in Titus 1:6–9, Paul gives the following recommendations for the appointment of elders to serve as leaders in the church: "An elder must blameless, the husband of but one wife, a man whose children believe and are not open to the charge of being wild and disobedient. Since an overseer is entrusted with God's work, he must be blameless—not overbearing, not quick-tempered, not given to drunkenness, not violent, not pursuing dishonest gain. Rather he must be hospitable, one who loves what is good, who is self-controlled, upright, holy and disciplined. He must hold firmly to the trustworthy message as it has been taught, so that he can encourage others by sound doctrine and refute those who oppose it."

Another relevant passage in the Bible that defines a standard of character for Christians is Galatians 5:22–23, which describes the "fruit of the Spirit" that reflects the work of the Holy Spirit in the lives of Christians: "But the fruit of the Spirit is love, joy, peace, patience, kindness, goodness, faithfulness, gentleness, and self-control. Against such things there is no law." I think we would all agree that these are admirable character traits in any individual. In 2 Peter 1:3–11, there is a list of character traits that we are instructed to "possess in increasing measure." Included in this list are faith, goodness, knowledge, self-control, perseverance, godliness, brotherly kindness, and love.

The writer of Proverbs was thoughtful enough to include a list of several characteristics that God particularly condemns: "There are six things that the Lord hates, seven that are detestable to him: haughty eyes, a lying tongue, hands that shed innocent blood, a heart that devises wicked schemes, feet that are quick to rush into evil, a false witness that pours out lies and a man who stirs up dissension among brothers" (Prov. 6:16–19), and, according to Proverbs 8:13, we can see that God also hates "pride, arrogance, evil behavior and perverse speech." There are many more principles of godly character and action that are scattered throughout the scriptures. Many are included below for your convenience, and I encourage you to comb the scriptures in search of other principles to guide your character development. In doing so, you will find that these principles will tug on your heart and compel you be obedient through the work of the Holy Spirit.

Some key points to consider include:

- God has established standards for character and behavior (1 Kings 9:4–5; Prov. 6:16–19; 12:4; Gal. 5:22–23; 1 Tim. 3:1–13; Titus 1:6–9; 2 Peter 1:3–11).
- An individual's godly character is apparent to others (Ruth 3:11; Prov. 20:11; 1 Tim. 3:7).
- God places a high value on integrity (Neh. 7:2; Job 2:3; 27:5; Prov. 10:9; 11:3; 13:6).
- God places a high value on honesty (Prov. 11:1; 16:11; 16:13; 20:10; 20:17; 20:23; 21:6; 22:28; 23:10–11; 24:26; 25:14).
- God places a high value on trustworthiness (Prov. 11:13; 13:17; 25:9–10; 25:13; 25:19; Ec. 5:4–5; James 5:12).
- Individuals with integrity and a godly character are often persecuted by those who lack integrity (Prov. 29:10; 29:27).
- Adversity often strengthens our character (Rom. 5:3–4; James 1:2–4).
- Our character can be influenced by individuals with whom we associate (Prov. 13:20; 1 Cor. 15:33).

The *Wise @ Heart* will strive to attain a godly character. Other verses to consider include:

- Ruth 3:11—"All my fellow townsmen know that you are a woman of noble character."
- 1 Kings 9:4–5—"As for you, if you walk before me in integrity of heart and uprightness, as David your father did, and do all I command and observe my decrees and laws, I will establish your royal throne over Israel forever, as

I promised David your father when I said, 'You shall never fail to have a man on the throne of Israel.'"

- Nehemiah 7:2—"I put in charge of Jerusalem my brother Hanani, along with Hananiah the commander of the citadel, because he was a man of integrity and feared God more than most men do."
- Job 2:3—"Then the Lord said to Satan, 'Have you considered my servant Job? There is no one on earth like him; he is blameless and upright, a man who fears God and shuns evil. And he still maintains his integrity, though you incited me against him without any reason.'"
- Job 27:5—"I will never admit you are in the right; till I die, I will not deny my integrity."
- Proverbs 6:16–19—"There are six things that the Lord hates, seven that are detestable to him: haughty eyes, a lying tongue, hands that shed innocent blood, a heart that devises innocent schemes, feet that are quick to rush into evil, a false witness who pours out lies and a man who stirs up dissension among brothers."
- Proverbs 8:13—"To fear the Lord is to hate evil; I hate pride and arrogance, evil behavior and perverse speech."
- Proverbs 10:9—"The man of integrity walks securely, but he who takes crooked paths will be found out."
- Proverbs 11:1—"The Lord abhors dishonest scales, but accurate weights are his delight."
- Proverbs 11:3—"The integrity of the upright guides them, but the unfaithful are destroyed by their duplicity."
- Proverbs 11:13—"A gossip betrays a confidence, but a trustworthy man keeps a secret."
- Proverbs 12:4—"A wife of noble character is her husband's crown, but a disgraceful wife is like decay in his bones."

- Proverbs 13:6—"Righteousness guards the man of integrity, but wickedness overthrows the sinner."
- Proverbs 13:17—"A wicked messenger falls into trouble, but a trustworthy envoy brings healing."
- Proverbs 13:20—"He who walks with the wise grows wise, but a companion of fools suffers harm."
- Proverbs 15:27—"A greedy man brings trouble to his family, but he who hates bribes will live."
- Proverbs 16:11—"Honest scales and balances are from the Lord; all the weights in the bag are of his making."
- Proverbs 16:13—"Kings take pleasure in honest lips; they value a man who speaks the truth."
- Proverbs 17:26—"It is not good to punish an innocent man, or to flog officials for their integrity."
- Proverbs 20:10—"Differing weights and differing measures—the Lord detests them both."
- Proverbs 20:11—"Even a child is known by his actions, by whether his conduct is pure and right."
- Proverbs 20:17—"Food gained by fraud tastes sweet to a man, but he ends up with a mouth full of gravel."
- Proverbs 20:23—"The Lord detests differing weights, and dishonest scales do not please Him."
- Proverbs 21:6—"A fortune made by a lying tongue is a fleeting vapor and a deadly snare."
- Proverbs 22:28—"Do not move an ancient boundary stone set up by your forefathers."
- Proverbs 23:10–11—"Do not move an ancient boundary stone or encroach on the fields of the fatherless, for their Defender is strong; he will take up their case against you."
- Proverbs 24:26—"An honest answer is like a kiss on the lips."
- Proverbs 25:9–10—"If you argue your case with a

neighbor, do not betray another man's confidence, or he who hears it may shame you and you will never lose your bad reputation."

- Proverbs 25:13—"Like the coolness of snow at harvest time is a trustworthy messenger to those who send him; he refreshes the spirit of his masters."
- Proverbs 25:14—"Like clouds and wind without rain is a man who boasts of gifts he does not give."
- Proverbs 25:19—"Like a bad tooth or a lame foot is reliance on the unfaithful in times of trouble."
- Proverbs 29:10—"Bloodthirsty men hate a man of integrity and seek to kill the upright."
- Proverbs 29:27—"The righteous detest the dishonest; the wicked detest the upright."
- Proverbs 31:10—"A wife of noble character who can find? She is worth far more than rubies."
- Ecclesiastes 5:4–5—"When you make a vow to God, do not delay in fulfilling it. He has no pleasure in fools; fulfill your vow. It is better not to vow than to make a vow and not fulfill it."
- Romans 5:3–4—"Not only so, but we also rejoice in our sufferings, because we know that suffering produces perseverance; perseverance, character; and character, hope."
- 1 Corinthians 15:33—"Do not be misled, 'Bad, company corrupts good character.'"
- 1 Timothy 3:7—"He must also have a good reputation with outsiders, so that he will not fall into disgrace and into the Devil's trap."
- Titus 2:7–8—"In everything set them an example by doing what is good. In your teaching show integrity,

seriousness and soundness of speech that cannot be condemned, so that those who oppose you may be ashamed because they have nothing bad to say about us."

- James 1:2–4—"Consider it pure joy, my brothers, whenever you face trials of many kind, because you know that the testing of your faith develops perseverance. Perseverance must finish its work so that you may be mature and complete, not lacking in anything."
- James 5:12—"Above all, my brothers, do not swear—not by heaven or by earth or by anything else. Let your 'Yes' be yes, and your 'No,' no, or you will be condemned."
- 2 Peter 1:3–11:

His divine power has given us everything we need for life and godliness through our knowledge of him who called us by his own glory and goodness. Through these he has given us his very great and precious promises, so that through them you may participate in the divine nature and escape the corruption in the world caused by evil desires. For this very reason, make every effort to add to your faith goodness; and to goodness, knowledge; and to knowledge, self-control; and to self-control, perseverance; and to perseverance, godliness and to godliness, brotherly kindness; and to brotherly kindness, love. For if you possess these qualities in increasing measure, they will keep you from being ineffective and unproductive in your knowledge of our Lord Jesus Christ. Therefore, my brothers, be all the more eager to make your calling and election sure. For if you do these things, you will never fall, and you will receive a rich welcome into the eternal kingdom of our Lord and Savior Jesus Christ.

# CHAPTER THIRTEEN

# WISE @ HEART
# IN DISCIPLINE AND
# SELF-CONTROL

When I was an intern, I was assigned to work with a group of nephrologists (kidney specialists) for one month. It was one of my favorite rotations. I loved the rigorous intellectual challenge of managing these complex diseases. There was one nephrologist, Dr. Newman, which I worked with more closely than the others. Our typical routine was to meet in the hospital doctor's lounge for coffee at 6 a.m. to discuss the patients we were about to see. As the intern assigned to Dr. Newman, I was responsible for managing all of the patients in the hospital that were under his care. In order for me to be prepared for these discussions, I would arrive about two hours before our meeting—usually at about 4 a.m.

Each morning, I would review each patient's chart, note any lab results, and prepare a brief summary of their status. Another one of my responsibilities was to be on call to see any patients that came in during the night. I would often end up spending the night in the hospital so that I could take care of the admissions from the night before and be prepared for morning rounds. I would present each of these new admissions during our morning rounds. After hospital rounds, we would head to Dr. Newman's office or to a dialysis center to see patients. We would do rounds again in the evening. It was typically a sixteen- to eighteen-hour workday. This was considered an "easy" rotation since most other rotations consisted of working twenty-four to thirty-six hours at a time with twelve hours off between shifts.

There was one patient, Mr. Prince, on our service who had severe kidney disease due to diabetes and high blood pressure. His heart was failing because it could not keep up with the fluid overload that resulted from poorly functioning kidneys. Mr. Prince was not yet on dialysis, and our goal was to keep him off dialysis for as long as possible. I was struggling to keep his fluid status under control and "dry him out" by giving him strong medications to stimulate what little kidney function he had left. Nothing seemed to be working. In fact, he seemed to be getting worse.

One morning on rounds, after explaining my frustration to Dr. Newman, he quietly entered Mr. Prince's room. After exchanging pleasant greetings, Dr. Newman asked Mr. Prince if he had been following the diet that we had prescribed for him. He had been placed on a very strict low salt and low fluid diet. Mr. Prince assured Dr. Newman that, of course, he had. Dr. Newman asked him if anyone had been bringing him food or if he had been adding salt to his food or drinking more water than was permitted. No, Mr. Prince assured us, he had not. As Dr. Newman was asking these questions, he was scanning the room with his eyes. He casually moved over to a cabinet in the room and slowly opened it. I noticed that Mr. Prince suddenly became very attentive.

Dr. Newman looked into the cabinet, reached in, and extracted a large, nearly empty bottle of soy sauce with a red cap, which was definitely not the low-sodium variety. He held it out for Mr. Prince and me to see. Mr. Prince looked sheepish. "Well, the food just doesn't taste very good," he said as he started to wither under Dr. Newman's glare. "Mr. Prince, you are not required to follow any of our recommendations," Dr. Newman said slowly. "You are free to leave this hospital anytime and seek care elsewhere," he continued. "Eating this," Dr. Newman held up the bottle, "will kill you. You already know this. We have been over this before. It is your lack of discipline that has created your illness, and it is your lack of discipline that is making your illness worse. If you would like for us to continue to care for you, then you will need to do your part to help yourself." Dr. Newman then dropped the soy sauce in the trashcan and walked out of the room. The mystery had been solved. Mr. Prince had been consuming massive quantities of salt contained in the soy sauce—over seven hundred milligrams per teaspoon! That is why he continued to retain fluid despite the aggressive therapy that I had ordered. Sadly, but predictably, his lack of self-discipline caused his kidney failure to get worse. He soon was placed on kidney dialysis.

Self-discipline, or self-control, is an important factor in our physical health. I have seen the example above repeated in the lives of many patients in my twenty years of medical practice. Many of the illnesses we experience are a direct result of an unhealthy, undisciplined lifestyle. Self-discipline is also an important factor in our spiritual health. Self-discipline is an important ingredient in a healthy relationship with God. Self-discipline is required for high achievement and effectiveness. Self-discipline is also included in the list of characteristics that God requires for leadership in the church (Titus 1:8). The importance of self-discipline in the life of a Christian cannot be overestimated. You will see this demonstrated quite clearly in the verses included below.

Self-discipline begins with disciplined thought. Engaging in disciplined spiritual thought starts with examining our beliefs and aligning them with God's will. If we align our beliefs and thinking with the instructions and principles provided in the Bible, then we are more likely to make decisions that are consistent with those beliefs. When our thoughts and behaviors are consistent with God's will, the results are predictable. For example, Ephesians 6:1–3 instructs us: "Children, obey your parents in the Lord, for this is right. Honor your father and mother—which is the first commandment with a promise—that it may go well with you and that you may enjoy long life on the earth." Our lives are much more likely to "go well" when we demonstrate self-discipline. In contrast, Proverbs 5:11–14 gives us some insight into the consequences of poor discipline: "At the end of your life you will groan, when your flesh and body are spent. You will say, 'How I hated discipline! How my heart spurned correction! I would not obey my teachers or listen to my instructors. I have come to the brink of utter ruin in the midst of the assembly.'"

Self-discipline is required to *transform* our thinking in order to be aligned with God's teaching rather than that of *our* desires and self-interest. In order to do so, we must *conform* our beliefs to God's principles. As we read in Romans 12:2, "Do not conform any longer to the pattern of this world, but be transformed by the renewing of your mind. Then you will be able to test and approve what God's will is—his good, pleasing and perfect will." This verse points out that, in order to discern God's will, we must think in conformance with God's principles. Without a clear understanding of God's will—and a commitment to obeying His will—we are likely to make decisions that lead to outcomes that are less than satisfactory. In other words, our flawed beliefs will lead to flawed decisions and the consequences will be unacceptable. In order to experience different consequences, we must transform beliefs and our thinking. As the verse above suggests, the "pattern of this world" is a flawed belief system. Following the pattern of this world will lead you astray.

Discipline can be either self-imposed or externally imposed. As Christians, we are commanded to be *self*-controlled (2 Peter 1:6). When self-discipline, or self-control, is lacking then we may experience *externally* imposed discipline from God, our parents, our teacher, our employer, the government, or any other individual in a position of authority over us. Whether self-imposed or externally imposed, effective discipline *generally* leads to greater knowledge, wisdom, and maturity. On the other hand, withholding discipline, either from others or yourself, is counterproductive to the process of gaining knowledge, wisdom, and maturity. Hebrews 12:10–11 instructs: "Our fathers disciplined us for a little while as they thought best; but God disciplines us for our good, that we may share in his holiness. No discipline seems pleasant at the time, but painful. Later on, however, it produces a harvest of righteousness and peace for those who have been trained by it."

A great example of growth and maturity through discipline is the relationship between a parent and child. When the child is very young, discipline is, almost exclusively, externally imposed by the parent. Parents have a responsibility to discipline their children: "Discipline your son, for in that there is hope; do not be a willing party to his death" (Prov. 19:18). Discipline is required for the child's safety and development. As the child grows in knowledge and maturity, he is able to make disciplined decisions in keeping with the lessons learned through the discipline imposed upon him. Through this process of maturity, he accepts increasing responsibility for self-discipline and less parental discipline is required to produce disciplined behavior. The parent is able to observe this process of maturity and discern when more or less externally imposed discipline is required. A disciplined child is a pleasure to be around and makes their parents proud as stated in Proverbs 23:24: "The father of a righteous man has great joy; he who has a wise son delights in him."

As an aside, read how the Israelites were instructed to deal with a rebellious son: "If a man has a stubborn and rebellious son who does not obey his father and mother and will not listen to them when they discipline him, his father and mother shall take hold of him and bring him to the elders at the gate of his town. They shall say to the elders, 'This son of ours is stubborn and rebellious. He will not obey us. He is a profligate and a drunkard.' Then all the men of his town shall stone him to death. You must purge the evil from among you. All Israel will hear of it and be afraid" (Deut. 21:18–21). I bet that made quite an impression on the other children! The lesson here is that God takes discipline *very* seriously.

Just as the level of maturity in a child is evident to his parents by his behavior and how he handles responsibility, our level of spiritual maturity is also evident to those around us. Our spiritual maturity is a reflection of the discipline that we have achieved in our lives. We might be able to fake some people out for a while, but, sooner or later, the chink in our armor will become obvious.

Discipline is a *learned* behavior that is taught by example and practiced until it becomes a habit. Note that the root word for *disciple* is the same as for *discipline*. The practice of medicine is sometimes referred to as a *discipline* or a branch of learning. The practice of Christianity is also a discipline. A disciple is a follower of a leader, a teacher, or a philosophy. A disciple of Christ is a follower of Christ and is recognized by the discipline that they exhibit in their lives as a reflection of their obedience to Christ.

Here are some key points about discipline summarized from the verses following:

- The Wise accept discipline (Prov. 12:1; 15:4; 15:32; 23:23).
- Fools do not accept discipline (Prov. 1:7; 3:11–12; 5:11–14; 5:22–23; 9:13; 12:1; 15:4; 15:32).
- Discipline leads to good consequences (Prov. 5:11–14; 5:22–23; 6:20–23; 10:17; 13:18).
- Lack of discipline leads to bad consequences (Prov. 6:20–23; 10:17; 13:18; 15:10).
- Loving parents discipline their children (Prov. 3:11–12; 13:24; 19:18; 22:15; 23:13–14; 29:15; 29:17).
- God disciplines us because he loves us (Deut. 4:36; Job 5:17; Prov. 3:11–12; Ps. 39:11; 94:12; 1 Cor. 11:32; Heb. 12:5–11; Rev. 3:19).
- God wants us to be self-disciplined (Gal. 5:22–23; 1 Thess. 5:6, 8; 1 Tim. 3:2; Titus 1:7–8; 2:2; 4–6; 1 Peter 1:13; 4:7; 5:8; 2 Peter 1:5–7).

The *Wise @ Heart* accept discipline and are self-disciplined. Here are some verses to consider:

- Deuteronomy 4:36—"From heaven he made you hear his voice to discipline you."
- Job 5:17—"Blessed is the man whom God corrects; so do not despise the discipline of the Almighty."
- Proverbs 1:7—"The fear of the Lord is the beginning of knowledge, but fools despise wisdom and discipline."
- Proverbs 3:11–12—"My son, do not despise the Lord's discipline and do not resent his rebuke, because the Lord disciplines those he loves, as a father the son he delights in."

- Proverbs 5:11–14—"At the end of your life you will groan, when your flesh and body are spent. You will say, 'How I hated discipline! How my heart spurned correction! I would not obey my teachers or listen to my instructors. I have come to the brink of utter ruin in the midst of the assembly.'"
- Proverbs 5:22–23—"The evil deeds of a wicked man ensnare him; the cords of sin hold him fast. He will die for lack of discipline, led astray by his own great folly."
- Proverbs 6:20–23—"My son, keep your father's commands and do not forsake your mother's teaching. Bind them upon your heart forever; fasten them around your neck. When you walk, they will guide you; when you sleep, they will watch over you; when you awake, they will speak to you. For these commands are a lamp, this teaching is a light, and the corrections of discipline are the way to life."
- Proverbs 9:13—"The woman Folly is loud; she is undisciplined and without knowledge."
- Proverbs 10:17—"He who heeds discipline shows the way to life, but whoever ignores correction leads others astray."
- Proverbs 12:1—"Whoever loves discipline loves knowledge, but he who hates correction is stupid."
- Proverbs 13:18—"He who ignores discipline comes to poverty and shame, but whoever heeds correction is honored."
- Proverbs13:24—"He who spares the rod hates his son, but he who loves him is careful to discipline him."
- Proverbs 15:4—"A fool spurns his father's discipline, but whoever heeds correction shows prudence."
- Proverbs 15:10—"Stern discipline awaits him who leaves the path; he who hates correction will die."

- Proverbs 15:32—"He who ignores discipline despises himself, but whoever heeds correction gains understanding."
- Proverbs 19:18—"Discipline your son, for in that there is hope; do not be a willing party to his death."
- Proverbs 22:15—"Folly is bound up in the heart of a child, but the rod of discipline will drive it far from him."
- Proverbs 23:13–14—"Do not withhold discipline from a child; if you punish him with a rod, he will not die. Punish him with a rod and save his soul from death."
- Proverbs 23:23—"Buy the truth and do not sell it; get wisdom, discipline and understanding."
- Proverbs 29:15—"The rod of correction imparts wisdom, but a child left to himself disgraces his mother."
- Proverbs 29:17—"Discipline your son, and he will give you peace; he will bring delight to your soul."
- Psalm 39:11—"You rebuke and discipline men for their sin."
- Psalm 94:12—"Blessed is the man you discipline, O Lord, the man you teach from your law."
- Jeremiah 30:11b—"I will discipline you but only with justice; I will not let you go entirely unpunished."
- 1 Corinthians 11:32—"When we are judged by the Lord, we are being disciplined so that we will not be condemned with the world."
- Galatians 5:22–23—"But the fruit of the Spirit is love, joy, peace, patience, kindness, goodness, faithfulness, gentleness and self-control."
- 1 Thessalonians 5:6—"So then, let us not be like others, who are asleep, but let us be alert and self-controlled."
- 1 Thessalonians 5:8—"But since we belong to the day, let us be self-controlled."

- 1 Timothy 3:2—"Now the overseer must be...self-controlled."
- Titus 1:7–8—"Since an overseer is entrusted with God's work, he must be...self-controlled...disciplined."
- Titus 2:2—"Teach the older men to be...self-controlled."
- Titus 2:4–5—"...train the younger women to...be self-controlled."
- Titus 2:6—"Similarly, encourage the young men to be self-controlled."
- Titus 2:11–12—"For the grace of God that brings salvation has appeared to all men. It teaches us to say 'No' to ungodliness and worldly passions, and to live self-controlled, upright and godly lives in this present age."
- Hebrews 12:5–11:

And you have forgotten that word of encouragement that addresses you as sons: "My son, do not make light of the Lord's discipline, and do not lose heart when he rebukes you, because the Lord disciplines those he loves, and he punishes everyone he accepts as a son." Endure hardship as discipline; God is treating you as sons. For what son is not disciplined by his father? If you are not disciplined (and everyone undergoes discipline), then you are illegitimate children and not true sons. Moreover, we have all had human fathers who disciplined us and we respected them for it. How much more should we submit to the Father of our spirits and live! Our fathers disciplined us for a little while as they thought best; but God disciplines us for our good, that we may share in his holiness. No discipline seems pleasant at the time, but painful. Later on, however, it produces a harvest of righteousness and peace for those who have been trained by it.

- 1 Peter 1:13—"Therefore, prepare your minds for action; be self-controlled."
- 1 Peter 4:7—"The end of all things is near. Therefore be clear minded and self-controlled so that you can pray."
- 1 Peter 5:8—"Be self-controlled and alert."
- 2 Peter 1:5–7—"For this very reason, make every effort to add to your faith goodness; and to goodness, knowledge; and to knowledge, self-control; and to self-control, perseverance; and to perseverance, godliness; and to godliness, brotherly kindness; and to brotherly kindness, love."
- Revelation 3:19—"Those whom I love I rebuke and discipline."

# CHAPTER FOURTEEN

# WISE @ HEART
# IN SPEECH

For many years, I served as the medical director and department chairman of an emergency department. Early one morning as I was walking into the hospital, I ran into a surgeon colleague who was entering the hospital at the same time. He said hello and asked me if I was working that day. My joking response was that, no, I was taking care of some administrative duties, which we both know is not really work compared to caring for patients. We both laughed and then heard someone clear their throat behind us. The hospital administrator, who was not a practicing physician, had walked up behind us. He made it clear that he had heard my comment and our laughter when he said, "Hello doctors," and then said over his shoulder as he passed by us, "Well, I'm going to my office to 'not work' for the next twelve hours." That is just one of many examples of how my tongue has gotten me into trouble and a good example of Proverbs 10:19: "Where words are many, sin is not absent, but he who holds his tongue is wise." On another occasion, I asked a young woman patient with a protuberant abdomen if she was pregnant. She was not. That is something you only do one time!

The subject of controlling our speech (tongue) receives quite a bit of attention in the Bible. In my version of the NIV Life Application Study Bible, there is a great summary (on page 1335) entitled, "The Four Tongues." The following is an excerpt:

- The Controlled Tongue—Those with this speech pattern think before speaking, know when silence is best, and give wise advice.
- The Caring Tongue—Those with this speech pattern speak truthfully while seeking to encourage.
- The Conniving Tongue—Those with this speech pattern are filled with wrong motives, gossip, slander, and a desire to twist the truth.
- The Careless Tongue—Those with this speech pattern are filled with lies, curses, quick-tempered words, which can lead to rebellion and destruction.

The Controlled and Caring Tongues are the examples we are meant to follow and the Conniving and Careless Tongues are to be avoided. As you review the key points and the reference verses below, you will notice an emphasis on the admonition to use words sparingly as noted in Proverbs 10:19 above. You will also see that there is significant emphasis on avoiding gossip. Gossip leads to big trouble. And, of course, lying and deceitful speech are condemned and "hated" by God.

The apostle James makes this stunning statement: "If anyone is never at fault in what he says, he is a perfect man, able to keep his whole body in check" (James 3:2). Superficially and, perhaps, tongue-in-cheek—I know, bad pun—this verse implies that all we have to do is control our speech and we will be perfect. Maybe James is making a point of how difficult it is to control our tongue. Only a perfect person can control their tongue. Even if we are not perfect, it pays to keep a tight reign on our tongue.

In Psalm 15, King David provides us with a short list of characteristics that describe the ideal individual. As you read this psalm, note how many of these characteristics are related to speech. I have added emphasis where relevant: "Lord, who may dwell in your sanctuary? Who may live on your holy hill? He whose walk is blameless and who does what is righteous, who *speaks the truth* from his heart and has *no slander* on his tongue, who does his neighbor no wrong and *casts no slur* on his fellowman, who despises a vile man but honors those who fear the Lord, who *keeps his oath* even when it hurts, who lends his money without usury and does not accept a bribe against the innocent. He who does these things will never be shaken." The *Wise @ Heart* place a high priority on controlling their speech.

Here are some key points regarding speech:

- God created speech (Ex. 4:10–12; Prov. 22:12).
- God wants for you to have control over your speech (Prov. 4:24; 11:12; 13:3; 17:7; 18:13; 18:21; 19:1; 20:3; 20:15; 20:19; 21:23; 22:17–21; 23:15–16; 25:11; 28:23; 29:20; 30:32; Ec. 5:6; 10:20; Eph. 5:4; 1 Tim. 4:12; Titus 2:7–8; 3:1–2; 1 Peter 3:10; James 1:19–21; 1:22; 2:12–13; 3:2; 3:5–12).
- Controlled speech leads to good consequences (Ps. 15; Prov. 10:13; 10:20; 10:21; 10:31; 10:32; 12:6; 12:13; 12:14; 12:18; 12:19; 12:25; 13:2; 14:3; 14:25; 15:1–2; 15:4; 15:7; 15:23; 15:28; 16:10; 16:13; 16:21; 16:23; 16:24; 17:9; 17:27; 17:28; 18:20; 22:11; 24:26; 25:12; 25:15; Ec. 10:12–14).
- Uncontrolled speech leads to bad consequences (Prov. 5:3; 6:1–5; 10:8; 10:10; 10:11; 10:14; 10:31; 11:9; 11:11;

12:6; 12:13; 12:18; 14:3; 14:7; 15:1–2; 15:4; 15:28; 16:27; 16:28; 17:4; 17:9; 17:20; 18:6; 18:7; 18:13; 19:5; 19:9; 19:28; 25:20; 25:23; 27:14; Ec. 10:12–14; 10:20).

- God hates lying, slander, gossip as well as deceitful, evil, and perverse speech (Lev. 19:16; Prov. 6:16–19; 8:13; 10:18; 10:31; 10:32; 11:13; 12:17; 12:19; 12:22; 15:4; 18:8; 19:1; 19:5; 19:9; 19:22; 20:19; 21:6; 21:28; 24:28–29; 25:18; 26:20; 26:22–26; 26:28; 29:5; 1 Cor. 6:9–10, 2 Cor. 12:20; 1 Tim. 5:13; Titus 2:3; James 4:11).
- Avoid excessive talking and keep your promises (Ps. 15; Prov. 10:8; 10:10; 10:19; 11:12; Ec. 5:2–3; 5:7; 6:11; 10:12–14).

Some verses for your consideration include:

- Exodus 4:10–12—"Moses said to the Lord, 'O Lord, I have never been eloquent, neither in the past nor since you have spoken to your servant. I am slow of speech and tongue.' The Lord said to him, 'Who gave man his mouth? Who makes him deaf or mute? Who gives him sight or makes him blind? Is it not I, the Lord? Now go; I will help you speak and will teach you what to say.'"
- Leviticus 19:16—"Do not go about spreading slander among your people."
- Psalm 15—"Lord, who may dwell in your sanctuary? Who may live on your holy hill? He whose walk is blameless and who does what is righteous, who speaks the truth from his heart and has no slander on his tongue, who does his neighbor no wrong and casts no slur on his fellowman, who despises a vile man but honors those who fear the

Lord, who keeps his oath even when it hurts, who lends his money without usury and does not accept a bribe against the innocent. He who does these things will never be shaken."

- Proverbs 4:24—"Put away perversity from your mouth; keep corrupt talk far from your lips."
- Proverbs 5:3—"For the lips of the adulteress drip honey, and her speech is smoother than oil; but in the end she is bitter as gall, sharp as a double-edged sword."
- Proverbs 6:1–5—"My son, if you have put up security for your neighbor, if you have struck hands in pledge for another, if you have been trapped by what you said, ensnared by the words of your mouth, then do this, my son, to free yourself, since you have fallen into your neighbor's hands: Go and humble yourself, press your plea with your neighbor! Allow no sleep to your eyes, no slumber to your eyelids. Free yourself, like a gazelle from the hand of the hunter, like a bird from the snare of the fowler."
- Proverbs 6:16–19—"There are six things that the Lord hates, seven that are detestable to him: haughty eyes, a lying tongue, hands that shed innocent blood, a heart the devises wicked schemes, feet that are quick to rush into evil, a false witness who pours out lies, and a man who stirs up dissension among brothers."
- Proverbs 8:13—"To fear the Lord is to hate evil; I hate pride and arrogance, evil behavior and perverse speech."
- Proverbs 10:8—"The wise in heart accept commands, but a chattering fool comes to ruin."
- Proverbs 10:10—"He who winks maliciously causes grief and a chattering fool comes to ruin."

- Proverbs 10:11—"The mouth of the righteous is a fountain of life, but violence overwhelms the mouth of the wicked."
- Proverbs 10:13—"Wisdom is found on the lips of the discerning, but a rod is for the back of him who lacks judgment."
- Proverbs 10:14—"Wise men store up knowledge, but the mouth of a fool invites ruin."
- Proverbs 10:18—"He who conceals his hatred has lying lips, and whoever spreads slander is a fool."
- Proverbs 10:19—"When words are many, sin is not absent, but he who holds his tongue is wise."
- Proverbs 10:20—"The tongue of the righteous is choice silver, but the heart of the wicked is of little value."
- Proverbs 10:21—"The lips of the righteous nourish many, but fools die for lack of judgment."
- Proverbs 10:31—"The mouth of the righteous brings forth wisdom, but a perverse tongue will be cut out."
- Proverbs 10:32—"The lips of the righteous knows what is fitting, but the mouth of the wicked only what is perverse."
- Proverbs 11:9—"With his mouth the godless destroys his neighbor, but through knowledge the righteous escape."
- Proverbs 11:11—"Through the blessing of the upright a city is exalted, but by the mouth of the wicked it is destroyed."
- Proverbs 11:12—"A man who lacks judgment derides his neighbor, but a man of understanding holds his tongue."
- Proverbs 11:13—"A gossip betrays a confidence, but a trustworthy man keeps a secret."
- Proverbs 12:6—"The words of the wicked lie in wait for blood, but the speech of the upright rescues them."

- Proverbs 12:13—"An evil man is trapped by his sinful talk, but a righteous man escapes trouble."
- Proverbs 12:14—"From the fruit of his lips a man is filled with good things as surely as the work of his hands rewards him."
- Proverbs 12:17—"The truthful witness gives honest testimony, but a false witness tells lies."
- Proverbs 12:18—"Reckless words pierce like a sword, but the tongue of the wise brings healing."
- Proverbs 12:19—"Truthful lips endure forever, but a lying tongue lasts only a moment."
- Proverbs 12:22—"The Lord detests lying lips, but he delights in men who are truthful."
- Proverbs 12:25—"An anxious heart weighs a man down, but a kind word cheers him up."
- Proverbs 13:2—"From the fruit of his lips a man enjoys good things, but the unfaithful have a craving for violence."
- Proverbs 13:3—"He who guards his lips guards his life, but he who speaks rashly will come to ruin."
- Proverbs 14:3—"A fool's talk brings a rod to his back, but the lips of the wise protect them."
- Proverbs 14:7—"Stay away from a foolish man, for you will not find knowledge on his lips."
- Proverbs 14:25—"A truthful witness saves lives, but a false witness is deceitful."
- Proverbs 15:1—"A gentle answer turns away wrath, but a harsh word stirs up anger."
- Proverbs 15:2—"The tongue of the wise commends knowledge, but the mouth of the fool gushes folly."
- Proverbs 15:4—"The tongue that brings healing is a tree of life, but a deceitful tongue crushes the spirit."

- Proverbs 15:7—"The lips of the wise spread knowledge; not so the hearts of fools."
- Proverbs 15:23—"A man finds joy in giving an apt reply—and how good is a timely word!"
- Proverbs 15:28—"The heart of the righteous weighs its answers, but the mouth of the wicked gushes evil."
- Proverbs 16:10—"The lips of a king speak as an oracle, and his mouth should not betray justice."
- Proverbs 16:13—"Kings take pleasure in honest lips; they value a man who speaks the truth."
- Proverbs 16:21—"The wise in heart are called discerning, and pleasant words promote instruction."
- Proverbs 16:23—"A wise man's heart guides his mouth, and his lips promote instruction."
- Proverbs 16:24—"Pleasant words are a honeycomb, sweet to the soul and healing to the bones."
- Proverbs 16:27—"A scoundrel plots evil, and his speech is like a scorching fire."
- Proverbs 16:28—"A perverse man stirs up dissension and a gossip separates close friends."
- Proverbs 17:4—"A wicked man listens to evil lips; a liar pays attention to a malicious tongue."
- Proverbs 17:7—"Arrogant lips are unsuited to a fool—how much worse lying lips to a ruler."
- Proverbs 17:9—"He who covers over an offense promotes love, but whoever repeats a matter separates close friends."
- Proverbs 17:20—"A man of perverse heart does not prosper; he whose tongue is deceitful falls into trouble."
- Proverbs 17:27—"A man of knowledge uses words with restraint, and a man of understanding is even-tempered."

- Proverbs 17:28—"Even a fool is thought wise if he keeps silent, and discerning if he holds his tongue."
- Proverbs 18:4—"The words of a man's mouth are deep waters, but the fountain of wisdom is a bubbling brook."
- Proverbs 18:6—"A fool's lips bring him strife and his mouth invites a beating."
- Proverbs 18:7—"A fool's mouth is his undoing and his lips are a snare to his soul."
- Proverbs 18:8—"The words of a gossip are like choice morsels; they go down to a man's inmost parts."
- Proverbs 18:13—"He who answers before listening—that is his folly and his shame."
- Proverbs 18:20—"From the fruit of his mouth a man's stomach is filled; with the harvest from his lips he is satisfied."
- Proverbs 18:21—"The tongue has the power of life and death, and those who love it will eat its fruit."
- Proverbs 19:1—"Better a poor man whose walk is blameless than a fool whose lips are perverse."
- Proverbs 19:5—"A false witness will not go unpunished, and he who pours out lies will not go free."
- Proverbs 19:9—"A false witness will not go unpunished, and he who pours out lies will perish."
- Proverbs 19:22—"What a man desires is unfailing love; better to be poor than a liar."
- Proverbs 19:28—"The corrupt witness mocks at justice, and the mouth of the wicked gulps down evil."
- Proverbs 20:3—"It is to a man's honor to avoid strife, but every fool is quick to quarrel."
- Proverbs 20:15—"Gold there is, and rubies in abundance, but lips that speak knowledge are a rare jewel."

- Proverbs 20:19—"A gossip betrays a confidence; so avoid a man who talks too much."
- Proverbs 21:6—"A fortune made by a lying tongue is a fleeting vapor and a deadly snare."
- Proverbs 21:23—"He who guards his mouth and his tongue keeps himself from calamity."
- Proverbs 21:28—"A false witness will perish, and whoever listens to him will be destroyed forever."
- Proverbs 22:11—"He who loves a pure heart and whose speech is gracious will have the king for his friend."
- Proverbs 22:12—"The eyes of the Lord keep watch over knowledge, but he frustrates the words of the unfaithful."
- Proverbs 22:17–21—"Pay attention and listen to the sayings of the wise; apply your heart to what I teach, for it is pleasing when you keep them in your heart and have all of them ready on your lips. So that your trust may be in the Lord, I teach you today, even you. Have I not written thirty sayings for you, sayings of counsel and knowledge, teaching you true and reliable words so that you can give sound answers to him who sent you?"
- Proverbs 23:15–16—"My son, if your heart is wise, then my heart will be glad; my inmost being will rejoice when your lips speak what is right."
- Proverbs 24:26—"An honest answer is like a kiss on the lips."
- Proverbs 24:28–29—"Do not testify against your neighbor without cause, or use your lips to deceive. Do not say, 'I'll do to him as he has done to me; I'll pay that man back for what he did.'"
- Proverbs 25:11—"A word aptly spoken is like apples of gold in settings of silver."

- Proverbs 25:12—"Like an earring of gold or an ornament of fine gold is a wise man's rebuke to a listening ear."
- Proverbs 25:15—"Through patience a ruler can be persuaded and a gentle tongue can break a bone."
- Proverbs 25:18—"Like a club or a sword or a sharp arrow is the man who gives false testimony against his neighbor."
- Proverbs 25:20—"Like one who takes away a garment on a cold day, or like vinegar poured on soda, is one who sings songs to a heavy heart."
- Proverbs 25:23—"As a north wind brings rain, so a sly tongue brings angry looks."
- Proverbs 26:20—"Without wood a fire goes out; without gossip a quarrel dies down."
- Proverbs 26:22—"The words of a gossip are like choice morsels; they go down to a man's inmost parts."
- Proverbs 26:23—"Like a coating of glaze over earthenware are fervent lips with an evil heart."
- Proverbs 26:24–26—"A malicious man disguises himself with his lips, but in his heart he harbors deceit. Though his speech is charming, do not believe him, for seven abominations fill his heart. His malice may be concealed by deception, but his wickedness will be exposed in the assembly."
- Proverbs 26:28—"A lying tongue hates those it hurts, and a flattering mouth works ruin."
- Proverbs 27:14—"If a man loudly blesses his neighbor in the morning, it will be taken as a curse."
- Proverbs 28:23—"He who rebukes a man will in the end gain more favor than he who has a flattering tongue."
- Proverbs 29:5 —"Whoever flatters his neighbor is spreading a net for his feet."

- Proverbs 29:20—"Do you see a man who speaks in haste? There is more hope for a fool than for him."
- Proverbs 30:32—"If you have played the fool and exalted yourself, or if you have planned evil, clap your hand over your mouth!"
- Ecclesiastes 5:2–3—"Do not be quick with your mouth, do not be hasty in your heart to utter anything before God. God is in heaven and you are on earth, so let your words be few. As a dream comes when there are many cares, so the speech of a fool when there are many words."
- Ecclesiastes 5:6—"Do not let your mouth lead you into sin."
- Ecclesiastes 5:7—"Much dreaming and many words are meaningless. Therefore stand in awe of God."
- Ecclesiastes 6:11—"The more words, the less meaning, and how does that profit anyone?"
- Ecclesiastes 10:12–14—"Words from a wise man's mouth are gracious, but a fool is consumed by his own lips. At the beginning his words are folly; at the end they are wicked madness—and the fool multiplies words."
- Ecclesiastes 10:20—"Do not revile the king even in your thoughts, or curse the rich in your bedroom, because a bird of the air may carry your words, and a bird on the wing may report what you say."
- 2 Corinthians 12:20—"For I am afraid that when I come I may not find you as I want you to be, and you may not find me as you want me to be. I fear that there may be quarreling, jealousy, outbursts of anger, factions, slander, gossip, arrogance, and disorder."
- Ephesians 5:4—"Nor should there be obscenity, foolish talk or coarse joking, which are out of place, but rather thanksgiving."

- 1 Timothy 4:12—"Don't let anyone look down on you because you are young, but set an example for the believers in speech, in life, in love, in faith and in purity."
- 1 Timothy 5:13—"And not only do they become idlers, but also gossips and busybodies, saying things they ought not to."
- Titus 2:3—"Likewise, teach the older women to be reverent in the way they live, not to be slanderers or addicted to much wine, but to teach what is good."
- Titus 2:7–8—"In everything set them an example by doing what is good. In your teaching show integrity, seriousness and soundness of speech that cannot be condemned, so that those who oppose you may be ashamed because they have nothing bad to say about us."
- Titus 3:1–2—"Remind the people to be subject to rulers and authorities, to be obedient, to be ready to do whatever is good, to slander no one, to be peaceable and considerate, and to show true humility toward all men."
- 1 Peter 3:10—"For, 'Whoever would love life and see good days must keep his tongue from evil and his lips from deceitful speech.'"
- James 1:19–21—"My dear brothers, take note of this: Everyone should be quick to listen, slow to speak, and slow to become angry, for man's anger does not bring about the righteous life that God desires. Therefore get rid of all moral filth and the evil that is so prevalent and humbly accept the word planted in you, which can save you."
- James 1:26—"If anyone considers himself religious and yet does not keep a tight rein on his tongue, he deceives himself and his religion is worthless."
- James 2:12–13—"Speak and act as those who are going to

be judged by the law that gives freedom, because judgment without mercy will be shown to anyone who has not been merciful. Mercy triumphs over judgment!"

- James 3:2—"We all stumble in many ways. If anyone is never at fault in what he says, he is a perfect man, able to keep his whole body in check."
- James 3:5–12:

Likewise, the tongue is a small part of the body, but it makes great boasts. Consider what a great forest is set on fire by a small spark. The tongue is also a fire, a world of evil among the parts of the body. It corrupts the whole person. All kinds of animals, birds, reptiles and creatures of the sea are being tamed and have been tamed by man, but no man can tame the tongue. It is a restless evil, full of deadly poison. With the tongue we praise our Lord and Father, and with it we curse men, who have been made in God's likeness. Out of the same mouth come praise and cursing. My brothers, this should not be. Can both fresh water and salt water flow from the same spring? My brothers, can a fig tree bear olives, or a grapevine bear figs? Neither can a salt spring produce fresh water.

- James 4:11—"Brothers, do not slander one another."

# CHAPTER FIFTEEN

# Wise @ Heart
# in Conflict

During my career as an administrator, I was confronted with a dilemma. Like most large organizations, the one I was working for had an established system for resolving conflict. Virtually every organization of any significant size has written policies of how conflicts are handled. Our policy was probably very similar to what most organizations develop. The problem I experienced was that conflicts seemed to escalate when the policy was followed. The escalation was not *in spite of the policy,* conflicts seemed to escalate *because of the policy.*

Basically, our policy said that if there was a conflict between two employees, then the manager or supervisor was to be involved in settling the dispute. One employee could actually levy an anonymous complaint about another employee. You can imagine the hostility and hurt that can arise when someone is presented with an anonymous third party complaint about something that they did that was thought to be inappropriate. Here is an example of what would typically happen.

One day, the nurse manager with whom I worked closely informed me that one of the doctors under my supervision had spoken harshly to a nurse. The nurse had brought this to her manager's attention and the manager brought it to my attention. This process followed the policy to the letter. The expectation was that I would confront the physician, hear his side of the story, and attempt to resolve the issue. As you can imagine, the physician was quite surprised that this issue had been elevated to this level. He was angry and defensive. He felt that the event was blown out of proportion. His presentation of the details was somewhat different from those of the nurse.

To make a long story short, there were hurt feelings on all sides and the conflict had been broadened to include many other parties. Sadly, both of the original parties are both hard-working, valuable members of the staff and neither had a history of repetitive poor behavior. Later, both agreed that they probably could have resolved this issue between themselves. If the nurse would have confronted the doctor about her concerns, then the doctor most likely would have apologized and their relationship would have been stronger instead of strained further by the escalation of the conflict. Later in this chapter, we will look at a method taught by Jesus to resolve conflict and how that process, if properly employed, can resolve conflict in a much healthier fashion. The goal of conflict resolution is just that: resolve the conflict! Not escalate the conflict. If managed properly the involved parties should have a stronger relationship after the conflict than before.

God prefers peace over conflict. In contrast, we live in a culture that not only permits conflict, but it also promotes conflict. Movies glorify the hero who engages in violence to avenge an injustice. Video games glorify violence and killing. We have rights, and we are taught and encouraged to fight for those rights. If we believe that someone has wronged us in some way, not only must the injustice be corrected, but the individual must also pay damages to compensate for our "mental suffering." Political campaigns—the most recent hard-fought presidential election, for example—very quickly degenerate into "mudslinging." This type of behavior is not what God wants. However, Christians should not be naïve about the world and the culture that surrounds them. You must be aware that if you aspire to be spiritually wise regarding conflict, then you also must accept that you will be swimming against a powerful current of cultural opposition. This, in itself, will create conflict. It is ironic, but it should not be a surprise.

Any attempted transformational change incites conflict. Jesus stated in Matthew 10:34: "Do not suppose that I have come to bring peace to the earth. I did not come to bring peace, but a sword." My guess is that Jesus was referring to the conflict that predictably occurs when the gospel collides with the culture of the world, other religions, or misdirected theology. There is a predictable conflict when righteousness confronts wickedness. There are many examples in the Bible of Jesus coming in conflict with the religious leaders of His day (see Matthew 23).

Christians are held to a different standard of principles and behavior than the world around us. If we follow Jesus' teaching, then the way in which we resolve conflict will set us apart from the common practices of the world we live in, the schools we attend, and the places where we work. Unresolved conflicts fester and grow like an abscess. An unresolved conflict will destroy a relationship. An unresolved conflict can cause division in a church or any organization. This is not what God intends for his people. In 1 Corinthians 6:15b, it says, "God has called us to live in peace." And, in 1 Corinthians 14:33, it reads, "For God is not a God of disorder but of peace." Proverbs 16:7 teaches: "When a man's ways are pleasing to the Lord, he makes even his enemies live at peace with him." It is God's will that we do our best to live in peace with those around us. In order to do this, we must accept and apply what the Bible teaches about resolving conflict even if it does not make "sense" to us. It should come as no surprise that God's way of resolving conflict is different than the world's way of resolving conflict.

The best way to resolve conflict is to avoid it whenever it is in our power to do so. Proverbs 19:11 instructs: "A man's wisdom gives him patience; it is to his glory to overlook an offense." Proverbs 20:3 is more direct: "It is to a man's honor to avoid strife, but every fool is quick to quarrel." I confess that I have been personally responsible for creating many conflicts. I could have sidestepped many conflicts that I did not initiate by employing patience and wisdom. My first impulse is usually to fight doggedly for my *rights*, defend my opinion, and counterattack when attacked. I often pull out the *pride* club before I pull out the *patience* club.

Prideful behavior undermines effectiveness, especially if you are a leader. The apostle Paul makes it clear in 1 Timothy 3:2–3 that a leader in the church must be "self-controlled...not violent but gentle...not quarrelsome." A chronically argumentative individual is difficult to tolerate. They can cause tremendous trouble in the church, family, community, or any other relationship or organization. That is why an argumentative individual is disqualified from leadership in the church.

As a manager, there have been many times that I have been a called upon to resolve conflicts. James 4:1–2 identifies the generic cause of most conflicts: "What causes fights and quarrels among you? Don't they come from your desires that battle within you? You want something but don't get it. You kill and covet, but you cannot have what you want. You quarrel and fight." I have certainly found this to be true in the conflicts that I have observed or in which I have been involved.

In order to avoid conflict and to resolve conflict in a spiritual fashion, we must understand and agree that it is usually our selfish desire, or the selfish desire of others, that is at the root of most conflicts. When a conflict occurs, our first action should be to look inward. Once we have assured ourselves that we are not the source of the conflict, we can then engage in the steps that Jesus outlines in Matthew 18:15–20: "If a brother sins against you, go and show him his fault, just between the two of you. If he listens to you, you have won your brother over. But if he will not listen, take one or two others along, so that every matter may be established by the testimony of two or three witnesses. If he refuses to listen to them, tell it to the church; and if he refuses to listen even to the church, treat him as you would a pagan or tax collector."

Until you have engaged in the process of conflict resolution described by Jesus, you will not believe its effectiveness. In fact, I have found a modified version of this process useful in resolving conflicts that occur in most secular situations. My experience in employing and encouraging this process of conflict resolution in this arena has been very favorable. Here is a summary of my recommendations for healthy conflict resolution in the workplace, school, community organizations, and other secular relationships:

- If an individual feels that they have been wronged by another individual, then they should first take time to decide if they, themselves, are the source of the conflict. In other words, is their selfish desire the source of the conflict? Even if the individual believes that they are not the source of the conflict, is it possible for them to avoid the conflict in order to keep the peace? Is continued conflict worth any potential gain?

- If the individual chooses to actively resolve the conflict, then they should speak directly to the individual involved—and only to the individual involved—and express their concern *respectfully and privately.* This should be done prior to speaking to any other individual about the conflict. This is crucial since once the audience has been broadened by gossip, it is very difficult to reach a satisfactory resolution to the conflict. You may not think of this as gossip, but it is. Anytime you engage in a discussion that disparages another individual when they are not present, it is gossip. And, God hates gossip. As it says in Proverbs 17:9: "He who covers over an offense promotes love, but whoever repeats the matter separates close friends." And, Proverbs 16:28 says, "A perverse man stirs up dissension, and a gossip separates close friends," while Proverbs 26:20 states, "Without wood a fire goes out; without gossip a quarrel dies down."

- If the conflict is successfully resolved after confronting the individual privately and directly, then the matter should not be discussed further ever again.

- If the conflict is not successfully resolved, then the offended party should ask one or two *unbiased* peers to participate in a discussion with the offending party. If the matter is resolved, then it should not be discussed further ever again.

- If the conflict is not successfully resolved at this point, then the matter should be brought to a supervisor for resolution. The supervisor should understand that their role is to facilitate a resolution of the conflict and not necessarily to decide who is right and who is wrong. The goal is for the involved parties to heal through the process of resolution.

In my experience, if this process is followed, then there is rarely a need to proceed past the first step. It turns out that most people prefer to resolve a conflict at the level at which it occurred—between the two involved parties—with no other supervisor, manager, or Human Resources staff involved. Many times, an individual is not even aware that they have offended someone and they are quick to apologize when confronted or explain how their actions were misinterpreted.

Contrast this process with the scenario that I described at the beginning of this chapter. Unfortunately, many organizations foster lingering and toxic conflicts by endorsing a system that triangulates the conflict. Employee A has an issue with Employee B. Employee A complains to the Manager. The Manager confronts Employee B. Employee B is blindsided and, if the complaint is anonymous, then the conflict is never fully resolved. Many organizations have policies that direct grievances to the manager or HR department prior to an attempt at "conflict level" resolution between the parties involved. In my experience, this establishes an adversarial climate in the workplace. Sadly, this happens all too often in the church. Think about how you would prefer to have a concern about you brought to your attention. This is a great opportunity for Christians to set themselves apart by their behavior in the workplace by not engaging in gossip and by resolving conflicts in a healthy fashion. A note of caution, however, is that your HR department may not be very supportive of your efforts and your coworkers may not reciprocate.

Jesus said, "So in everything, do to others what you would have them do to you, for this sums up the Law and the Prophets" (Matt. 7:12). This principle, often referred to as the Golden Rule, is important for us to keep in mind as we seek to avoid and resolve conflict in a spiritually mature fashion. A lot of people do not carry the implications of the Golden Rule far enough. If you think that the Golden Rule means that you should treat people in the exact same way that you would want to be treated in the exact same circumstance, then I think you are missing the point. I believe the real value in employing the Golden Rule is in taking the time to understand what and how an individual would prefer to have you "*do to them*" and honoring their preference. After all, don't we want people to treat us the way *we* want to be treated and not how *they* would want us to treat them?

I think that most of us would much prefer that if an individual felt that we had offended them in some way, then that individual should come to us first with their concerns rather than presenting the matter to a pastor, elder, or manager or gossiping to a coworker or friend. But, to truly honor another person, it is wise to find out how they would want their conflicts to be resolved.

Proverbs 26:17 says, "Like one who seizes a dog by the ears is a passer-by who meddles in a quarrel not his own." This is another very important lesson to learn. We need to be very careful about getting involved in other people's quarrels. Even if we think we are helping, we can make matters worse and even get hurt ourselves. This point was made clear to me one day during a shift in the ER. Here is what happened.

Two men were arguing outside of a convenience store. One man pulled out a knife and both men began to grapple. In the course of the fight, a bystander jumped in and tried to stop the fight. The knife wielder ended up cutting off the finger of his opponent and the nose of the bystander! So, now I had two patients in the ER—

one with an amputated nose and one with an amputated finger. Fortunately, both of the amputated parts were able to be re-implanted. As each man was being wheeled out of the ER into surgery, I could not resist telling the one with the amputated finger, "From now on, I hope you will keep your fingers to yourself!" And, to the one with the amputated nose, I quipped, "You should keep your nose out of other people's business!"

The *Wise @ Heart* will *avoid* conflict—if possible—and *resolve* conflict in a godly fashion when necessary.

Here are some verses to consider:

- Numbers 6:24–26—"The Lord bless you and keep you; the Lord make his face to shine upon you and be gracious to you; the Lord turn his face toward you and give you peace."
- Psalm 34:14—"Turn from evil and do good; seek peace and pursue it."
- Psalm 85:10—"Love and faithfulness meet together; righteousness and peace kiss each other."
- Proverbs 10:12—"Hatred stirs up dissension, but love covers over all wrongs."
- Proverbs 14:30—"A heart at peace gives life to the body, but envy rots the bones."
- Proverbs 15:18—"A hot-tempered man stirs up dissension, but a patient man calms a quarrel."
- Proverbs 16:7—"When a man's ways are pleasing to the Lord, he makes even his enemies live at peace with him."
- Proverbs 16:28—"A perverse man stirs up dissension, and a gossip separates close friends."
- Proverbs 17:1—"Better a dry crust with peace and quiet than a house full of feasting with strife."

- Proverbs 17:9—"He who covers over an offense promotes love, but whoever repeats the matter separates close friends."
- Proverbs 17:14—"Starting a quarrel is like breaching a dam; so drop the matter before a dispute breaks out."
- Proverbs 17:19—"He who loves a quarrel loves sin; he who builds a high gate invites destruction."
- Proverbs 18:18—"Casting the lot settles disputes and keeps strong opponents apart."
- Proverbs 18:19—"An offended brother is more unyielding than a fortified city, and disputes are like the barred gates of a citadel."
- Proverbs 19:11—"A man's wisdom gives him patience; it is to his glory to overlook an offense."
- Proverbs 19:13—"...a quarrelsome wife is like a constant dripping."
- Proverbs 20:3—"It is to a man's honor to avoid strife, but every fool is quick to quarrel."
- Proverbs 26:17—"Like one who seizes a dog by the ears is a passer-by who meddles in a quarrel not his own."
- Proverbs 26:20—"Without wood a fire goes out; without gossip a quarrel dies down."
- Proverbs 26:21—"As charcoal to embers and as wood to fire, so is a quarrelsome man for kindling strife."
- Proverbs 27:3—"Stone is heavy and sand a burden, but provocation by a fool is heavier than both."
- Proverbs 30:33—"For as churning the milk produces butter, and as twisting the nose produces blood, so stirring up anger produces strife."
- Matthew 7:12—"So in everything, do to others what you

would have them do to you, for this sums up the Law and the Prophets."

- Matthew 10:34—"Do not suppose that I have come to bring peace to the earth. I did not come to bring peace, but a sword."
- Matthew 18:15–20—"If a brother sins against you, go and show him his fault, just between the two of you. If he listens to you, you have won your brother over. But if he will not listen, take one or two others along, so that every matter may be established by the testimony of two or three witnesses. If he refuses to listen to them, tell it to the church; and if he refuses to listen even to the church, treat him as you would a pagan or tax collector."
- Luke 17:3–4—"If your brother sins, rebuke him, and if he repents, forgive him. If he sins against you seven times in a day, and seven times comes back to you and says, 'I repent,' forgive him."
- 1 Corinthians 6:15b—"God has called us to live in peace."
- 1 Corinthians 14:33—"For God is not a God of disorder but of peace."
- Galatians 5:22—"But the fruit of the Spirit is love, joy, peace, patience, kindness, gentleness and self-control. Against such things there is no law."
- 1 Timothy 3:2–3—"Now the overseer must be above reproach, the husband of but one wife, temperate, self-controlled, respectable, hospitable, able to teach, not given to drunkenness, not violent but gentle, not quarrelsome, not a lover of money."
- 2 Timothy 2:22–24—"Flee the evil desires of youth, and pursue righteousness, faith, love, and peace, along with

those who call on the Lord out of a pure heart. Don't have anything to do with foolish and stupid arguments, because you know they produce quarrels. And the Lord's servant must not quarrel; instead, he must be kind to everyone, able to teach, not resentful."

- 1 Peter 3:8–12—"Finally, all of you, live in harmony with one another; be sympathetic, love as brothers, be compassionate and humble. Do not repay evil with evil or insult with insult, but with blessing, because to this you were called so that you may inherit a blessing. For, 'Whoever would love life and see good days must keep his tongue from evil and his lips from deceitful speech. He must turn from evil and do good; he must seek peace and pursue it. For the eyes of the Lord are on the righteous and his ears are attentive to their prayer, but the face of the Lord is against those who do evil.'"

- James 4:1–2—"What causes fights and quarrels among you? Don't they come from your desires that battle within you? You want something but don't get it. You kill and covet, but you cannot have what you want. You quarrel and fight."

# WISE @ HEART IN MANAGING WEALTH (STEWARDSHIP)

*Of what use is money in the hand of a fool,*
*since he has no desire to get wisdom?*
—PROVERBS 17:16

*Stewardship* seems like such an outdated and "churchy" term to me. A steward is someone who manages someone else's property, finances, or other affairs. To be wise in stewardship is to be wise in the management of property, finances, or other such affairs. A steward, then, is a *manager.* In the context of this book, wise stewardship means to be wise in the management of the wealth that God has entrusted to you.

"What wealth?" you might be thinking. God has given you various gifts—spiritual, physical, material—that he expects you to use in His service and in the service of others. Our life as Christians is a sacred stewardship (management) of all that God has entrusted to us.

The *Wise @ Heart* are wise in stewardship.

# CHAPTER SIXTEEN

# WISE @ HEART IN WORK AND REST

**M**ary worked full-time in the cafeteria at our hospital. She also cleaned houses and worked at Wal-Mart as a cashier part-time. Every time that I saw Mary, she was smiling and happy. She always gave great service. She told me once that, even though she was a single mother, all three of her children had attended college and one daughter was set to graduate from law school. When I first met Mary many years ago, she let me know that she was a Christian and felt that God had blessed her in many ways. She promised to pray for me. She prayed for all of the doctors and nurses at our hospital. Mary was a great example of someone who worked hard and maintained a great attitude while doing so.

People who work hard with a good attitude are attractive to others. We like being around them. They radiate energy and enthusiasm. Lazy people are much less attractive. We tend to avoid them. Proverbs 10:26 points out, "As vinegar to the teeth and smoke to the eyes, so is a sluggard to those who send him." Lazy people are irritating to those around them. Here are some even stronger words about laziness from Proverbs 18:9: "One who is slack in his work is brother to one who destroys." I think you get the point.

What many lazy people do not realize is that their laziness is obvious. Their slowness in attending to responsibilities, their whining attitude, and the poor quality of their work all give evidence to their inherent laziness. Lazy people often try to make excuses for their laziness. Their excuses are often quite ridiculous and only serve to call more attention to their laziness. A good example of a ridiculous excuse for laziness is seen in Proverbs 22:13: "The sluggard says, 'There is a lion outside!' or, 'I will be murdered in the streets!'" Often, lazy people think that they are getting away with these excuses when really they are just being left to their laziness. Hard workers have very little time to spend trying to rehabilitate lazy people. A Christian who is lazy is not living the life that God intends.

God expects us to work so hard that our hard work is evident to others (1 Thess. 4:11–12). God also wants us to some take time out to rest (Ex. 23:12). It may seem strange to you that God would mandate that we rest. God knew that some of us would become addicted to hard work. Hard work is addictive not only because it produces tangible rewards, but hard work is also inherently rewarding. In other words, there is a "rush" that is experienced by those who exhaust themselves physically, mentally, and spiritually in pursuit of a worthy endeavor. God knew that we would become addicted to this experience and likely overdo it. That is the way we are. If something is worth doing, then it is worth overdoing! If some is good, then more is better and too much is still not enough! God knew that some of us would kill ourselves working too hard if he let us.

In order for us to remain balanced physically, mentally, and spiritually, we must rest. God tells us to rest at least one day out of seven. Some of you are probably thinking, "That is not nearly enough rest!" There is some variability to each person's tolerance for work, but I think, in general, most of us are quite capable of working hard six days a week and remaining healthy. Now, that does not mean that we are driving ourselves to exhaustion all six days. What it means is that we work hard within reasonable boundaries while being respectful of our health. As it says in Proverbs 23:4, "Do not wear yourself out to get rich; have the wisdom to show restraint." If we develop the wisdom to show restraint, then we will be able to maintain balance in our lives.

Here are some key points to consider regarding work and rest:

- It is God's will that we work hard (Gen. 3:17b–19; Col. 3:23; 2 Thess. 3:10).
- It is God's will that we rest (Gen. 2:2–3; Ex. 23:12; 31:15a; Deut. 5:13–14).
- True rest comes from God (Ps. 62:1; 91:1; Jer. 6:16; Matt. 11:28–29; Heb. 4:9; Rev. 14:13).
- Hard work is rewarded; laziness results in negative consequences (Prov. 10:4–5; 12:11; 12:14; 12:24; 13:4; 14:23; 15:19; 19:15; 20:4; 20:13; 21:5; 21:25; 24:30–34; 28:19; Ec. 4:5; 10:18; 11:6; Jer. 48:10; Matt. 25:26–29; 1 Thess. 5:12–13; 2 Thess. 3:10).
- A lazy person is despised by others (Prov. 10:26; 18:9; 19:24; 22:29; Jer. 48:10).
- A lazy person often makes excuses to conceal their laziness (Prov. 22:13; 26:13).
- Working hard brings satisfaction (Ec. 2:10; 2:24–26; 3:22; 5:18–20).
- The most important work we do is God's work (Luke 10:2; John 6:27–28; 9:4).
- We will be held accountable for the results of our work and be rewarded accordingly by God (Matt. 25:26–29; 1 Cor. 3:12–15; Col. 3:23; Heb. 6:10; James 2:24, 26; Rev. 14:13).

- It is God's will that we have a good attitude and do not complain about our work so that we set a good example for others (Phil. 2:14–16).

The *Wise @ Heart* will work hard when appropriate and rest when appropriate.

Verses to consider include:

- Genesis 2:2–3—"By the seventh day God had finished the work he had been doing; so on the seventh day he rested from all his work. And God blessed the seventh day and made it holy, because on it he rested from all the work of creating that he had done."
- Genesis 3:17b–19—"Cursed is the ground because of you; through painful toil you will eat of it all the days of your life. It will produce thorns and thistles for you, and you will eat the plants of the field. By the sweat of the brow you will eat your food until you return to the ground, since from it you were taken; for dust you are and to dust you will return."
- Exodus 23:12—"Six days do your work, but on the seventh day do not work, so that your ox and donkey may rest and the slave born in your household, and the alien as well, may be refreshed."
- Exodus 31:15a—"For six days, work is to be done, but the seventh day is a Sabbath day of rest, holy to the Lord."
- Deuteronomy 5:13–14—"Six days you shall labor and do all your work, but the seventh day is a Sabbath to the Lord your God. On it you shall not do any work, neither you, nor your son or daughter, nor your manservant or maidservant, nor your ox, your donkey or any of your

animals, nor the alien within your gates, so that your manservant and maidservant may rest, as you do."

- Psalm 62:1—"My soul finds rest in God alone; my salvation comes from him."
- Psalm 91:1—"He who dwells in the shelter of the Most High will rest in the shadow of the Almighty."
- Proverbs 6:6–11—"Go to the ant you sluggard; consider its ways and be wise! It has no commander, no overseer or ruler, yet it stores its provisions in summer and gathers its food at harvest. How long will you lie there, you sluggard? When will you get up from your sleep? A little sleep, a little slumber, a little folding of the hands to rest—and poverty will come on you like a bandit and scarcity like an armed man."
- Proverbs 10:4—"Lazy hands make a man poor but diligent hands bring wealth."
- Proverbs 10:5—"He who gathers crops in summer is a wise son, but diligent hands bring wealth."
- Proverbs 10:26—"As vinegar to the teeth and smoke to the eyes, so is a sluggard to those who send him."
- Proverbs 12:11—"He who works his land will have abundant food, but he who chases fantasies lacks judgment."
- Proverbs 12:14—"From the fruit of his lips a man is filled with good things as surely as the work of his hands rewards him."
- Proverbs 12:24—"Diligent hands will rule, but laziness ends in slave labor."
- Proverbs 12:27—"The lazy man does not roast his game, but the diligent man prizes his possessions."
- Proverbs 13:4—"The sluggard craves and gets nothing, but the desires of the diligent are fully satisfied."

- Proverbs 14:23—"All hard work brings a profit, but mere talk leads only to poverty."
- Proverbs 15:19—"The way of the sluggard is blocked with thorns, but the path of the upright is a highway."
- Proverbs 16:26—"The laborer's appetite works for him; his hunger drives him on."
- Proverbs 18:9—"One who is slack in his work is brother to one who destroys."
- Proverbs 19:15—"Laziness brings on deep sleep, and the shiftless man goes hungry."
- Proverbs 19:24—"The sluggard buries his hand in the dish; he will not even bring it back to his mouth!"
- Proverbs 20:4—"A sluggard does not plow in season; so at harvest time he looks and finds nothing."
- Proverbs 20:13—"Do not love sleep or you will grow poor; stay awake and you will have food to spare."
- Proverbs 21:5—"The plans of the diligent leads to profit as surely as haste leads to poverty."
- Proverbs 21:25—"The sluggard's craving will be the death of him, because his hands refuse to work. All day long he craves for more but the righteous give without sparing."
- Proverbs 22:13—"The sluggard says, 'There is a lion outside!' or, 'I will be murdered in the streets!'"
- Proverbs 22:29—"Do you see a man skilled in his work? He will serve before kings; he will not serve before obscure men."
- Proverbs 24:30–34—"I went past the field of the sluggard, past the vineyard of the man who lacks judgment; thorns had come up everywhere, the ground was covered with weeds, and the stone wall was in ruins. I applied my heart to what I observed and learned a lesson from what I saw:

A little sleep, a little slumber, a little folding of the hands to rest—and poverty will come on you like a bandit and scarcity like an armed man."

- Proverbs 26:13—"The sluggard says, 'There is a lion in the road, a fierce lion roaming in the streets!'"
- Proverbs 26:14—"As a door turns on its hinges, so a sluggard turns on his bed."
- Proverbs 26:15—"The sluggard buries his hand in the dish; he is too lazy to bring it back to his mouth."
- Proverbs 26:16—"The sluggard is wiser in his own eyes than seven men who answer discreetly."
- Proverbs 28:19—"He who works his land will have abundant food, but the one who chases fantasies will have his fill of poverty."
- Ecclesiastes 2:10—"My heart took delight in all my work, and this was the reward for all my labor."
- Ecclesiastes 2:24–26—"A man can do nothing better than to eat and drink and find satisfaction in his work. This too I see is from the hand of God, for without him, who can eat or find enjoyment? To the man who pleases him, God gives wisdom, knowledge, and happiness, but to the sinner he gives the task of gathering and storing up wealth to hand it over to the one who pleases God."
- Ecclesiastes 3:22—"So I saw that there is nothing better for a man than to enjoy his work, because that is his lot."
- Ecclesiastes 4:4—"And I saw that all labor and all achievement spring from man's envy of his neighbor. This too is meaningless, a chasing after the wind."
- Ecclesiastes 4:5—"The fool folds his hands and ruins himself."
- Ecclesiastes 5:12—"The sleep of a laborer is sweet,

whether he eats little or much, but the abundance of a rich man permits him no sleep."

- Ecclesiastes 5:18–20—"Then I realized that it is good and proper for a man to eat and drink and to find satisfaction in his toilsome labor under the sun during the few days of life God has given him—for this is his lot. Moreover, when God gives any man wealth and possessions, and enables him to enjoy them, to accept his lot and be happy in his work—this is a gift of God. He seldom reflects on the days of his life, because God keeps him occupied with gladness of heart."
- Ecclesiastes 10:18—"If a man is lazy, the rafters sag; if his hands are idle, the house leaks."
- Ecclesiastes 11:6—"Sow your seed in the morning, and at evening let not your hands be idle, for you do not know which will succeed, whether this or that, or whether both will do equally well."
- Jeremiah 6:16—"This is what the Lord says: 'Stand at the crossroads and look; ask for the ancient paths, ask where the good way is, and walk in it, and you will find rest for your souls.'"
- Jeremiah 48:10—"A curse on him who is lax in doing the Lord's work!"
- Matthew 11:28–29—"Come to me, all you who are weary and burdened, and I will give you rest. Take my yoke upon you and learn from me, for I am gentle and humble in heart, and you will find rest for your souls. For my yoke is easy and my burden is light."
- Matthew 25:26–29—"His master replied, 'You wicked, lazy servant! So you knew that I harvest where I have not sown and gather where I have not scattered seed? Well

then, you should have put my money on deposit with the
bankers, so that when I returned I would have received it
back with interest. Take the talent from him and give it to
the one who has the ten talents. For everyone who has will
be given more, and he will have an abundance. Whoever
does not have, even what he has will be taken from him.'"

- Luke 10:2—"He told them, 'The harvest is plentiful, but
the workers are few. Ask the Lord of the harvest, therefore,
to send out workers into his harvest field.'"

- John 6:27—"Do not work for food that spoils, but for
food that endures to eternal life, which the Son of Man
will give you. On him God the Father has placed his seal of
approval."

- John 6:28—"Then they asked him, 'What must we do to
do the works God requires?' Jesus answered, 'The work of
God is this: to believe in the one he has sent.'"

- John 9:4—"As long as it is day, we must do the work of
him who sent me. Night is coming, when no one can
work."

- 1 Corinthians 3:12–15—"If any man builds on this
foundation using gold, silver, costly stones, wood, hay, or
straw, his work will be shown for what it is, because the
Day will bring it to light. It will be revealed with fire, and
the fire will test the quality of each man's work. If what he
has built survives, he will receive his reward. If it is burned
up, he will suffer loss; he himself will be saved, but only as
one escaping through the flames."

- Ephesians 4:11–13—"It was he who gave some to be
apostles, some to be prophets, some to be evangelists,
and some to be pastors and teachers, to prepare God's
people for works of service, so that the body of Christ

may be built up until we all reach unity in faith and in the knowledge of the Son of God and become mature, attaining to the whole measure of the fullness of Christ."

- Philippians 2:14–16—"Do everything without complaining or arguing, so that you may become blameless and pure, children of God without fault in a crooked and depraved generation, in which you shine like stars in the universe as you hold out the word of life—in order that I may boast on the day of Christ that I did not run or labor for nothing."

- Colossians 3:23—"Whatever you do, work at it with all your heart, as working for the Lord, not for men, since you know that you will receive an inheritance from the Lord as a reward."

- 1 Thessalonians 4:11–12—"Make it your ambition to lead a quiet life, to mind your own business and to work with your hands, just as we told you, so that your daily life may win the respect of outsiders and so that you will not be dependent on anybody."

- 1 Thessalonians 5:12–13—"Now we ask you brothers, to respect those who work hard among you, who are over you in the Lord and who admonish you. Hold them in the highest regard in love because of their work."

- 1 Thessalonians 5:14—"...warn those who are idle."

- 2 Thessalonians 3:10—"For even when we were with you, we gave you this rule: 'If a man will not work, he shall not eat.'"

- Hebrews 4:9—"There remains, then, a Sabbath-rest for the people of God; for anyone who enters God's rest also rests from his own work, just as God did from his."

- Hebrews 6:10—"God is not unjust; he will not forget your

work and the love you have shown him as you have helped his people and continue to help them."

- James 2:24—"You see that a person is justified by what he does and not by faith alone."
- James 2:26—"As the body without the spirit is dead, so faith without deeds is dead."
- Revelation 14:13—"Then I heard a voice from heaven say, 'Write: Blessed are the dead who die in the Lord from now on.' 'Yes,' says the Spirit, 'they will rest from their labor, for their deeds will follow them.'"

# CHAPTER SEVENTEEN

# WISE @ HEART IN
# MANAGING WEALTH

At the time of this writing, many Americans are experiencing a sudden and severe decline in their financial wealth. Home values began dropping gradually and then precipitously around the country earlier this year. As the media reported mounting numbers of foreclosures, it became clear that some of the largest financial institutions were in dire trouble. Stock market prices have now taken a dive, and the global economy is showing convincing signs of recession. There is tremendous uncertainty in the future of the US and the world economy. There is a saying: "When the US economy sneezes, the world economy catches a cold." To top it off, we have just experienced one of the most hotly contested presidential elections in history. Barrack Obama is now the President of the United States. So far, there is no cohesive strategy promoted to address the financial instability in our economy.

Efforts to acquire wealth consume the majority of time, thought, energy, and talents of many individuals and organizations around the world. The culture of the world honors those who have amassed great wealth. Savvy investors—particularly at this time in our history—

are being consulted for wisdom and guidance. An individual's power and influence are generally proportional to the amount of wealth that they control. Given the earthly rewards available to those who are rich, it is hard to resist the temptation to proceed down the very well-traveled path of accumulating wealth.

However, caution is in order. God speaks clearly about the dangers of the headlong pursuit of wealth. In Matthew 6:24, it says, "No one can serve two masters. Either he will hate the one and love the other, or he will be devoted to the one and despise the other. You cannot serve both God and Money." In 1 Timothy 6:10, Paul says, "For the love of money is a root of all kinds of evil. Some people, eager for money, have wandered from the faith and pierced themselves with many griefs." In 1 Timothy 3:3, we are told that an overseer (elder) should be "not a lover of money." And, in Hebrews 13:5, the advice reads, "Keep your lives free from the love of money and be content with what you have, because God has said, 'Never will I leave you; never will I forsake you.'" There are three important lessons here for us. First, financial wealth can be an obstacle in our relationship with God. Second, being a lover of money disqualifies an individual from leadership in the church. And, third, God promises to take care of our financial needs.

As you will see in the verses included below and in **Appendix G**, God has much to say about money. Perhaps the most important concept that God imparts to us is that *spiritual wisdom has a greater value than monetary wealth*. That is why Christians are to have a life that is driven by the pursuit of wisdom rather than one lived in pursuit of *wealth*. As we read in Proverbs 3:13–15, "Blessed is the man who finds wisdom, the man who gains understanding, for she is more profitable than silver and yields better returns than gold. She is more precious than rubies; nothing you desire can compare with her."

The concept that wisdom is to be valued above wealth is critical to understanding what the Bible teaches about wealth. Developing spiritual wisdom is a prerequisite for managing our wealth according to God's expectations as well as avoiding the pitfalls and perils often associated with money. In addition, we are told that those who develop spiritual wisdom may be rewarded with financial wealth. For example, Proverbs 8:18–21, referring to wisdom, says, "With me are riches and honor, enduring wealth and prosperity. My fruit is better than fine gold; what I yield surpasses choice silver. I walk in the way of righteousness, along the paths of justice, bestowing wealth on those who love me and making their treasuries full." Note that the accumulation of wealth without wisdom is condemned by God as we see in Proverbs 17:16: "Of what use is money in the hand of a fool, since he has no desire to get wisdom?"

Here is another important point to consider. In God's economy, wealth is not accompanied by the stress and strain that we often see in the lives of the wealthy or in those who are in a strenuous head-long pursuit of wealth. Proverbs 10:22 instructs us that "the blessing of the Lord brings wealth, and he adds no trouble to it." And, we are urged in Proverbs 23:4–5: "Do not wear yourself out to get rich; have the wisdom to show restraint. Cast but a glance at riches, and they are gone, for they will surely sprout wings and fly off to the sky like an eagle." Now, contrast the thoughts in this scripture with the multitude of examples that we hear and read about of individuals whose lives are consumed or destroyed by the pursuit of money. Stories also abound about the damage done to lives from the sudden acquisition of wealth through receiving an inheritance, winning a lottery, or gambling.

It takes wisdom and maturity to understand that it is better to have less wealth with "peace" than to experience the stress and spiritual decline that can be associated with the unwise accumulation of wealth. As noted in Proverbs 15:16, "Better a little with the fear of the Lord than great wealth with turmoil," and in Proverbs 17:1 where it reads, "Better a dry crust with peace and quiet than a house full of feasting with strife." King Solomon, the wisest and richest man of his time and any time before him, tells us in Ecclesiastes 5:10: "Whoever loves money never has money enough; whoever loves wealth is never satisfied with his income."

Many people, who have traveled to third-world countries as I have, comment on how much happier the residents of these countries often seem despite having so few material possessions compared to their American counterparts. Even if we do not act like it, most of us know that happiness is not something that can be purchased. The generosity that I have witnessed in the midst of poverty is quite convicting.

For example, a few weeks after the Asian tsunami that struck on December 26, 2004, I traveled with a medical team from Hawaii to provide medical support to the victims in Banda Aceh, Indonesia. The devastation was appalling. There were open mass graves filled with bodies in bags every mile or so along the roads. One of our interpreters had narrowly escaped death by frantically driving his motor scooter to higher ground. He was able to save his sister, mother, and father. All of their possessions, except for their scooter and the clothes on their backs, were lost. He invited me and my team to meet his parents who were staying in an Internally Displaced Persons (IDP) camp a few miles from the hospital where we were working. He said that his mother very much wanted to meet us.

The accommodations at the IDP camp consisted of a plastic tarp under which about fifty metal frame portable cots were arranged. We met our interpreter's mother, sister, and father. The mother expressed her appreciation to us for hiring her son as an interpreter. That is the only income that they were receiving. She proceeded to bring out a small brown paper-wrapped bundle from under her cot. She removed the wrapping paper and there was a small square of plain yellow cake. She divided it up and gave each of us what amounted to a small bite. I tried to refuse, but it was clear that she very much wanted to honor us with this gift. It was all that she had to give. I had to turn away because of the tears that were filling my eyes. This woman had given all that she had out of her poverty.

On another occasion in Banda Aceh, I met a group of Indonesian Christians who had left their jobs in Jakarta to assist with the tsunami relief. We had hired several of them to help us out in the hospital and work as interpreters since they spoke a little English. Keep in mind that these were Christians who volunteered to work in a heavily conservative Muslim area where Christians had been persecuted. In fact, I met one young man that I nicknamed Daniel. Daniel was eighteen-years old. He had been raised by Christian parents in a village not far from where we were working. When Daniel was about twelve, his family was attacked in their home by Muslim extremists. His parents and his younger sister where killed by machete-armed terrorists. The attackers dragged Daniel outside, hacked his arms and legs with their machetes, covered him with brush, poured gasoline over him, and set fire to the brush. They left him for dead. Miraculously, he survived because the brush that covered him was wet and he was somewhat protected although he was still badly burned.

After his attackers left the scene, Daniel crawled into the jungle, bleeding and burned. He told me that he lay in the jungle for at least two weeks, mostly delirious. His wounds became infested with maggots. He remembers that one night he was crying out to God for mercy and then he fell asleep. While he slept, he had the sensation that someone had placed their hand firmly on his back and held it there while he slept. He believes that God sent an angel to comfort him in the night. The next morning, he was discovered by villagers who helped him to safety and nursed him back to health. Orphaned, he was sent to Jakarta to live in an orphanage with other Christian children. As Daniel told me this story and showed me the horrible scars on his body, once again, I had to turn away because of the tears that were filling my eyes. Daniel was giving his life to bring the gospel to the very people who had killed his family and who had tried to take his life only a few years before. Daniel gave all that he had to give out of his poverty.

I do not mean to suggest that it is necessarily wrong to exert ourselves in some endeavor that results in the accumulation of financial wealth. As we saw in a previous chapter, we are expected to work (Gen. 2:15). God makes it clear that He is very much in favor of diligent work and opposed to laziness. Proverbs 24:30–34 reads: "I went past the field of the sluggard, past the vineyard of the man who lacks judgment; thorns had come up everywhere, the ground was covered with weeds, and the stone wall was in ruins. I applied my heart to what I observed and learned a lesson from what I saw; A little sleep, a little slumber, a little folding of the hands to rest—and poverty will come on you like a bandit and scarcity like an armed man." In Proverbs 10:4–5, it says, "Lazy hands make a man poor, but diligent hands bring wealth. He who gathers crops in summer is a wise son, but he who sleeps during harvest is a disgraceful son." And, in Colossians 3:23–24, we are advised, "Whatever you do, work at it with all your heart, as working for the Lord, not for men, since you know that you will receive an inheritance from the Lord as a reward. It is the Lord Christ you are serving." The lesson to keep in mind is that our focus should be on serving God and growing in spiritual wisdom rather than on the accumulation of wealth.

Many Christians struggle with the issue of giving money to the church. Here is my belief based on my study of the scriptures. We are all to give as much as we are able from the wealth that God has given us. In 2 Corinthians 8:2–5, Paul describes an inspiring example of the type of giving that honors God: "And now, brothers, we want you to know about the grace that God has given the Macedonian churches. Out of the most severe trial, their overflowing joy and their extreme poverty welled up in rich generosity. For I testify that they gave as much as they were able, and even beyond their ability." Note that there is no mention of a certain percentage of their net worth that was given.

In Mark 12:41–44, Jesus gave us another example of acceptable giving: "Jesus sat down opposite the place where the offerings were put and watched the crowd putting their money into the temple treasury. Many rich people threw in large amounts. But a poor widow came and put in two very small copper coins, worth only a fraction of a penny. Calling his disciples to him, Jesus said, 'I tell you the truth, this poor widow has put more into the treasury than all the others. They all gave out of their wealth; but she out of her poverty, put in everything—all she had to live on.'" Once again, there is no mention of a specific amount or percentage. The common theme is that we give as much as we are able.

It is also important that when we give, we give with the proper attitude and with the proper motives. In 2 Corinthians 9:7, it says, "Each man should give what he has decided in his heart to give, not reluctantly or under compulsion, for God loves a cheerful giver." We are instructed to give anonymously in Matthew 6:1: "Be careful not to do your 'acts of righteousness' before men, to be seen by them. If you do, you will have no reward from your Father in heaven."

The *attitude* of giving is much more important to God than the *amount* that is given. Remember what Jesus said about our financial priorities: "Do not store up for yourselves treasures on earth, where moth and rust destroy, and where thieves break in and steal. But store up for yourselves treasures in heaven, where moth and rust do not destroy, and where thieves do not break in and steal. For where your treasure is, there your heart will be" (Matt. 6:21). When we truly value the treasure that we have in our salvation, we will develop a heart for giving.

So far, I have been focusing on financial wealth. In addition to financial wealth—money—God blesses each of us with many other forms of wealth: time, talents, opportunity, health, and relationships. In the Parable of the Talents (Matt. 25:14–30), Jesus makes it clear that we have a responsibility to demonstrate a return on the investment of all of the wealth that God has entrusted to us. This is the essence of stewardship. In the reference verses below, try replacing the word "wealth" with these other terms. For example, Proverbs 3:9–10 would read: "Honor the Lord with your wealth [time, talents, opportunities, health, and relationships], with the first fruits of all your crops; then your barns will be filled to overflowing, and your vats will brim over with new wine."

Out of all the wealth that is available to us, *time* is our most valuable possession. How we manage our time impacts our success in managing the other components of our wealth. It is through the *disciplined management of our time* that we can fulfill our obligations to grow in our relationship to God, be available to provide service to others, strengthen our interpersonal relationships, develop greater spiritual wisdom, work to provide for our physical needs, manage our health, develop and use our talents, and capitalize on opportunities. If we are undisciplined in our use of time, then we will be continually frustrated by our "lack of time" and inability to meet our obligations in the important areas listed above. It is vital that all Christians be experts and role models in time management.

Many times in my career as an emergency physician, I have been present at the time of a person's death. I have also provided care to many individuals who were terminally ill and in the end-stages of their illness. While this is, perhaps, the most unpleasant and emotionally taxing role of an emergency physician, it has given me the opportunity and privilege to learn something very important. There are three things that most of my dying patients say that they wish they had placed more value on during their lives: health, relationships, and spiritual matters. Many also say that if they could do their life over, they would spend less of it working. Take a moment to reflect on the priorities of your life that are reflected in how you spend your time. What makes you think that you are going to feel any differently at the time of your death? What can you do now to make sure that you do not have the same regrets? I, for one, am guilty of spending far too much time building a career and far less time constructing a legacy that my family can look to as an example.

This book is evidence that I am trying to spend more time on the important things in life—eternal life. The sudden death of my father-in-law, Jake, was a wake-up call for me and Diane. I took a break—a sabbatical—from the hectic pace of corporate medicine in order to work on this book. During this sabbatical, I was able to travel around the world with my wife and teenage daughters, take my son on a surf trip to Indonesia, visit all of my family and some that my daughters had never met, assist with mission work, visit a close friend who is suffering from leukemia, and reflect on how I can be a better steward of the wealth that God has entrusted to me. I was also able to make myself available to fully enjoy my son's wedding without being distracted by work. We are now committed to spending more time in ministry, with family, and using our wealth (money, time, opportunities, health, and relationships) to serve God.

Here are some key points about stewardship:

- All wealth comes from and belongs to God (1 Chron. 29:11–13).
- Accumulating wealth should not have a higher priority than our service to God and service to others. We should use our wealth to honor God and serve others (Prov. 3:9–10; 11:26; 22:4; 28:20; 30:8–9).
- Wisdom is more valuable in God's economy than monetary wealth (Prov. 3:13–14; 4:7; 8:10–11; 8:18–21; 16:16; 17:16; 19:8; 19:10; 21:20; 22:4; 24:3–4; 28:11; Ec. 7:11–12; 9:16, Luke 16:15).
- We should be generous and not greedy with our wealth (Prov. 3:27–28; 11:24–26; 14:21; 19:17; 21:13; 22:8; 27:20; 28:22; 28:25; 28:27; Ec. 6:7; 2 Cor. 8:2–5; 14–15; 9:6–7; James 2:14–17; 4:17).
- Our wealth should not be used to gain glory for ourselves or enhance our reputation or ego (Prov. 12:9; 13:7).
- Some of our wealth should be saved for the future (Prov. 13:22; 21:20).
- We should behave respectfully and compassionately towards the poor (Prov. 14:21; 14:31; 17:5; 18:23; 19:1; 19:7; 19:17; 21:13; 22:2; 22:16; 22:22–23; 28:11; 29:7; 29:13; 31:8–9; James 2:5–7).
- We should not be prideful about our wealth nor ashamed about our lack of wealth (Prov. 12:9; 13:7; 13:8; 18:11; James 1:9–11; 5:1–6).
- Wealth that is accumulated wisely does not have trouble or strife associated with it (Prov. 10:22; 15:16–17; 17:1; 23:4–5; 28:20; Ec. 4:6–8; 5:12; 5:18–20; 6:2–3).
- Our reputation is more valuable than our wealth. Wealth should not be obtained through immoral or illegal means. Do not accept bribes (Prov. 1:19; 10:2; 10:16; 11:18;

13:11; 15:6; 16:8; 16:19; 17:23; 19:1; 19:22; 21:6; 21:21; 22:1; 28:6; 28:8; 28:16).

- Wealth is wisely accumulated through discipline and hard work (Prov. 10:4; 10:5; 12:11; 12:14; 13:18; 14:23; 20:4; 20:13; 20:21; 21:5; 24:30–34; 28:19; Ec. 10:18–19).
- Debt should be avoided (Prov. 6:1–5; 17:18; 22:7; 22:26–27).
- We should avoid gluttony and excess (Prov. 21:17; 21:20; 22:16; 23:19–21; 29:3).
- Wealth should be guarded against sudden adverse circumstances (Prov. 27:23–27; Ec. 11:1–2).

**Appendix G** contains several reference verses on the subject of wealth and stewardship. Here are some of my favorites:

- 1 Chronicles 29:11–13—"Yours, O Lord, is the greatness and the power and the glory and the majesty and the splendor, for everything in heaven and earth is yours. Yours, O Lord, is the kingdom; you are exalted as head over all. Wealth and honor come from you; you are the ruler of all things. In your hands are strength and power to exalt and give strength to all. Now, our God, we give you thanks, and praise your glorious name."
- Psalm 127:1–2—"Unless the Lord builds the house, its builders labor in vain. Unless the Lord watches over the city, the watchmen stand guard in vain. In vain you rise early and stay up late, toiling for food to eat—for he grants sleep to those he loves."
- Proverbs 1:19—"Such is the end of all who go after ill-gotten gain; it takes away the lives of those who get it."
- Proverbs 3:9–10—"Honor the Lord with your wealth,

with the first fruits of all your crops; then your barns will be filled to overflowing, and your vats will brim over with new wine."

- Proverbs 3:13–14—"Blessed is the man who finds wisdom, the man who gains understanding, for she is more profitable than silver and yields better returns than gold. She is more precious than rubies; nothing you desire can compare with her."
- Proverbs 3:27–28—"Do not withhold good from those who deserve it, when it is in your power to act. Do not say to your neighbor, 'Come back later; I'll give it tomorrow'—when you now have it with you."
- Proverbs 10:4—"Lazy hands make a man poor, but diligent hands bring wealth."
- Proverbs 10:5—"He who gathers crops in summer is a wise son, but he who sleeps during harvest is a disgraceful son."
- Proverbs 10:22—"The blessing of the Lord brings wealth, and he adds no trouble to it."
- Proverbs 11:24—"One man gives freely, yet gains even more; another withholds unduly, but comes to poverty."
- Proverbs 11:25—"A generous man will prosper; he who refreshes others will himself be refreshed."
- Proverbs 11:28—"Whoever trusts in his riches will fall, but the righteous will thrive like a green leaf."
- Proverbs 12:11—"He who works his land will have abundant food, but he who chases fantasies lacks judgment."
- Proverbs 14:21—"He who despises his neighbor sins, but blessed is he who is kind to the needy."
- Proverbs 14:31—"He who oppresses the poor shows

contempt for their Maker, but whoever is kind to the needy honors God."

- Proverbs 15:16—"Better a little with the fear of the Lord than great wealth with turmoil."
- Proverbs 17:16—"Of what use is money in the hand of a fool, since he has no desire to get wisdom?"
- Proverbs 19:17—"He who is kind to the poor lends to the Lord, and he will reward him for what he has done."
- Proverbs 20:21—"An inheritance quickly gained at the beginning will not be blessed at the end."
- Proverbs 21:6—"A fortune made by a lying tongue is a fleeting vapor and a deadly snare."
- Proverbs 21:13—"If a man shuts his ears to the cry of the poor, he too will cry out and not be heard."
- Proverbs 22:1—"A good name is more desirable than great riches; to be esteemed is better than silver or gold."
- Proverbs 22:8—"A generous man will himself be blessed, for he shares his food with the poor."
- Proverbs 22:4—"Humility and the fear of the Lord bring wealth and honor and life."
- Proverbs 22:26–27—"Do not be a man who strikes hands in pledge or puts up security for debts; if you lack the means to pay, your very bed will be snatched from under you."
- Proverbs 23:4–5—"Do not wear yourself out to get rich; have the wisdom to show restraint. Cast but a glance at riches, and they are gone, for they will surely sprout wings and fly off to the sky like an eagle."
- Proverbs 28:20—"A faithful man will be richly blessed, but one eager to get rich will not go unpunished."
- Proverbs 28:22—"A stingy man is eager to get rich and is unaware that poverty awaits him."

- Proverbs 28:27—"He who gives to the poor will lack nothing, but he who closes his eyes to them receives many curses."
- Proverbs 30:8–9—"…give me neither poverty nor riches, but give me only my daily bread. Otherwise, I may have too much and disown you and say, 'Who is the Lord?' Or I may become poor and steal, and so dishonor the name of my God."
- Matthew 6:19–21—"Do not store up for yourselves treasures on earth, where moth and rust destroy, and where thieves break in and steal. But store up for yourselves treasures in heaven, where moth and rust do not destroy, and where thieves do not break in and steal. For where your treasure is, there your heart will be also."
- Matthew 6:24—"No one can serve two masters. Either he will hate the one and love the other, or he will be devoted to the one and despise the other. You cannot serve both God and Money."
- Matthew 19:23–24—"Then Jesus said to his disciples, 'I tell you the truth, it is hard for a rich man to enter the kingdom of heaven. Again I tell you, it is easier for a camel to go through the eye of a needle than for a rich man to enter the kingdom of God.'"
- 1 Timothy 3:2–3—"Now the overseer must be above reproach, the husband of but one wife, temperate, self-controlled, respectable, hospitable, able to teach, not given to drunkenness, not violent but gentle, not quarrelsome, not a lover of money."
- 1 Timothy 6:10—"For the love of money is a root of all kinds of evil. Some people, eager for money, have

wandered from the faith and pierced themselves with many griefs."

- Hebrews 13:5—"Keep your lives free from the love of money and be content with what you have, because God has said, 'Never will I leave you; never will I forsake you.'"
- James 1:9–11—"The brother in humble circumstances ought take pride in his high position. But the one who is rich should take pride in his low position, because he will pass away like a wild flower...In the same way, the rich man will fade away even while he goes about his business."

# CHAPTER EIGHTEEN

# WISE @ HEART IN
# PLANNING FOR THE FUTURE

After completing my medical training, I started my practice of emergency medicine in Southern California. After many years of delayed gratification, Diane and I were ready to start living the American Dream! Within a year of starting my practice, we were able to purchase a small three-bedroom townhome in the North County area of San Diego. Since I had no savings, I had to borrow money from a friend at church to help with the down payment. I could have waited a few months to save the money, but I was impatient and my friend knew that he would be repaid with interest. Besides, the real estate market was in a phase of rapid acceleration at that time. It was a seller's market. Homes were already expensive and prices were going up, up, up. There were bidding wars for property, and sellers were selling for more than their asking price. It was a fast-moving train and I was determined to jump on it.

We loved our townhome. It was *perfect* for us. It had three bedrooms and two baths and was close to the beach. We were thrilled to be living there. At that time, we had one child, a three-year-old son. Soon after moving into our townhome, we were blessed with the arrival of our second child, a daughter. Our good fortune continued. About nine months after the birth of our second child, we discovered that we were expecting a third! Yes, we did finally figure out the cause of all those pregnancies. With the impending birth of our third child, we decided that we *needed* a larger home. It is clear in retrospect that we were confusing *needs* with *wants*.

When we began shopping for a larger home, the housing market in Southern California had begun to decline in value. Just like that. It had only been a couple of years since we had purchased our townhome. It was now a "buyer's market" and we were, once again, ready to buy. The only obstacle was that we had to sell our townhome in order to purchase a larger home. It gradually dawned on us that we had purchased our townhome at the very top of the market. Now, we were probably going to take a loss when we sold our townhome. This was disappointing since we were counting on making a profit on the sale of our townhome to help finance the purchase of the larger home.

We were not going to let that stop us though. We were determined to have our way. We found out that there are a lot of creative ways to buy something that you cannot afford! To make a long story short, because of our impatience and inexperience, we sold our townhome for a loss and then paid too much for a house that was much larger than we needed. That is not a formula for financial success by the way. Faster than you can say "moron," I had placed our family deeply into debt. Of course, I could manage the debt by working longer hours to make more money.

The consequences of our mistake soon became evident. I started to work long strenuous hours. I was working full-time at one ER and moonlighting at a couple of others. I would often work twelve hours at one facility and then drive to another to work another twelve to twenty-four hours. I was rarely home except to sleep. My wife began to experience symptoms of depression. It was exhausting for her to take care of our three young children with little help from me. We rarely attended church because our first move had taken us far from the church we attended and the second move was even farther away. I was either working or too tired to make the long drive in the mini-van with three kids strapped into their car seats. We had few friends since we had little time to build relationships. Those friends that we did have were struggling with the same issues we were struggling with and seemed to be making the same poor decisions that we were making. It became increasingly obvious that a positive change was needed. That is when I learned about a job opportunity in Hawaii.

The job in Hawaii was for much less pay in an area with an even higher cost of living than Southern California. It seemed like a move backwards and, yet, we seemed drawn to it. The community was similar to the community that my wife and I had grown up in—a rural environment that was unlike the hectic Southern California setting where we were struggling to succeed. It was not something that we had been striving for; it had just landed in our lap. In retrospect, I do not think we really thought it through very carefully—not that we ever did think things through very carefully in those days. It just seemed like a better place for us to be at that point in our lives. We had the restlessness that is typical of those who are unhappy and looking in all the wrong places for happiness. I took the job and have never regretted it. Mostly, by accident or through God's divine grace, it turned out to be the right decision. Even though the transition was difficult, the move to Hawaii made a tremendous positive impact on our family. Here is some more of the story:

When we put our California home on the market in preparation for our move to Hawaii, it became apparent that we had paid too much for it in a rapidly declining market. I had already signed the contract to accept the new job in Hawaii, and they were expecting me to start work in about a month. We decided to move even if our house was not sold. After living in Hawaii for about six months, we still had not sold our California home. We were having trouble keeping up with the payments on the house with my reduced salary. We eventually lost the home in foreclosure when a short-sell offer fell through. The irony is that the bank would not agree to a short-sale (an arrangement where the bank agrees to accept less than what is owed on the mortgage) until we were in default on the loan. When the short-sale negotiations fell apart, we were seriously behind on the payments and the bank moved to foreclose.

This is very similar to the situation that a lot of Americans are in at the time of this writing. Foreclosures are at a historical high. Many people have lost their homes and the trend is continuing. It was a very bitter time for us, and I have a great deal of empathy for anyone who has to go through it. The fault was mine for assuming such a large degree of debt. The best thing that came out of it was the valuable lesson that we learned: God will sometimes allow us to have what we want even when it will lead to negative consequences. If we had stayed in the townhome, we could have easily rented it if it did not sell. We would not have lost money on the sale if we had just waited a couple of years.

The situation was much different when we purchased our first home in Hawaii. A colleague and Christian, who lived in our neighborhood, approached me about purchasing his home. He was planning to relocate to the mainland. This was just after our California home was lost in foreclosure. We really had no interest in purchasing another home. We had already lost a lot of money on both of the properties we had purchased and were still bruised and reeling from the experience. We had pretty much decided that it would be many years before we were able to purchase another home. God had other plans.

My colleague made us an offer that we could not refuse. If we purchased his home with his offer of financing, our mortgage would be manageable on my current salary. We have never regretted that home purchase. We lived happily for many years in that neighborhood near our church, my wife's job, and our children's school. My colleague was able to transition to the mainland without leaving a vacant, unsold house behind. It was a blessing for all of us.

Over the years, we have learned that we must make our plans carefully, thoughtfully, and prayerfully as well as incorporate God's wisdom in our decisions and plans. We did not consider God in either of our first two real estate purchases. We did not bother seeking the advice of wiser, more experienced, individuals. Our only interest was in owning a home near the beach. We wanted what we wanted. We acted foolishly and naïvely. We paid a huge financial price for this decision. It could have been devastating. Fortunately, we have been able to recover.

Good stewardship requires that we make prudent plans for the future. Our future is made up of the unspent time that God has entrusted to us. As I pointed out in the previous chapter, time is our most valuable asset. As you might expect, the Bible instructs us through some important principles that we should keep in mind when making plans. In chapter 2, I introduced the concept that God has a plan for the world. His plan includes his generic will for you and for me. His generic will is customized for each of us in that he has given each of us specific gifts (Rom. 12:6). You get to choose how you will uniquely express your obedience—or disobedience—to God through your stewardship of these gifts. Of course, God has the power and authority to overrule any of our plans. Proverbs 16:9 says, "In his heart a man plans his course, but the Lord determines his steps."

We must accept that even if we believe we are acting in accordance with God's will for our lives, we may face adversity and unexpected obstacles. On two occasions, I have taken care of talented surfers with the potential for a career in professional surfing who either lost an arm or a leg due to a shark attack. Each of these individuals—both of them are Christians—demonstrated tremendous courage and perseverance in the face of this sudden setback. Both of these individuals returned to surfing after their injuries. Their faith in God and their determination to continue doing what they loved to do—what God had blessed them with the ability to do—was a great example to all.

When we plan, we should anticipate the possibility of adversity and obstacles to our success. In the example of my home purchase fiasco above, if I would have factored in the possibility of a housing slump in my plans, then I probably would have been reluctant to acquire so much debt. Now, in all my financial decisions, I do my best to determine a best case, worst case, and likely case scenario. I also invested in a formal graduate level management education that has helped me to be a better steward of resources in my professional career as well as in my personal life. This is not necessary for everyone or even most people; it is just what I chose to do.

It is very difficult to make predictions, particularly about the future! When our plans fail, it may be because our plans are not consistent with God's will. Or, it could be that we need to be patient and persevere through adversity. In James 1:2–4, it says "Consider it pure joy, my brothers, whenever you face trials of many kinds, because you know that the testing of your faith develops perseverance. Perseverance must finish its work so that you may be mature and complete, not lacking in anything." I realize that these are not necessarily comforting words and may seem trite when you are facing adversity. However, anyone who has triumphed over adversity will understand what James means. Adversity is an opportunity to grow and become stronger even though it seems unpleasant at the time.

There are circumstances when we may never understand why our perfectly laid plans are not successful. Sometimes, only God knows why; we may not have the capacity to understand. As it says in Isaiah 55:8, "'For my thoughts are not your thoughts, neither are your ways my ways,' declares the Lord." God is God, and we are not. The take-home message for you is that wise stewardship of the wealth, time, opportunities, health, and relationships that God entrusts us with requires thoughtful and wise planning. As Jesus pointed out in the Parable of Talents (Matt. 25:14–30), God expects a return on His investment—the wealth he has given us to manage. We can earn a return on God's investment by using that wealth to serve God and to serve others. 1 Peter 4:10 says, "Each one should use whatever gift he has received to serve others, faithfully administering God's grace in its various forms."

Here are some key points that summarize what the Bible teaches about making plans:

- God has a plan for the world (Job 42:2; Ps. 33:10–11; 40:5; Prov. 16:4; 16:9; 19:21; 20:24; 21:30–31; Is. 14:24; Is. 30:1; 46:11; Jer. 29:11–13; Eph. 1:11; Heb. 11:40).
- God can, and does, help us to succeed in our plans if we live according to His will (Ps. 37:23–24; Prov. 12:5; 16:3; Is. 32:8).
- It is wise to plan our future prudently and factor in the possibility of adversity (Prov. 14:8; 14:15; Ec. 11:1–2; 11:6; 2 Cor. 1:17).
- The plans that make perfect sense to us may not be consistent with God's will (Prov. 14:12; 16:1; 16:25; 20:24; 21:2; Is. 55:8–9).

- There may be positive or negative consequences to the plans we make (Prov. 14:22; 20:4; 21:5; 26:27; Ec. 10:8–9).
- It is good to seek wise advice when we make plans (Prov. 15:22; 20:18; 24:5–6).
- Our plans must include how we are going to utilize the gifts that God has given us to use in His service (Rom. 12:6; 1 Cor. 7:7; 12:4–7; 14:12; 2 Cor. 9:8–9; 1 Peter 4:10).
- We must have pure motives when we plan. God knows our true motives (Prov. 16:2; 21:2; Is. 29:15; James 4:3).
- When making plans, we must place a higher priority on the present than on the future (Prov. 24:7; 27:23–27; Ec. 3:1; 11:4; 11:6).
- We must not be boastful about our future plans or have prideful confidence that our future plans will prevail (Prov. 27:1; Ec. 7:13–14; 9:12; 10:14b; 11:1–2; 11:6; James 4:13–17).

The *Wise @ Heart* make wise plans for the future.
Some verses to consider include:

- Job 42:2—"I know that you can do all things; no plan of yours can be thwarted."
- Psalm 20:4—"May he give you the desire of your heart and make all your plans succeed."
- Psalm 33:10–11—"The Lord foils the plans of the nations; he thwarts the purposes of the peoples. But the plans of the Lord stand firm forever, the purposes of his heart through all generations."
- Psalm 37:23–24—"If the Lord delights in a man's way, he

makes his steps firm; though he stumble, he will not fall, for the Lord upholds him with his hand."

- Psalm 40:5—"Many, O Lord my God, are the wonders you have done. The things you planned for us no one can recount to you; were I to speak and tell of them, they would be too many to declare."
- Proverbs 12:5—"The plans of the righteous are just, but the advice of the wicked is deceitful."
- Proverbs 14:8—"The wisdom of the prudent is to give thought to their ways, but the folly of fools is deception."
- Proverbs14:12—"There is a way that seems right to a man, but in the end it leads to death."
- Proverbs 14:15—"A simple man believes anything, but a prudent man gives thought to his steps."
- Proverbs 14:22—"Do not those who plot evil go astray? But those who plan what is good find love and faithfulness."
- Proverbs 15:22—"Plans fail for lack of counsel, but with many advisers they succeed."
- Proverbs 16:1—"To man belong the plans of the heart, but from the Lord comes the reply of the tongue."
- Proverbs 16:2—"All a man's ways seem innocent to him, but motives are weighed by the Lord."
- Proverbs 16:3—"Commit to the Lord whatever you do, and your plans will succeed."
- Proverbs 16:4—"The Lord works out everything for his own ends—even the wicked for a day of disaster."
- Proverbs 16:9—"In his heart a man plans his course, but the Lord determines his steps."
- Proverbs 16:25—"There is a way that seems right to a man, but in the end it leads to death."

- Proverbs 19:21—"Many are the plans in a man's heart, but it is the Lord's purpose that prevails."
- Proverbs 20:4—"A sluggard does not plow in season; so at harvest time he looks but finds nothing."
- Proverbs 20:18—"Make plans by seeking advice; if you wage war, obtain guidance."
- Proverbs 20:24—"A man's steps are directed by the Lord. How then can anyone understand his own way?"
- Proverbs 21:2—"All a man's ways seem right to him, but the Lord weighs the heart."
- Proverbs 21:5—"The plans of the diligent lead to profit as surely as haste leads to poverty."
- Proverbs 21:30–31—"There is no wisdom, no insight, no plan that can succeed against the Lord. The horse is made ready for the day of battle, but victory rests with the Lord."
- Proverbs 24:5–6—"A wise man has great power, and a man of knowledge increases strength; for waging war you need guidance, and for victory many advisors."
- Proverbs 24:27—"Finish your outdoor work and get your fields ready; after that, build your house."
- Proverbs 26:27—"If a man digs a pit, he will fall into it; if a man rolls a stone, it will roll back on him."
- Proverbs 27:1—"Do not boast about tomorrow, for you do not know what a day may bring forth."
- Proverbs 27:23–27—"Be sure you know the condition of your flocks, give careful attention to your herds; for riches do not endure forever, and a crown is not secure for all generations. When the hay is removed and new growth appears and the grass from the hills is gathered in, the lambs will provide you with clothing, and the goats with

the price of a field. You will have plenty of goat's milk to feed you and your family and to nourish your servant girls."

- Ecclesiastes 3:1—"There is a time for everything, and a season for every activity under heaven."
- Ecclesiastes 7:13–14—"Consider what God has done: Who can straighten what he has made crooked? When times are good, be happy; but when times are bad, consider: God has made the one as well as the other. Therefore, a man cannot discover anything about his future."
- Ecclesiastes 9:12—"Moreover, no man knows when his hour will come: As fish are caught in a net, or birds are taken in a snare, so men are trapped by evil times that fall unexpectedly upon them."
- Ecclesiastes 10:8–9—"Whoever digs a pit may fall into it; whoever breaks through a wall may be bitten by a snake. Whoever splits logs may be endangered by them."
- Ecclesiastes 10:14b—"No one knows what is coming— who can tell what will happen after him?"
- Ecclesiastes 11:1–2—"Cast your bread upon the waters, for after many days you will find it again. Give portions to seven, yes to eight, for you do not know what disaster may come upon the land."
- Ecclesiastes 11:4—"Whoever watches the wind will not plant; whoever looks at the clouds will not reap."
- Ecclesiastes 11:6—"Sow your seed in the morning, and at evening let not your hands be idle, for you do not know which will succeed, whether this or that, or whether both will do equally well."

- Isaiah 14:24—"The Lord Almighty has sworn, 'Surely, as I have planned, so it will be, and as I have purposed, so it will stand.'"
- Isaiah 29:15—"Woe to those who go to great depths to hide their plans from the Lord, who do their work in darkness and think, 'Who sees us? Who will know?'"
- Isaiah 30:1—"'Woe to the obstinate children,' declares the Lord, 'to those who carry out plans that are not mine, forming an alliance, but not by my Spirit, heaping sin upon sin.'"
- Isaiah 32:8—"But the noble man makes noble plans, and by noble deeds he stands."
- Isaiah 46:11—"From the east I summon a bird of prey; from a far off land, a man to fulfill my purpose. What I have said, that will I bring about; what I have planned, that will I do."
- Isaiah 55:8–9—"For my thoughts are not your thoughts, neither are your ways my ways. As the heavens are higher than the earth, so are my ways higher than your ways and my thoughts than your thoughts."
- Jeremiah 29:11–13—"'For I know the plans I have for you,' declares the Lord, 'plans to prosper you and not harm you, plans to give you hope and a future. Then you will call upon me and come and pray to me, and I will listen to you. You will seek me and find me when you seek me with all your heart.'"
- Romans 11:33—"Oh the depth of the riches of the wisdom and knowledge of God! How unsearchable his judgments, and his path beyond tracing out."
- 2 Corinthians 1:17—"When I planned this, did I do it

lightly? Or do I make my plans in a worldly manner so that in the same breath I say, 'Yes, yes' and 'No, no'?"

- 2 Corinthians 9:8–9—"And God is able to make all grace abound to you, so that in all things at all times, having all that you need, you will abound in every good work. As it is written: 'He has scattered abroad his gifts to the poor; his righteousness endures forever.'"

- Ephesians 1:11—"In him we were also chosen, having been predestined according to the plan of him who works out everything in conformity with the purpose of his will."

- Hebrews 11:40—"God had planned something better for us so that only together with us would they be made perfect."

- James 4:3—"When you ask, you do not receive, because you ask with wrong motives, that you may spend what you get on your pleasures."

- James 4:13–17—"Now listen, you who say, 'Today or tomorrow we will go to this or that city, spend a year there, carry on business and make money.' Why, you do not even know what will happen tomorrow. What is your life? You are a mist that appears for a little while and then vanishes. Instead you ought to say, 'If it is the Lord's will, we will live and do this or that.' As it is, you boast and brag. All such boasting is evil. Anyone, then, who knows the good he ought to do and doesn't do it, sins."

- 1 Peter 4:10—"Each one should use whatever gift he has received to serve others, faithfully administering God's grace in its various forms."

# CHAPTER NINETEEN

# THE CONCLUSION OF THE MATTER

*"Now all has been heard; here is the conclusion of the matter:*
*Fear God and keep his commandments, for this is the whole*
*duty of man. For God will bring every deed into judgment,*
*including every hidden thing, whether it is good or evil."*

—ECCLESIASTES 12:13–14

At the time of this writing, the economy of the United States and much of the world is in the throes of the worst recession since the Great Depression. Many people have lost their homes as a result of an inability to pay their mortgages or because they have chosen to stop paying for a home that is worth less than the amount of the mortgage. The housing meltdown initiated a cascade of events, including a massive meltdown in the stock market, further impoverishing many individuals who had invested their hard-earned money with the expectation of growing their wealth.

In an effort to minimize the damage of this economic tsunami, the U.S. government has, so far, issued nearly a trillion dollars of bailout money to failing financial institutions and other key industries as well as programs to restructure personal debt as part of a prescription for economic recovery. Sadly, it appears that some of this money may have been used to pay lavish bonuses to some of the very individuals who were responsible for the demise of these critical institutions. Fraud and abuse have been discovered in our financial system, and many of us have lost confidence in the government's ability to protect our savings and investment dollars.

There are very few people who have not been adversely impacted by this economic recession. Retirements and plans for college have been put on hold by many. Thousands of individuals have lost jobs and the expectation is that the worst may be yet to come. We have a newly elected president who is grappling with this economic devastation as well as dealing with two wars and a health care system that is unraveling. If there was ever a time that wisdom is needed, it is now.

It is my prayer that the leaders of our world will take pause and reflect on the economic consequences that we are all experiencing that appear to be fundamentally a result of greed, selfishness, irresponsibility, and just plain foolishness on the part of those who knew, or should have known, better. I count myself as one of the guilty as I have also made foolish—or, at the very least, less than wise— financial decisions as a result of the unfounded belief that the good times would continue indefinitely. I hope this book has made this very clear: foolishness always has negative consequences. So, we really should not be terribly surprised at the current state of affairs. The prescription for the economic, social, spiritual, financial, political, and relational ills is, and always will be, *wisdom*.

At the end of the day, we all have to give an account for what we have accomplished, or failed to accomplish, on this earth during the few brief days of our lives. For my part, I know that I have fallen short of what God expects of me. I strive for more wisdom and yet often engage in the most unwise activities and make mystifyingly foolish decisions. There appears to be no end to the amount of trouble that I can create for myself by disregarding God's wisdom in my relationships, my marriage, my parenting, my career, my finances, my health, and my spiritual life.

I would very much like to hear from you. Your feedback is important to me—good or bad. If this book has been helpful to you in any way, please write an e-mail to me or the publisher and share your thoughts. Likewise, if you have any suggestions for improvements, I would very much appreciate your input.

Most of all, it is my sincere hope that you will commit to a lifelong pursuit of wisdom. It is also my desire that you will make an investment in those around you and endeavor to impart the wisdom of your experiences to others. Fear God and keep his commandments for this is your whole duty. If you do this, then you will become *Wise @ Heart.*

# Heart Verses

- Exodus 4:21—"The Lord said to Moses, 'When you return to Egypt, see that you perform before Pharaoh all the wonders I have given you the power to do. But I will harden his heart so that he will not let the people go.'"
- Leviticus 19:17—"Do not hate your brother in your heart."
- Deuteronomy 6:5—"Love the Lord your God with all your heart and with all your soul and with all your strength."
- Deuteronomy 10:16—"Circumcise your hearts, therefore, and do not be stiff-necked any longer."
- Deuteronomy 11:18—"Fix these words of mine in your hearts and minds; tie them as symbols on your hands and bind them on your foreheads."
- 1 Samuel 13:14—"But now your kingdom will not endure; the Lord has sought out a man after his own heart and appointed him leader of his people, because you have not kept the Lord's command."
- 1 Samuel 16:7—"But the Lord said to Samuel, 'Do not consider his appearance or his height, for I have rejected him. The Lord does not look at the things man looks at.

Man looks at the outward appearance, but the Lord looks at the heart.'"

- 1 Chronicles 28:9—"And you, my son Solomon, acknowledge the God of your father, and serve him with wholehearted devotion and with a willing mind, for the Lord searches every heart and understands every motive behind the thoughts. If you seek him, he will be found by you; but if you forsake him, he will reject you forever."
- Psalms 14:1—"The fool says in his heart, 'There is no God.'"
- Psalms 51:10—"Create in me a pure heart, O God."
- Psalms 90:12—"Teach us to number our days aright, that we may gain a heart of wisdom."
- Proverbs 1:23—"If you had responded to my rebuke, I would have poured out my heart to you and made my thoughts known to you."
- Proverbs 2:1–5—"My son, if you accept my words and store up my commands within you, turning your ear to wisdom and applying your heart to understanding, and if you call out for insight and cry aloud for understanding, and if you look for it as for silver and search for it as for hidden treasure, then you will understand the fear of the Lord and find the knowledge of God."
- Proverbs 3:1–2—"My son, do not forget my teaching, but keep my commands in your heart, for they will prolong your life many years and bring you prosperity."
- Proverbs 3:3–4—"Let love and faithfulness never leave you; bind them on the tablet of your heart. Then you will win favor and a good name in the sight of God and man."
- Proverbs 3:5–6—"Trust in the Lord with all your heart

and lean not on your own understanding; in all your ways acknowledge him, and he will make your paths straight."

- Proverbs 4:4—"Lay hold of my words with all your heart; keep my commands and you will live."
- Proverbs 4:21—"Do not let them out of your sight; keep them within your heart."
- Proverbs 4:23—"Above all else, guard your heart, for it is the wellspring of life."
- Proverbs 5:12—"…How my heart spurned correction."
- Proverbs 6:16—"There are six things the Lord hates, seven that are detestable to him:

haughty eyes, a lying tongue, hands that shed innocent blood, a *heart* that devises wicked schemes, feet that are quick to rush into evil, a false witness who pours out lies and a man who stirs up dissension among brothers."

- Proverbs 6:21—"Bind them upon your heart forever; fasten them around your neck."
- Proverbs 6:25—"Do not lust in your heart after her beauty or let her captivate you with her eyes."
- Proverbs 7:3—"Bind them on your fingers; write them on the tablet of your heart."
- Proverbs 7:25—"Do not let your heart turn to her ways or stray into her paths."
- Proverbs 10:8—"The wise in heart accept commands, but a chattering fool comes to ruin."
- Proverbs 10:20—"The tongue of the righteous is choice silver, but the heart of the wicked is of little value."
- Proverbs 11:20—"The Lord detests men of perverse heart but he delights in those whose ways are blameless."

- Proverbs 12:20—"There is deceit in the hearts of those who plot evil, but joy for those who promote peace."
- Proverbs 12:23—"A prudent man keeps his knowledge to himself, but the heart of fools blurts out folly."
- Proverbs 12:25—"An anxious heart weighs a man down, but a kind word cheers him up."
- Proverbs 13:12—"Hope deferred makes the heart sick, but a longing fulfilled is a tree of life."
- Proverbs 14:10—"Each heart knows its own bitterness, and no one else can share its joy."
- Proverbs 14:13—"Even in laughter, the heart may ache, and joy may end in grief."
- Proverbs 14:30—"A heart at peace gives life to the body, but envy rots the bones."
- Proverbs 14:33—"Wisdom reposes in the heart of the discerning and even among fools she lets herself be known."
- Proverbs 15:7—"The lips of the wise spread knowledge; not so the hearts of fools."
- Proverbs 15:11—"Death and Destruction lie open before the Lord—how much more the hearts of men!"
- Proverbs 15:13—"A happy heart makes the face cheerful, but heartache crushes the spirit."
- Proverbs 15:14—"The discerning heart seeks knowledge, but the mouth of a fool feeds on folly."
- Proverbs 15:15—"All the days of the oppressed are wretched, but the cheerful heart has a continual feast."
- Proverbs 15:28—"The heart of the righteous weighs its answers, but the mouth of the wicked gushes evil."
- Proverbs 15:30—"A cheerful look brings joy to the heart, and good news gives health to the bones."

- Proverbs 16:1—"To man belong the plans of the heart, but from the Lord comes the reply of the tongue."
- Proverbs 16:5—"The Lord detests all the proud of heart. Be sure of this: They will not go unpunished."
- Proverbs 16:9—"In his heart a man plans his course, but the Lord determines his steps."
- Proverbs 16:21—"The wise in heart are called discerning, and pleasant words promote instruction."
- Proverbs 16:23—"A wise man's heart guides his mouth, and his lips promote instruction."
- Proverbs 17:3—"The crucible for silver and the furnace for gold, but the Lord tests the heart."
- Proverbs 17:20—"A man of perverse heart does not prosper; he whose tongue is deceitful falls into trouble."
- Proverbs 17:22—"A cheerful heart is good medicine, but a crushed spirit dries up the bones."
- Proverbs 18:12—"Before his downfall a man's heart is proud, but humility comes before honor."
- Proverbs18:15—"The heart of the discerning acquires knowledge; the ears of the wise seek it out."
- Proverbs 19:3—"A man's own folly ruins his life, yet his heart rages against the Lord."
- Proverbs 19:21—"Many are the plans in a man's heart, but it is the Lord's purpose that prevails."
- Proverbs 20:5—"The purposes of a man's heart are deep waters, but a man of understanding draws them out."
- Proverbs 20:9—"Who can say, 'I have kept my heart pure; I am clean and without sin'?"
- Proverbs 20:27—"The lamp of the Lord searches the spirit of a man; it searches out his inmost being."

- Proverbs 21:1—"The king's heart is in the hand of the Lord; he directs it like a watercourse wherever he pleases."
- Proverbs 21:2—"All a man's ways seem right to him, but the Lord weighs the heart."
- Proverbs 21:4—"Haughty eyes and a proud heart, the lamp of the wicked are sin!"
- Proverbs 22:11—"He who loves a pure heart and whose speech is gracious will have the king for his friend."
- Proverbs 22:15—"Folly is bound up in the heart of a child, but the rod of discipline will drive it far from him."
- Proverbs 22:17–21—"Pay attention and listen to the sayings of the wise; apply your heart to what I teach, for it is pleasing when you keep them in your heart and have all of them ready on your lips. So that your trust may be in the Lord, I teach you today, even you. Have I not written thirty sayings for you, sayings of counsel and knowledge, teaching you true and reliable words, so that you can give sound answers to him who sent you?"
- Proverbs 23:12—"Apply your heart to instruction and your ears to words of knowledge."
- Proverbs 23:15–16—"My son, if your heart is wise, then my heart will be glad; my inmost being will rejoice when your lips speak what is right."
- Proverbs 23:17–18—"Do not let your heart envy sinners but always be zealous for the fear of the Lord. There is surely a future hope for you, and your hope will not be cut off."
- Proverbs 23:19–21—"Listen, my son, and be wise, and keep your heart on the right path. Do not join those who drink too much wine or gorge themselves on meat, for drunkards and gluttons become poor, and drowsiness clothes them in rags."

- Proverbs 23:26–28—"My son, give me your heart and let your eyes keep to my ways, for a prostitute is a deep pit and a wayward wife is a narrow well. Like a bandit she lies in wait, and multiplies the unfaithful among men."
- Proverbs 24:1—"Do not envy wicked men, do not desire their company; for their hearts plot violence, and their lips talk about making trouble."
- Proverbs 24:11–12—"Rescue those being led away to death; hold back those staggering toward slaughter. If you say, 'But we knew nothing about this,' does not he who weighs the heart perceive it? Will he not repay each person according to what he has done?"
- Proverbs 24:17–18—"Do not gloat when your enemy falls; when he stumbles, do not let your heart rejoice, or the Lord will see and disapprove and turn his wrath away from him."
- Proverbs 24:30–34—"I went past the field of the sluggard, past the vineyard of the man who lacks judgment; thorns had come up everywhere, the ground was covered with weeds, and the stone wall was in ruins. I applied my heart to what I observed and learned a lesson from what I saw: A little sleep, a little slumber, a little folding of the hands to rest—and poverty will come on you like a bandit and scarcity like an armed man."
- Proverbs 25:3—"As the heavens are high and the earth is deep, so the hearts of kings are unsearchable."
- Proverbs 25:20—"Like one who takes away a garment on a cold day, or like vinegar poured on soda, is one who sings songs to a heavy heart."
- Proverbs 26:23–26—"Like a coating of glaze over earthenware are fervent lips with an evil heart. A malicious

man disguises himself with his lips, but in his heart he harbors deceit. Though his speech is charming, do not believe him, for seven abominations fill his heart. His malice may be concealed by deception, but his wickedness will be exposed in the assembly."

- Proverbs 27:9—"Perfume and incense bring joy to the heart, and the pleasantness of one's friend springs from his earnest counsel."
- Proverbs 27:11—"Be wise, my son, and bring joy to my heart; then I can answer anyone who treats me with contempt."
- Proverbs 27:19—"As water reflects a face, so a man's heart reflects the man."
- Proverbs 28:14—"Blessed is the man who always fears the Lord, but he who hardens his heart falls into trouble."
- 1 Kings 9:3–4—"The Lord said to him: 'I have heard the prayer and plea you have made before me; I have consecrated this temple, which you have built, by putting my name there forever. My eyes and my heart will always be there. As for you [Solomon], if you walk before me in integrity of heart and uprightness, as David your father did, and do all I command and observe my decrees and laws, I will establish your royal throne over Israel forever, as I promised David your father when I said, 'You shall never fail to have a man on the throne of Israel.'"
- Ecclesiastes 3:10–11—"I have seen the burden that God has laid on men. He has made everything beautiful in its time. He has also set eternity in the hearts of men; yet they cannot fathom what God has done from beginning to end."
- Ecclesiastes 5:20—"He seldom reflects on the days of his

life, because God keeps him occupied with gladness of heart."

- Ecclesiastes 7:3—"Sorrow is better than laughter, because a sad face is good for the heart."
- Ecclesiastes 7:4—"The heart of the wise is in the house of mourning, but the heart of fools is in the house of pleasure."
- Ecclesiastes 7:7—"Extortion turns a wise man into a fool, and a bribe corrupts the heart."
- Ecclesiastes 7:26—"I find more bitter than death the woman who is a snare, whose heart is a trap and whose hands are chains. The man who pleases God will escape her, but the sinner she will ensnare."
- Ecclesiastes 8:5—"…the wise heart will know the proper time and procedure."
- Ecclesiastes 8:11—"When the sentence for a crime is not quickly carried out, the hearts of the people are filled with schemes to do wrong."
- Ecclesiastes 9:3b—"The hearts of men, moreover, are full of evil and there is madness in their hearts while they live, and afterward they join the dead."
- Ecclesiastes 11:9–10—"Be happy, young man, while you are young, and let your heart give you joy in the days of your youth. Follow the ways of your heart and whatever your eyes see, but know that for all these things God will bring you to judgment. So then, banish anxiety from your heart and cast off the troubles of your body, for youth and vigor are meaningless."
- Jeremiah 17:5—"This is what the Lord says: 'Cursed is the one who trusts in man, who depends on flesh for his strength and whose heart turns away from the Lord.'"

- Jeremiah 17:9—"The heart is deceitful above all things and beyond cure. Who can understand it?"
- Jeremiah 17:10—"I the Lord search the heart and examine the mind, to reward a man according to his conduct, according to what his deeds deserve."
- Jeremiah 24:7—"I will give them a heart to know me, that I am the Lord. They will be my people, and I will be their God, for they will return to me with all their heart."
- Jeremiah 29:13—"You will seek me and find me when you seek me with all your heart."
- Ezekiel 18:31—"Rid yourselves of all the offenses you have committed, and get a new heart and a new spirit."
- Ezekiel 36:26—"I will give you a new heart and put a new spirit in you; I will remove from you your heart of stone and give you a heart of flesh."
- Malachi 4:5–6—"See, I will send you the prophet Elijah before that great and dreadful day of the Lord comes. He will turn the hearts of the fathers to their children, and the hearts of the children to their fathers; or else I will come and strike the land with a curse."
- Matthew 5:8—"Blessed are the pure in heart, for they will see God."
- Matthew 6:21—"For where your treasure is, there your heart will be also."
- Matthew 12:34—"You brood of vipers, how can you who are evil say anything good? For out of the overflow of the heart the mouth speaks."
- Matthew 15:18—"But the things that come out of the mouth come from the heart, and these make a man 'unclean.'"
- Matthew 22:37—"Jesus replied: 'Love the Lord your God

with all your heart and with all your soul and with all your mind. This is the first and greatest commandment.'"

- Luke 16:15—"He said to them, 'You are the ones who justify yourselves in the eyes of men, but God knows your hearts. What is highly valued among men is detestable in God's sight.'"
- John 5:41–42—"I do not accept praise from men, but I know you. I know that you do not have the love of God in your hearts."
- John 14:1—"Do not let your hearts be troubled. Trust in God; trust also in me."
- Acts 4:32—"All the believers were one in heart and mind. No one claimed that any of his possessions was his own, but they shared everything they had."
- Acts 16:14—"One of those listening was a woman named Lydia, a dealer in purple cloth from the city of Thyatira, who was a worshiper of God. The Lord opened her heart to respond to Paul's message."
- Romans 2:15—"…the requirements of the law are written on their hearts."
- Romans 2:29—"No, a man is a Jew if he is one inwardly; and circumcision is circumcision of the heart, by the Spirit, not by the written code. Such a man's praise is not from men, but from God."
- 2 Corinthians 1:21–22—"Now it is God who makes both us and you stand firm in Christ. He anointed us, set his seal of ownership on us, and put his Spirit in our hearts as a deposit, guaranteeing what is to come."
- Ephesians 1:18—"I pray also that the eyes of your heart may be enlightened."
- Ephesians 5:19—"Sing and make music in your heart

to the Lord, always giving thanks to God the Father for everything, in the name of our Lord Jesus Christ."

- Colossians 3:1—"Since, then, you have been raised with Christ, set your hearts on things above, where Christ is seated at the right hand of God."
- Colossians 3:15—"Let the peace of Christ rule in your hearts, since as members of one body you were called to peace."
- Colossians 3:23–24—"Whatever you do, work at it with all your heart, as working for the Lord, not for men, since you know that you will receive an inheritance from the Lord as a reward. It is the Lord Christ you are serving."
- Hebrews 8:10—"This is the covenant I will make with the house of Israel after that time, declares the Lord. I will put my laws in their minds and write them on their hearts. I will be their God and they will be my people."
- James 3:13–18:

Who is wise and understanding among you? Let him show it by his good life, by deeds done in the humility that comes from wisdom. But if you harbor bitter envy and selfish ambition in your hearts, do not boast about it or deny the truth. Such "wisdom" does not come down from heaven but is earthly, unspiritual, of the devil. For where you have envy and selfish ambition, there you find disorder and every evil practice. But the wisdom that comes from heaven is first of all pure; then peace-loving, considerate, submissive, full of mercy and good fruit, impartial and sincere. Peacemakers who so in peace raise a harvest of righteousness.

- James 4:8—"Wash your hands you sinners, and purify your hearts, you double minded."
- 1 John 3:19–24:

This then is how we know that we belong to the truth, and how we set our hearts at rest in his presence whenever our hearts condemn us. For God is greater than our hearts, and he knows everything. Dear friends, if our hearts do not condemn us, we have confidence before God and receive from him anything we ask, because we obey his commands and do what pleases him. And this is his command: to believe in the name of his Son, Jesus Christ, and to love one another as he commanded us. Those who obey his commands live in him, and he in them. And this is how we know that he lives in us: We know it by the Spirit he gave us.

# WISDOM VERSES

- Proverbs 1:7—"The fear of the Lord is the beginning of knowledge, but fools despise wisdom and discipline."
- Proverbs 1:22–33:

Wisdom calls aloud in the street, she raises her voice in the public squares; at the head of the noisy streets she cries out, in the gateways of the city she makes her speech: "How long will you simple ones love your simple ways? How long will mockers delight in mockery and fools hate knowledge? If you had responded to my rebuke, I would have poured out my heart to you and made my thoughts known to you. But since you rejected me when I called and no one gave heed when I stretched out my hand, since you ignored all my advice and would not accept my rebuke, I in turn will laugh at your disaster; I will mock when calamity overtakes you—when calamity overtakes you like a storm, when disaster sweeps over you like a whirlwind, when distress and trouble overwhelm you. Then they will call out to me but I will not answer; they will look for me but will not find me. Since they hated knowledge and did not choose to fear the

Lord, since they would not accept my advice and spurned my rebuke, they will eat the fruit of their ways and be filled with the fruit of their schemes. For the waywardness of the simple will kill them, and the complacency of fools will destroy them; but whoever listens to me will live in safety and be at ease, without fear of harm."

- Proverbs 2:1–22:

My son, if you accept my words, and store up my commands within you, turning your ear to wisdom and applying your heart to understanding, and if you call out for insight and cry aloud for understanding, and if you look for it as for silver and search for it as for hidden treasure, then you will understand the fear of the Lord and find the knowledge of God. For the Lord gives wisdom, and from his mouth come knowledge and understanding. He holds victory in store for the upright, he is a shield to those whose walk is blameless, for he guards the course of the just and protects the way of the faithful ones. Then you will understand what is right and just and fair—every good path. For wisdom will enter your heart, and knowledge will be pleasant to your soul. Discretion will protect you, and understanding will guard you. Wisdom will save you from the ways of wicked men. Wisdom will save you from the adulteress. Thus you will walk in the ways of good men and keep to the paths of the righteous. For the upright will live in the land, and the blameless will remain in it; but the wicked will be cut off from the land, and the unfaithful will be torn from it.

- Proverbs 3:7–8—"Do not be wise in your own eyes; fear the Lord and shun evil. This will bring health to your body and nourishment to your bones."
- Proverbs 3:13–18—"Blessed is the man who finds wisdom, the man who gains understanding for she is more profitable than silver and yields better returns than gold. She is more precious than rubies; nothing you desire can compare with her. Long life is in her right hand; in her left hand are riches and honor. Her ways are pleasant ways, and all her paths are peace. She is a tree of life to those who embrace her; those who lay hold of her will be blessed."
- Proverbs 3:19–20—"By wisdom the Lord laid the earth's foundations, by understanding he set the heavens in place; by his knowledge the deeps were divided, and the clouds let drop the dew."
- Proverbs 3:35—"The wise inherit honor, but fools he holds up to shame."
- Proverbs 4:5—"Get wisdom, get understanding; do not forget my words or swerve from them."
- Proverbs 4:6—"Do not forsake wisdom, and she will protect you; love her and she will watch over you."
- Proverbs 4:7—"Wisdom is supreme; therefore get wisdom. Though it cost all you have, get understanding. Esteem her, and she will exalt you. She will set a garland of grace on your head and present you with a crown of splendor."
- Proverbs 4:11—"I guide you in the way of wisdom and lead you along straight paths. When you walk, your steps will not be hampered; when you run, you will not stumble."
- Proverbs 5:1–2—"My son, pay attention to my wisdom,

listen well to my words of insight, that you may maintain discretion and your lips may preserve knowledge."

- Proverbs 7:4–6—"Say to wisdom, 'You are my sister,' and call understanding your kinsman; they will keep you from the adulteress, from the wayward wife with her seductive words."
- Proverbs 9:1–6—"Wisdom has built her house; she has hewn out its seven pillars. She has prepared her meat and mixed her wine; she has also set her table. She has sent out her maids, and she calls from the highest point of the city. 'Let all who are simple come in here!' she says to those who lack judgment. 'Come, eat my food and drink the wine I have mixed. Leave your simple ways and you will live; walk in the way of understanding.'"
- Proverbs 9:8—"Do not rebuke a mocker or he will hate you; rebuke a wise man and he will love you."
- Proverbs 9:9—"Instruct a wise man and he will be wiser still; teach a righteous man and he will add to his learning."
- Proverbs 9:10–11—"The fear of the Lord is the beginning of wisdom, and knowledge of the Holy One is understanding. For through me your days will be many, and years will be added to your life."
- Proverbs 9:12—"If you are wise, your wisdom will reward you; if you are a mocker, you alone will suffer."
- Proverbs 10:1—"A wise son brings joy to his father, but a foolish son grief to his mother."
- Proverbs 10:8—"The wise in heart accept commands, but a chattering fool comes to ruin."
- Proverbs 10:13—"Wisdom is found on the lips of the discerning, but a rod is for the back of him who lacks judgment."

- Proverbs 10:14—"Wise men store up knowledge, but the mouth of a fool invites ruin."
- Proverbs 10:19—"When words are many, sin is not absent, but he who holds his tongue is wise."
- Proverbs 10:23—"A fool finds pleasure in evil conduct, but a man of understanding delights in wisdom."
- Proverbs 10:31—"The mouth of the righteous brings forth wisdom, but the perverse tongue will be cut out."
- Proverbs 11:2—"When pride comes, then comes disgrace, but with humility comes wisdom."
- Proverbs 11:29—"He who brings trouble on his family will inherit only wind, and the fool will be servant to the wise."
- Proverbs 11:30—"The fruit of the righteous is a tree of life, and he who wins souls is wise."
- Proverbs 12:8—"A man is praised according to his wisdom, but men of warped minds are despised."
- Proverbs 12:18—"Reckless words pierce like a sword, but the tongue of the wise brings healing."
- Proverbs 13:1—"The wise son heeds his father's instruction, but a mocker does not listen to rebuke."
- Proverbs 13:10—"Pride only breeds quarrels, but wisdom is found in those who take advice."
- Proverbs 13:14—"The teaching of the wise is a fountain of life, turning a man from the snares of death."
- Proverbs 13:20—"He who walks with the wise grows wise, but a companion of fools suffers harm."
- Proverbs 14:1—"The wise woman builds her house, but with her own hands the foolish one tears hers down."
- Proverbs 14:3—"A fool's talk brings a rod to his back, but the lips of the wise protect them."

- Proverbs 14:6—"The mocker seeks wisdom and finds none, but knowledge comes easily to the discerning."
- Proverbs 14:8—"The wisdom of the prudent is to give thought to their ways, but the folly of fools is deception."
- Proverbs 14:16—"A wise man fears the Lord and shuns evil, but a fool is hotheaded and reckless."
- Proverbs 14:24—"The wealth of the wise is their crown, but the folly of fools yields folly."
- Proverbs 14:33—"Wisdom reposes in the heart of the discerning and even among fools she lets herself be known."
- Proverbs 14:35—"A king delights in a wise servant, but a shameful servant incurs his wrath."
- Proverbs 15:2—"The tongue of the wise commends knowledge, but the mouth of the fool gushes folly."
- Proverbs 15:7—"The lips of the wise spread knowledge; not so the hearts of fools."
- Proverbs 15:12—"A mocker resents correction; he will not consult the wise."
- Proverbs 15:20—"A wise son brings joy to his father, but a foolish man despises his mother."
- Proverbs 15:24—"The path of life leads upward for the wise to keep him from going down to the grave."
- Proverbs 15:31—"He who listens to a life-giving rebuke will be at home among the wise."
- Proverbs 15:33—"The fear of the Lord teaches a man wisdom, and humility comes before honor."
- Proverbs 16:14—"A king's wrath is a messenger of death, but a wise man will appease it."
- Proverbs 16:16—"How much better to get wisdom than gold, to choose understanding rather than silver."

- Proverbs 16:21—"The wise in heart are called discerning, and pleasant words promote instruction."
- Proverbs 16:23—"A wise man's heart guides his mouth, and his lips promote instruction."
- Proverbs 17:2—"A wise servant will rule over a disgraceful son, and will share the inheritance as one of the brothers."
- Proverbs 17:16—"Of what use is money in the hand of a fool, since he has no desire to get wisdom?"
- Proverbs 17:24—"A discerning man keeps wisdom in view, but a fool's eyes wander to the ends of the earth."
- Proverbs 17:28—"Even a fool is thought wise if he keeps silent, and discerning if he holds his tongue."
- Proverbs 18:4—"The words of a man's mouth are deep waters, but the fountain of wisdom is a bubbling brook."
- Proverbs 18:15—"The heart of the discerning acquires knowledge; the ears of the wise seek it out."
- Proverbs 19:8—"He who gets wisdom loves his own soul; he who cherishes understanding prospers."
- Proverbs 19:11—"A man's wisdom gives him patience; it is to his glory to overlook an offense."
- Proverbs 19:20—"Listen to advice and accept instruction, and in the end, you will be wise."
- Proverbs 20:1—"Wine is a mocker and beer a brawler; whoever is led astray by them is not wise."
- Proverbs 20:26—"A wise king winnows out the wicked; he drives the threshing wheel over them."
- Proverbs 21:11—"When a mocker is punished, the simple gain wisdom; when a wise man is instructed, he gets knowledge."
- Proverbs 21:20—"In the house of the wise are stores of choice food and oil, but a foolish man devours all he has."

- Proverbs 21:22—"A wise man attacks the city of the mighty and pulls down the stronghold in which they trust."
- Proverbs 21:30—"There is no wisdom, no insight, no plan that can succeed against the Lord."
- Proverbs 22:17–21—"Pay attention and listen to the sayings of the wise; apply your heart to what I teach, for it is pleasing when you keep them in your heart and have all of them ready on your lips. So that your trust may be in the Lord, I teach you today, even you. Have I not written thirty sayings for you, sayings of counsel and knowledge, teaching you true and reliable words, so that you can give sound answers to him who sent you?"
- Proverbs 23:19–21—"Listen, my son, and be wise, and keep your heart on the right path. Do not join those who drink too much wine or gorge themselves on meat, for drunkards and gluttons become poor, and drowsiness clothes them in rags."
- Proverbs 24:3–4—"By wisdom a house is built, and through understanding it is established; through knowledge its rooms are filled with rare and beautiful treasures."
- Proverbs 24:5–6—"A wise man has great power, and a man of knowledge increases strength; for waging war you need guidance, and for victory many advisors."
- Proverbs 24:7—"Wisdom is too high for a fool; in the assembly at the gate he has nothing to say."
- Proverbs 24:13–14—"Eat honey, my son, for it is good; honey from the comb is sweet to your taste. Know also that wisdom is sweet to your soul; if you find it, there is future hope for you, and your hope will not be cut off."

- Proverbs 25:12—"Like an earring of gold or an ornament of fine gold is a wise man's rebuke to a listening ear."
- Proverbs 26:12—"Do you see a man wise in his own eyes? There is more hope for a fool than for him."
- Proverbs 27:11—"Be wise, my son, and bring joy to my heart; then I can answer anyone who treats me with contempt."
- Proverbs 28:11—"A rich man may be wise in his own eyes, but a poor man who has discernment sees through him."
- Proverbs 28:26—"He who trusts in himself is a fool, but he who walks in wisdom is kept safe."
- Proverbs 29:3—"A man who loves wisdom brings joy to his father, but a companion of prostitutes squanders his wealth."
- Proverbs 29:8—"Mockers stir up a city, but wise men turn away anger."
- Proverbs 29:9—"If a wise man goes to court with a fool, the fool rages and scoffs, and there is no peace."
- Proverbs 29:11—"A fool gives full vent to his anger, but a wise man keeps himself under control."
- Proverbs 29:15—"The rod of correction imparts wisdom, but the child left to himself disgraces his mother."
- Proverbs 30:2–3—"I am the most ignorant of men; I do not have a man's understanding. I have not learned wisdom, nor have I knowledge of the holy one."
- Proverbs 30:24–28—"Four things on earth are small, yet they are extremely wise: ants are creatures of little strength, yet they store up their food in the summer; coneys are creatures of little power, yet they make their home in the crags; locusts have no king, yet they advance together in ranks; a lizard can be caught with the hand, yet it is found in king's palaces."

- Ecclesiastes 2:26—"To the man who pleases him, God gives wisdom, knowledge and happiness, but to the sinner he gives the task of gathering and storing up wealth to hand it over to the one who pleases God."
- Ecclesiastes 4:13—"Better a poor but wise youth than an old but foolish king who no longer knows how to take warning."
- Ecclesiastes 7:5—"It is better to heed the wise man's rebuke than to listen to the song of fools."
- Ecclesiastes 7:7—"Extortion turns a wise man into a fool, and a bribe corrupts the heart."
- Ecclesiastes 7:10—"Do not say, 'Why were the old days better than these?' For it is not wise to ask such questions."
- Ecclesiastes 7:11–12—"Wisdom, like an inheritance, is a good thing and benefits those who see the sun. Wisdom is a shelter as money is a shelter, but the advantage of knowledge is this: that wisdom preserves the life of its possessor."
- Ecclesiastes 7:16–18—"Do not be overrighteous, neither be overwise—why destroy yourself? Do not be overwicked, and do not be a fool—why die before your time? It is good to grasp the one and not let go of the other. The man who fears God will avoid all extremes."
- Ecclesiastes 7:19—"Wisdom makes one wise man more powerful than ten rulers in a city."
- Ecclesiastes 8:1—"Who is like the wise man? Who knows the explanation of things? Wisdom brightens a man's face and changes its hard appearance."
- Ecclesiastes 9:16—"Wisdom is better than strength. But the poor man's wisdom is despised, and his words are no longer heeded."

- Ecclesiastes 9:17—"The quiet words of the wise are more to be headed than the shouts of a ruler of fools."

- Ecclesiastes 9:18—"Wisdom is better than weapons of war, but one sinner destroys much good."

- Ecclesiastes 10:1—"As dead flies give perfume a bad smell, so a little folly outweighs wisdom and honor."

- Ecclesiastes10:2—"The heart of the wise inclines to the right but, the heart of the fool to the left."

- Ecclesiastes 10:12–14—"Words from a wise man's mouth are gracious, but a fool is consumed by his own lips. At the beginning his words are folly; at the end they are wicked madness—and the fool multiplies words."

- Ecclesiastes 12:11–12—"The words of the wise are like goads, their collected sayings like firmly embedded nails—given by one Shepherd. Be warned, my son, of anything in addition to them. Of making many books there is no end, and much study wearies the body."

- James 1:5–8—"If any of you lacks wisdom, he should ask God, who gives generously to all without finding fault, and it will be given to him. But when he asks, he must believe and not doubt, because he who doubts is like a wave of the sea, blown and tossed by the wind. That man should not think that he will receive anything from the Lord; he is a double-minded man, unstable in all he does."

- James 3:13–18:

Who is wise and understanding among you? Let him show it by his good life, by deeds done in the humility that comes from wisdom. But if you harbor bitter envy and selfish ambition in your hearts, do not boast about it or deny the truth. Such "wisdom" does not come down from heaven but is earthly, unspiritual, of the devil. For where you have envy and selfish ambition, there you find disorder and every evil practice. But the wisdom that comes from heaven is first of all pure; then peace-loving, considerate, submissive, full of mercy and good fruit, impartial and sincere. Peacemakers who sow in peace raise a harvest of righteousness.

- Job 12:12—"Is not wisdom found among the aged? Does not long life bring understanding?"
- Job 12:13—"To God belong wisdom and power; counsel and understanding are his."
- Job 13:5—"If only you would be altogether silent! For you, that would be wisdom."
- Job 28:12–28:

But where can wisdom be found? Where does understanding dwell? Man does not comprehend its worth; it cannot be found in the land of the living. The deep says, "It is not in me"; the sea says, "It is not with me." It cannot be bought with the finest gold, nor can its price be weighed in silver. It cannot be bought with the gold of Ophir, with precious onyx or sapphires. Neither gold nor crystal can compare with it, nor can it be had for jewels of gold. Coral and jasper are not worthy of mention; the price of wisdom is beyond rubies. The topaz of Cush cannot compare with it; it cannot be bought with pure gold. Where then does wisdom come from? Where does understanding dwell? It is hidden from the eyes of every living thing, concealed even from the birds of the air. Destruction and Death say, "Only a rumor of it has reached our ears." God understands the way to it and he alone knows where it dwells for he views the ends of the earth and sees everything under the heavens. When he established the force of the wind and measured out the waters, when he made a decree for the rain and a path for the thunderstorm, then he looked at wisdom and appraised it; he confirmed it and tested it. And he said to man, "The fear of the Lord—that is wisdom, and to shun evil is understanding."

- Colossians 1:9—"For this reason, since the day we heard about you, we have not stopped praying for you and asking God to fill you with the knowledge of his will through all spiritual wisdom and understanding."

# VERSES FOR THE BUILDING BLOCKS OF WISDOM

*Knowledge:*

- 2 Chronicles 1:10—"Give me wisdom and knowledge, that I [Solomon] may lead this people, for who is able to govern this great people of yours?"
- Job 38:2—"Who is this that darkens my [God's] counsel with words without knowledge?"
- Psalm 19:1–2—"The heavens declare the glory of God; the skies proclaim the works of hands. Day after day they pour forth speech; night after night they display knowledge."
- Proverbs 1:7—"The fear of the Lord is the beginning of knowledge, but fools despise wisdom and discipline."
- Proverbs 1:22—"How long will you simple ones love your simple ways? How long will mockers delight in mockery and fools hate knowledge?"
- Proverbs 2:6—"For the Lord gives wisdom, and from his mouth come knowledge and understanding."
- Proverbs 3:19–20—"By wisdom the Lord laid the earth's foundations, by understanding he set the heavens in place;

by his knowledge the deeps were divided, and the clouds let drop the dew."

- Proverbs 5:1–2—"My son, pay attention to my wisdom, listen well to my words of insight, that you may maintain discretion and your lips may preserve knowledge."
- Proverbs 8:10—"Choose my instruction instead of silver, knowledge rather than choice gold."
- Proverbs 9:10—"The fear of the Lord is the beginning of wisdom, and knowledge of the Holy One is understanding."
- Proverbs 9:13—"The woman Folly is loud; she is undisciplined and without knowledge."
- Proverbs 10:14—"Wise men store up knowledge, but the mouth of a fool invites ruin."
- Proverbs 11:9—"With his mouth the godless destroys his neighbor, but through knowledge the righteous escape."
- Proverbs 12:1—"Whoever loves discipline loves knowledge, but he who hates correction is stupid."
- Proverbs 12:23—"A prudent man keeps his knowledge to himself, but the heart of fools blurts out folly."
- Proverbs 13:16—"Every prudent man acts out of knowledge, but a fool exposes his folly."
- Proverbs 14:6—"The mocker seeks wisdom and finds none, but knowledge comes easily to the discerning."
- Proverbs 14:7—"Stay away from the foolish man, for you will not find knowledge on his lips."
- Proverbs 14:18—"The simple inherit folly, but the prudent are crowned with knowledge."
- Proverbs 15:2—"The tongue of the wise commends knowledge, but the mouth of the fool gushes folly."

- Proverbs 15:7—"The lips of the wise spread knowledge; not so the hearts of fools."
- Proverbs 15:14—"The discerning heart seeks knowledge, but the mouth of a fool feeds on folly."
- Proverbs 17:27—"A man of knowledge uses words with restraint, and a man of understanding is even-tempered."
- Proverbs 18:15—"The heart of the discerning acquires knowledge; the ears of the wise seek it out."
- Proverbs 19:2—"It is not good to have zeal without knowledge, nor to be hasty and miss the way."
- Proverbs 19:25—"Flog a mocker, and the simple will learn prudence; rebuke a discerning man, and he will gain knowledge."
- Proverbs 19:27—"Stop listening to instruction, my son, and you will stray from the words of knowledge."
- Proverbs 20:15—"Gold there is, and rubies in abundance, but lips that speak knowledge are a rare jewel."
- Proverbs 21:11—"When a mocker is punished, the simple gain wisdom; when a wise man is instructed, he gets knowledge."
- Proverbs 22:12—"The eyes of the Lord keep watch over knowledge, but he frustrates the words of the unfaithful."
- Proverbs 23:12—"Apply your heart to instruction and your ears to words of knowledge."
- Proverbs 24:3–4—"By wisdom a house is built, and through understanding it is established; through knowledge its rooms are filled with rare and beautiful treasures."
- Proverbs 24:5–6—"A wise man has great power, and a man of knowledge increases strength; for waging war you need guidance, and for victory many advisors."

- Ecclesiastes 2:26—"To the man who pleases him, God gives wisdom, knowledge and happiness, but to the sinner he gives the task of gathering and storing wealth to hand it over to the one who pleases God."
- Ecclesiastes 7:12—"Wisdom is a shelter as money is a shelter, but the advantage of knowledge is this: that wisdom preserves the life of its possessor."
- Hosea 4:6—"...my people are destroyed from lack of knowledge."
- Habakkuk 2:14—"For the earth will be filled with the knowledge of the glory of the Lord, as the waters cover the sea."
- Matthew 13:11–12—"He [Jesus] replied, 'The knowledge of the secrets of the kingdom of heaven has been given to you, but not to them. Whoever has will be given more, and he will have an abundance. Whoever does not have, even what he has will be taken from him.'"
- Romans 1:28—"Furthermore, since they did not think it worthwhile to retain the knowledge of God, he gave them over to a depraved mind, to do what ought not to be done."
- Romans 10:2—"For I can testify about them that they are zealous for God, but their zeal is not based on knowledge."
- 1 Corinthians 8:1—"Knowledge puffs up, but love builds up."
- 1 Corinthians 13:2—"If I have the gift of prophecy and can fathom all mysteries and all knowledge, and if I have a faith that can move mountains, but have not love, I am nothing."
- Colossians 2:2—"My purpose is that they may be encouraged in heart and united in love, so that they may

have the full riches of complete understanding, in order that they may know the mystery of God, namely, Christ, in whom are hidden all the treasures of wisdom and knowledge."

- 1 Timothy 6:20—"Turn away from godless chatter and the opposing ideas of what is falsely called knowledge, which some have professed and in so doing have wandered from the faith."
- 2 Peter 3:18—"But grow in the grace and knowledge of our Lord and Savior Jesus Christ."

*Understanding:*
- Job 12:12–13—"Is not wisdom found among the aged? Does not long life bring understanding? To God belong wisdom and power, counsel and understanding are his."
- Job 28:12—"But where can wisdom be found? Where does understanding dwell?"
- Job 28:23—"God understands the way to it and he alone knows where it dwells."
- Job 28:28—"And He said to man, 'The fear of the Lord— that is wisdom, and to shun evil is understanding.'"
- Job 36:26—"How great is God—beyond our understanding!"
- Psalm 119:130—"The unfolding of your word gives light; it gives understanding to the simple."
- Psalm 147:5—"Great is our Lord and mighty in power; his understanding has no limit."
- Proverbs 2:6—"For the Lord gives wisdom, and from his mouth come knowledge and understanding."
- Proverbs 2:9–11—"Then you will understand what is right and just and fair—every good path. For wisdom will enter

your heart and knowledge will be pleasant to your soul. Discretion will protect you, and understanding will guard you."

- Proverbs 3:5—"Trust in the Lord with all your heart and lean not on your own understanding."
- Proverbs 3:13—"Blessed is the man who finds wisdom, the man who gains understanding."
- Proverbs 3:19–20—"By wisdom the Lord laid the earths foundations, by understanding he set the heavens in place; by his knowledge the deeps were divided, and the clouds let drop the dew."
- Proverbs 4:5—"Get wisdom, get understanding; do not forget my words or swerve from them."
- Proverbs 7:4–6—"Say to wisdom, 'You are my sister,' and call understanding your kinsman."
- Proverbs 10:23—"A fool finds pleasure in evil conduct, but a man of understanding delights in wisdom."
- Proverbs 11:12—"A man who lacks judgment derides his neighbor, but a man of understanding holds his tongue."
- Proverbs 13:15—"Good understanding wins favor, but the way of the unfaithful is hard."
- Proverbs 14:29—"A patient man has great understanding, but a quick-tempered man displays folly."
- Proverbs 15:21—"Folly delights a man who lacks judgment, but a man of understanding keeps a straight course."
- Proverbs 15:32—"He who ignores discipline despises himself, but whoever heeds correction gains understanding."
- Proverbs 16:16—"How much better to get wisdom than gold, to choose understanding rather than silver!"

- Proverbs 16:22—"Understanding is a fountain of life to those who have it, but folly brings punishment to fools."
- Proverbs 17:27—"A man of knowledge uses words with restraint, and a man of understanding is even-tempered."
- Proverbs 18:2—"A fool finds no pleasure in understanding but delights in airing his own opinions."
- Proverbs 19:8—"He who gets wisdom loves his own soul; he who cherishes understanding prospers."
- Proverbs 20:5—"The purposes of a man's heart are deep waters, but a man of understanding draws them out."
- Proverbs 21:16—"A man who strays from the path of understanding comes to rest in the company of the dead."
- Proverbs 24:3–4—"By wisdom a house is built, and through understanding it is established; through knowledge its rooms are filled with rare and beautiful treasures."
- Ecclesiastes 11:5—"As you do not know the path of the wind, or how the body is formed in a mother's womb, so you cannot understand the work of God, the Maker of all things."
- Isaiah 11:2—"The spirit of the Lord will rest on him—the Spirit of wisdom and of understanding, the Spirit of counsel and power, the Spirit of knowledge and of the fear of the Lord—and he will delight in the fear of the Lord."
- Matthew 13:15—"For this people's heart has become calloused; they hardly hear with their ears, for they have closed their eyes. Otherwise they might see with their eyes, hear with their ears, understand with their hearts and turn, and I would heal them."
- Ephesians 1:7–8—"In him we have redemption through his blood, the forgiveness of sins, in accordance with

the riches of God's grace that he lavished on us with all wisdom and understanding."

- Ephesians 5:17—"Therefore do not be foolish, but understand what the Lord's will is."
- James 1:22–25—"Do not merely listen to the word, and so deceive yourselves. Do what it says. Anyone who listens to the word but does not do what it says is like a man who looks at his face in a mirror and, after looking at himself, goes away and immediately forgets what he looks like. But the man who looks intently into the perfect law that gives freedom, and continues to do this, not forgetting what he has heard, but doing it—he will be blessed in what he does."

*Discernment:*
- 1 Kings 3:9–12—"So give your servant a discerning heart to govern your people and to distinguish between right and wrong...The Lord was pleased that Solomon had asked for this. So God said to him, 'Since you have asked for this and not for long life or wealth for yourself, nor have you asked for the death of your enemies but for discernment in administering justice, I will do what you have asked. I will give you a wise and discerning heart.'"
- Proverbs 3:21—"My son, preserve sound judgment and discernment, do not let them out of your sight."
- Proverbs 8:8–9—"All the words of my mouth are just; none of them is crooked or perverse. To the discerning all of them are right; they are faultless to those who have knowledge."
- Proverbs 10:13—"Wisdom is found on the lips of the

discerning, but a rod is for the back of him who lacks judgment."

- Proverbs 14:6—"The mocker seeks wisdom and finds none, but knowledge comes easily to the discerning."
- Proverbs 14:33—"Wisdom reposes in the heart of the discerning and even among fools she lets herself be known."
- Proverbs 15:14—"The discerning heart seeks knowledge, but the mouth of a fool feeds on folly."
- Proverbs 16:21—"The wise in heart are called discerning, and pleasant words promote instruction."
- Proverbs 17:10—"A rebuke impresses a man of discernment more than a hundred lashes a fool."
- Proverbs 17:24—"A discerning man keeps wisdom in view, but a fool's eyes wander to the ends of the earth."
- Proverbs 17:28—"Even a fool is thought wise if he keeps silent, and discerning if he holds his tongue."
- Proverbs 18:15—"The heart of the discerning acquires knowledge; the ears of the wise seek it out."
- Proverbs 19:25—"Flog a mocker, and the simple will learn prudence; rebuke a discerning man, and he will gain knowledge."
- Proverbs 28:7—"He who keeps the law is a discerning son, but a companion of gluttons disgraces his father."
- Proverbs 28:11—"A rich man may be wise in his own eyes, but a poor man who has discernment sees through him."
- 1 Corinthians 2:14—"The man without the Spirit does not accept the things that come from the Spirit of God, for they are foolishness to him, and he cannot understand them, because they are spiritually discerned."
- Philippians 1:9–10—"And this is my prayer: that your love

- may abound more and more in knowledge and depth of insight, so that you may be able to discern what is best."
- Hebrews 5:14—"But solid food is for the mature, who by constant use have trained themselves to distinguish good from evil."

*Judgment:*
- 1 Samuel 25:33—"May you be blessed for your good judgment."
- Psalm 119:66—"Teach me knowledge and good judgment, for I believe in your commands."
- Proverbs 3:21–26—"My son, preserve sound judgment and discernment, do not let them out of your sight; they will be a life to you, an ornament to grace your neck. Then you will go on your way in safety, and your foot will not stumble; when you lie down, you will not be afraid; when you lie down, your sleep will be sweet. Have no fear of sudden disaster or of the ruin that overtakes the wicked, for the Lord will be your confidence and will keep your foot from being snared."
- Proverbs 6:32—"But a man who commits adultery lacks judgment; whoever does so destroys himself."
- Proverbs 9:4—"'Let all who are simple come in here!' she says to those who lack judgment."
- Proverbs 10:13—"Wisdom is found on the lips of the discerning, but a rod is for the back of him who lacks judgment."
- Proverbs 10:21—"The lips of the righteous nourish many, but fools die for lack of judgment."
- Proverbs 11:12—"A man who lacks judgment derides his neighbor, but a man of understanding holds his tongue."

- Proverbs 12:11—"He who works his land will have abundant food, but he who chases fantasies lacks judgment."
- Proverbs 12:21—"Folly delights a man who lacks judgment, but a man of understanding keeps a straight course."
- Proverbs 17:18—"A man lacking in judgment strikes hands in pledge and puts up security for his neighbor."
- Proverbs 18:1—"An unfriendly man pursues selfish ends; he defies all sound judgment."
- Proverbs 24:30–34—"I went past the field of the sluggard, past the vineyard of the man who lacks judgment; thorns had come up everywhere, the ground was covered with weeds, and the stone wall was in ruins. I applied my heart to what I observed and learned a lesson from what I saw: A little sleep, a little slumber, a little folding of the hands to rest—and poverty will come on you like a bandit and scarcity like an armed man."
- Proverbs 28:16—"A tyrannical ruler lacks judgment, but he who hates ill gotten gain will enjoy long life."
- John 7:24—"Stop judging by mere appearances, and make a right judgment."

*Prudence:*
- Proverbs 8:5—"You who are simple, gain prudence; you who are foolish, gain understanding."
- Proverbs 12:16—"A fool shows his annoyance at once, but a prudent man overlooks an insult."
- Proverbs 12:23—"A prudent man keeps his knowledge to himself, but the heart of fools blurts out folly."
- Proverbs 13:16—"Every prudent man acts out of knowledge, but a fool exposes his folly."

- Proverbs 14:8—"The wisdom of the prudent is to give thought to their ways, but the folly of fools is deception."
- Proverbs 14:15—"A simple man believes anything, but a prudent man gives thought to his steps."
- Proverbs 14:18—"The simple inherit folly, but the prudent are crowned with knowledge."
- Proverbs 15:5—"A fool spurns his father's discipline, but whoever heeds correction shows prudence."
- Proverbs 19:14—"Houses and wealth are inherited from parents, but a prudent wife is from the Lord."
- Proverbs 19:25—"Flog a mocker, and the simple will learn prudence; rebuke a discerning man, and he will gain knowledge."
- Proverbs 22:3—"A prudent man sees danger and takes refuge, but the simple keep going and suffer for it."
- Amos 5:13—"Therefore the prudent man keeps quiet in such times, for the times are evil."

*Discretion:*
- 1 Chronicles 22:12—"May the Lord give you discretion and understanding when he puts you in command over Israel, so that you may keep the law of the Lord your God."
- Proverbs 1:4—"...for giving prudence and discretion to the simple, knowledge and discretion to the young."
- Proverbs 2:11—"Discretion will protect you, and understanding will guard you."
- Proverbs 5:1–2—"My son, pay attention to my wisdom, listen well to my words of insight, that you may maintain discretion and your lips may preserve knowledge."
- Proverbs 11:22—"Like a gold ring in a pig's snout is a

beautiful woman who shows no discretion."

- Proverbs 25:20—"Like one who takes away a garment on a cold day, or like vinegar poured on soda, is one who sings songs to a heavy heart."
- Proverbs 26:17—"Like one who seizes a dog by the ears is a passer-by who meddles in a quarrel not his own."
- Proverbs 26:18—"Like a madman shooting firebrands or deadly arrows is a man who deceives his neighbor and says, 'I was only joking!'"
- Proverbs 27:14—"If a man loudly blesses his neighbor early in the morning, it will be taken as a curse."

# ALTERNATIVES TO WISDOM

*Reference Verses for Fools:*
- Proverbs 1:7—"The fear of the Lord is the beginning of knowledge but fools despise wisdom and discipline."
- Proverbs 1:22—"How long will you simple ones love your simple ways? How long will mockers delight in mockery and fools hate knowledge?"
- Proverbs 1:32—"…the complacency of fools will destroy them."
- Proverbs 3:35—"The wise inherit honor, but fools he holds up to shame."
- Proverbs 5:23—"He will die for lack of discipline, led astray by his own great folly."
- Proverbs 8:5—"You who are simple gain prudence; you who are foolish gain understanding."
- Proverbs 9:13–18—"The woman Folly is loud; she is undisciplined and without knowledge. She sits at the door of her house, on a seat at the highest point of the city, calling out to those who pass by, who go straight on their way. 'Let all who are simple come in here!' she says to those who lack judgment. 'Stolen water is sweet; food eaten in

secret is delicious!' But little do they know that the dead are there, that her guests are in the depths of the grave."

- Proverbs 10:1—"A wise son brings joy to his father, but a foolish son grief to his mother."
- Proverbs 10:8—"The wise in heart accept commands, but a chattering fool comes to ruin."
- Proverbs 10:10—"He who winks maliciously causes grief and a chattering fool comes to ruin."
- Proverbs 10:14—"Wise men store up knowledge, but the mouth of a fool invites ruin."
- Proverbs 10:18—"He who conceals his hatred has lying lips, and whoever spreads slander is a fool."
- Proverbs 10:21—"The lips of the righteous nourish many, but fools die for lack of judgment."
- Proverbs 10:23—"A fool finds pleasure in evil conduct, but a man of understanding delights in wisdom."
- Proverbs 11:29—"He who brings trouble on his family will inherit only the wind, and the fool will be servant to the wise."
- Proverbs 12:15—"The way of a fool seems right to him, but a wise man listens to advice."
- Proverbs 12:16—"A fool shows his annoyance at once, but a prudent man overlooks an insult."
- Proverbs 12:23—"A prudent man keeps his knowledge to himself, but the heart of fools blurts out folly."
- Proverbs 13:16—"Every prudent man acts out of knowledge, but a fool exposes his folly."
- Proverbs 13:19—"A longing fulfilled is sweet to the soul, but fools detest turning from evil."
- Proverbs 13:19—"He who walks with the wise grows wise, but a companion of fools suffers harm."

- Proverbs 14:3—"A fool's talk brings a rod to his back, but the lips of the wise protect them."
- Proverbs 14:7—"Stay away from a foolish man, for you will not find knowledge on his lips."
- Proverbs 14:8—"The wisdom of the prudent is to give thought to their ways, but the folly of fools is deception."
- Proverbs 14:9—"Fools mock at making amends for sin, but goodwill is found among the upright."
- Proverbs 14:16–17—"A wise man fears the Lord and shuns evil, but fool is hotheaded and reckless. A quick-tempered man does foolish things, and a crafty man is hated."
- Proverbs 14:18—"The simple inherit folly, but the prudent are crowned with knowledge."
- Proverbs 14:24—"The wealth of the wise is their crown, but the folly of fools yields folly."
- Proverbs 15:2—"The tongue of the wise commends knowledge, but the mouth of the fool gushes folly."
- Proverbs 15:4—"A fool spurns his father's discipline, but whoever heeds correction shows prudence."
- Proverbs 15:7—"The lips of the wise spread knowledge; not so the hearts of fools."
- Proverbs 15:14—"The discerning heart seeks knowledge, but the mouth of the fool feeds on folly."
- Proverbs 15:20—"A wise son brings joy to his father, but a foolish man despises his mother."
- Proverbs 15:21—"Folly delights a man who lacks judgment, but a man of understanding keeps a straight course."
- Proverbs 16:22—"Understanding is a fountain of life to those who have it, but folly brings punishment to fools."
- Proverbs 17:7—"Arrogant lips are unsuited to a fool—how much worse lying lips to a ruler."

- Proverbs 17:10—"A rebuke impresses a man of discernment, more than a hundred lashes a fool."
- Proverbs 17:12—"Better to meet a bear robbed of her cubs than a fool in his folly."
- Proverbs 17:16—"Of what use is money in the hand of a fool, since he has no desire to get wisdom?"
- Proverbs 17:24—"A discerning man keeps wisdom in view, but a fool's eyes wander to the ends of the earth."
- Proverbs 17:28—"Even a fool is thought wise if he keeps silent, and discerning if he holds his tongue."
- Proverbs 18:2—"A fool finds no pleasure in understanding but delights in airing his own opinions."
- Proverbs 18:6—"A fool's lips bring him strife, and his mouth invites a beating."
- Proverbs 18:7—"A fool's mouth is his undoing and his lips are a snare to his soul."
- Proverbs 18:13—"He who answers before listening—that is his folly and his shame."
- Proverbs 19:1—"Better a poor man whose walk is blameless than a fool whose lips are perverse."
- Proverbs 19:3—"A man's own folly ruins his life, yet his heart rages against the Lord."
- Proverbs 19:10—"It is not fitting for a fool to live in luxury—how much worse for a slave to rule over princes!"
- Proverbs 19:29—"Penalties are prepared for mockers, and beatings for the backs of fools."
- Proverbs 20:3—"It is to a man's honor to avoid strife, but every fool is quick to quarrel."
- Proverbs 21:20—"In the house of the wise are stores of choice food and oil, but a foolish man devours all he has."

- Proverbs 22:15—"Folly is bound up in the heart of a child, but the rod of discipline will drive it far from him."
- Proverbs 23:9—"Do not speak to a fool, for he will scorn the wisdom of your words."
- Proverbs 24:7—"Wisdom is too high for a fool; in the assembly at the gate he has nothing to say."
- Proverbs 24:8–9—"He who plots evil will be known as a schemer. The schemes of folly are sin, and men detest a mocker."
- Proverbs 26:1—"Like snow in summer or rain in harvest, honor is not fitting for a fool."
- Proverbs 26:3—"A whip for the horse, a halter for the donkey, and a rod for the backs of fools!"
- Proverbs 26:4–5—"Do not answer a fool according to his folly, or you will be like him yourself. Answer a fool according to his folly, or he will be wise in his own eyes."
- Proverbs 26:6—"Like cutting off one's feet or drinking violence is the sending of a message by the hand of a fool."
- Proverbs 26:7—"Like a lame man's legs that hang limp is a proverb in the mouth of a fool."
- Proverbs 26:8—"Like tying a stone in a sling is the giving of honor to a fool."
- Proverbs 26:9—"Like a thornbush in a drunkard's hand is a proverb in the mouth of a fool."
- Proverbs 26:10—"Like an archer who wounds at random is he who hires a fool or any passer-by."
- Proverbs 26:11—"As a dog returns to his vomit, so a fool repeats his folly."
- Proverbs 26:12—"Do you see a man wise in his own eyes? There is more hope for a fool than for him."

- Proverbs 27:3—"Stone is heavy and sand a burden, but provocation by a fool is heavier than both."
- Proverbs 27:22—"Though you grind a fool in a mortar, grinding him like grain with a pestle, you will not remove his folly from him."
- Proverbs 28:26—"He who trusts in himself is a fool, but he who walks in wisdom is kept safe."
- Proverbs 29:9—"If a wise man goes to court with a fool, the fool rages and scoffs, and there is no peace."
- Proverbs 29:11—"A fool gives full vent to his anger, but a wise man keeps himself under control."
- Proverbs 29:20—"Do you see a man who speaks in haste? There is more hope for a fool than for him."
- Proverbs 30:32—"If you have played the fool and exalted yourself, or if you have planned evil, clap your hand over your mouth!"
- Ecclesiastes 4:5—"The fool folds his hands and ruins himself."
- Ecclesiastes 5:1—"Guard your steps when you go to the house of God. Go near to listen rather than to offer the sacrifice of fools, who do not know that they do wrong."
- Ecclesiastes 5:3—"As a dream comes when there are many cares, so the speech of a fool when there are many words."
- Ecclesiastes 7:5—"It is better to heed a wise man's rebuke than to listen to the song of fools."
- Ecclesiastes 7:6—"Like the crackling of thorns under the pot, so is the laughter of fools."
- Ecclesiastes 7:7—"Extortion turns a wise man into a fool, and a bribe corrupts the heart."
- Ecclesiastes 7:8—"Do not be quickly provoked in your spirit, for anger resides in the lap of fools."

- Ecclesiastes 10:1—"As dead flies give perfume a bad smell, so a little folly outweighs wisdom and honor."
- Ecclesiastes 10:2—"The heart of the wise inclines to the right, but the heart of the fool to the left."
- Ecclesiastes 10:3—"Even as he walks along the road, the fool lacks sense and shows everyone how stupid he is."
- Ecclesiastes 10:12–14—"Words from a wise man's mouth are gracious, but a fool is consumed by his own lips. At the beginning his words are folly; at the end they are wicked madness—and the fool multiplies words."
- Ecclesiastes 10:15—"A fool's work worries him; he does not know the way to town."

*Reference Verses for Mockers:*
- Proverbs 1:22—"How long will you simple ones love your simple ways? How long will mockers delight in mockery and fools hate knowledge?"
- Proverbs 9:7–9—"Whoever corrects a mocker invites insult; whoever rebukes a wicked man incurs abuse. Do not rebuke a mocker or he will hate you; rebuke a wise man and he will love you. Instruct a wise man and he will be wiser still; teach a righteous man and he will add to his learning."
- Proverbs 13:1—"A wise son heeds his father's instruction, but a mocker does not listen to rebuke."
- Proverbs 14:6—"The mocker seeks wisdom and finds none, but knowledge comes easily to the discerning."
- Proverbs 15:12—"A mocker resents correction; he will not consult the wise."
- Proverbs 19:25—"Flog a mocker, and the simple will learn prudence; rebuke a discerning man, and he will gain knowledge."

- Proverbs 19:29—"Penalties are prepared for mockers, and beatings for the backs of fools."
- Proverbs 21:11—"When a mocker is punished, the simple gain wisdom; when a wise man is instructed, he gets knowledge."
- Proverbs 21:24—"The proud and arrogant man— 'Mocker' is his name; he behaves with overweening pride."
- Proverbs 22:10—"Drive out the mocker, and out goes strife; quarrels and insults are ended."
- Proverbs 24:8–9—"He who plots evil will be known as a schemer. The schemes of folly are sin, and men detest a mocker."
- Proverbs 29:8—"Mockers stir up a city, but wise men turn away anger."
- Proverbs 29:9—"If a wise man goes to court with a fool, the fool rages and scoffs [mocks], and there is no peace."

*Reference Verses for the Simple (Immature/Naïve):*
- Proverbs 1:22—"How long will you simple ones love your simple ways? How long will mockers delight in mockery and fools hate knowledge?"
- Proverbs 1:32—"For the waywardness of the simple will kill them."
- Proverbs 7:7—"I saw among the simple, I noticed among the young men, a youth who lacked judgment."
- Proverbs 8:5—"You who are simple gain prudence; you who are foolish, gain understanding."
- Proverbs 9:6—"Leave your simple ways and you will live; walk in the way of understanding."
- Proverbs 9:13–18 —"The woman Folly is loud; she is undisciplined and without knowledge. She sits at the door

of her house, on a seat at the highest point of the city, calling out to those who pass by, who go straight on their way. 'Let all who are simple come in here!' she says to those who lack judgment. 'Stolen water is sweet; food eaten in secret is delicious!' But little do they know that the dead are there, that her guests are in the depths of the grave."

- Proverbs 14:15—"A simple man believes anything, but a prudent man gives thought to his steps."
- Proverbs 14:18—"The simple inherit folly, but the prudent are crowned with knowledge."
- Proverbs 21:11—"When a mocker is punished, the simple gain wisdom; when a wise man is instructed, he gets knowledge."
- Proverbs 22:3—"A prudent man sees danger and takes refuge, but the simple keep going and suffer for it."
- Proverbs 27:12—"The prudent see danger and take refuge, but the simple keep going and suffer for it."

# VERSES FOR OBEDIENCE AND SUBMISSION

- Proverbs 3:1–2—"My son, do not forget my teaching but keep my commands in your heart, for they will prolong your life many years and bring you prosperity."
- Proverbs 3:7–8—"Do not be wise in your own eyes; fear the Lord and shun evil. This will bring health to your body and nourishment to your bones."
- Proverbs 4:10–12—"Listen, my son, accept what I say, and the years of your life will be many. I guide you in the way of wisdom and lead you along straight paths. When you walk, your steps will not be hampered; when you run, you will not stumble."
- Proverbs 5:21—"For a man's ways are in full view of the Lord, and he examines all his paths."
- Proverbs 10:8—"The wise in heart accept commands, but a chattering fool comes to ruin."
- Proverbs 10:27—"The fear of the Lord adds length to life, but the years of the wicked are cut short."
- Proverbs 10:29—"The way of the Lord is a refuge for the righteous, but it is the ruin of those who do evil."

- Proverbs 13:13—"He who scorns instruction will pay for it, but he who respects a command is rewarded."
- Proverbs 14:2—"He whose walk is upright fears the Lord, but he whose ways are devious despises him."
- Proverbs 14:16—"A wise man fears the Lord and shuns evil, but a fool is hotheaded and reckless."
- Proverbs 14:26—"He who fears the Lord has a secure fortress, and for his children it will be a refuge."
- Proverbs 14:27—"The fear of the Lord is a fountain of life, turning a man from the snares of death."
- Proverbs 16:12—"Kings detest wrongdoing, for a throne is established through righteousness."
- Proverbs 16:13—"Kings take pleasure in honest lips; they value a man who speaks the truth."
- Proverbs 16:14—"A king's wrath is a messenger of death, but a wise man will appease it."
- Proverbs 16:15—"When a king's face brightens, it means life; his favor is like a rain cloud in spring."
- Proverbs 19:16—"He who obeys instructions guards his life, but he who is contemptuous of his ways will die."
- Proverbs 19:20—"Listen to advice and accept instruction, and in the end you will be wise."
- Proverbs 19:23—"The fear of the Lord leads to life: Then one rests content, untouched by trouble."
- Proverbs 20:2—"A king's wrath is like the roar of a lion; he who angers him forfeits his life."
- Proverbs 21:1—"The king's heart is in the hand of the Lord; he directs it like a watercourse wherever he pleases."
- Proverbs 24:21–22—"Fear the Lord and the king, my son, and do not join with the rebellious, for those two will

send sudden destruction upon them, and who knows what calamities they can bring?"

- Proverbs 28:7—"He who keeps the law is a discerning son, but a companion of gluttons disgraces his father."
- Proverbs 28:9—"If anyone turns a deaf ear to the law, even his prayers are detestable."
- Proverbs 28:14—"Blessed is the man who always fears the Lord, but he who hardens his heart falls into trouble."
- Proverbs 29:18—"Where there is no revelation, the people cast off restraint; but blessed is he who keeps the law."
- Proverbs 29:25—"Fear of man will prove to be a snare, but whoever trusts in the Lord is kept safe."
- Proverbs 30:5–6—"Every word of God is flawless; he is a shield to those who take refuge in him. Do not add to his words or he will rebuke you and prove you a liar."
- Proverbs 30:17—"The eye that mocks a father, that scorns obedience to a mother, will be pecked out by the ravens of the valley, will be eaten by the vultures."
- Romans 1:5–6—"Through him and for his name's sake, we received grace and apostleship to call people from among all the Gentiles to the obedience that comes from faith. And you also are among those who are called to belong to Jesus Christ."
- Romans 6:16—"Don't you know that when you offer yourselves to someone to obey him as slaves, you are slaves to the one whom you obey—whether you are slaves to sin, which leads to death, or to obedience, which leads to righteousness?"
- Romans 13:1–7:

Everyone must submit himself to the governing authorities, for there is no authority for there is no authority except that which God has established. Consequently he who rebels against the authority is rebelling against what God has instituted, and those who do so will bring judgment on themselves. For rulers hold no terror for those who do right, but for those who do wrong. Do you want to be free from fear from the one in authority? Then do what is right and he will commend you. For he is God's servant to do you good. But if you do wrong, be afraid, for he does not bear the sword for nothing. He is God's servant, an agent of wrath to bring punishment on the wrongdoer. Therefore, it is necessary to submit to the authorities, not only because of possible punishment but also because of conscience. This is also why you pay taxes, for the authorities are God's servants, who give their full time to governing. Give everyone what you owe him: if you owe taxes, pay taxes; if revenue, then revenue; if respect, then respect; if honor, then honor.

- 1 Corinthians 14:34—"As in all congregations of the saints, women should remain silent in the churches. They are not allowed to speak, but must be in submission, as the Law says."
- 1 Corinthians 16:15–16—"You know that the household of Stephanas were the first converts in Achaia, and they have devoted themselves to the service of the saints. I urge you, brothers, to submit to such as these and to everyone who joins in the work, and labors at it."
- Ephesians 5:21—"Submit to one another out of reverence for Christ."
- Ephesians 5:22–24—"Wives, submit to your husbands

as to the Lord. For the husband is the head of the wife as Christ is the head of the church, his body, of which he is the Savior. Now as the church submits to Christ, so also wives should submit to their husbands in everything."

- Colossians 3:18—"Wives, submit to your husbands, as is fitting in the Lord."
- 1 Timothy 2:11–12—"A woman should learn in quietness and full submission. I do not permit a woman to teach or have authority over man; she must be silent."
- Titus 3:1–2—"Remind the people to be subject to rulers and authorities, to be obedient, to be ready to do whatever is good, to slander no one, to be peaceable and considerate and to show true humility toward all men."
- Hebrews 12:9—"Moreover, we have all had human fathers who disciplined us and we respected them for it. How much more should we submit to the Father of our spirits and live."
- Hebrews 13:17—"Obey your leaders and submit to their authority. They keep watch over you as men who must give an account. Obey them so that their work may be a joy, not a burden, for that would be of no advantage to you."
- James 1:21–25—"Therefore, get rid of all moral filth and the evil that is so prevalent and humbly accept the word planted in you, which can save you. Do not merely listen to the word, and so deceive yourselves. Do what it says. Anyone who listens to the word but does not do what it says is like a man who looks at his face in a mirror and, after looking at himself, goes away and immediately forgets what he looks like. But the man who looks intently into the perfect law that gives freedom, and continues to do

this, not forgetting what he has heard, but doing it—he
will be blessed in what he does."

- James 3:17—"But the wisdom that comes from heaven is
first of all pure; then peace-loving, considerate, submissive,
full of mercy and good fruit, impartial and sincere."

- James 4:7–8—"Submit yourselves, then, to God. Resist the
devil, and he will flee from you. Come near to God and he
will come near to you."

- 1 Peter 2:13–17—"Submit yourselves for the Lord's sake
to every authority instituted among men: whether to
the king, as the supreme authority, or to governors, who
are sent by him to punish those who do wrong and to
commend those who do right. For it is God's will that by
doing good you should silence the ignorant talk of foolish
men. Live as free men, but do not use your freedom as
a cover-up for evil; live as servants of God. Show proper
respect to everyone: Love the brotherhood of believers, fear
God, honor the king."

- 1 Peter 2:18–21—"Slaves, submit yourselves to your
masters with all respect, not only to those who are good
and considerate, but also to those who are harsh. For it is
commendable if a man bears up under the pain of unjust
suffering because he is conscious of God. But how is it
to your credit if you receive a beating for doing wrong
and endure it? But if you suffer for doing good and you
endure it, this is commendable before God. To this you
were called, because Christ suffered for you, leaving you an
example, that you should follow in His steps."

- 1 Peter 3:1—"Wives, in the same way be submissive
to your husbands so that, if any of them do not believe

the word, they may be won over without words by the behavior of their wives."

- 1 Peter 5:5—"Young men, in the same way be submissive to those who are older."
- 2 John 6—"And this is love: that we walk in obedience to his commands. As you have heard from the beginning, his command is that you walk in love."
- 2 Chronicles 31:21—"In everything that he undertook in the service of God's temple and in obedience to the law and the commands, he sought his God and worked wholeheartedly. And so he prospered."
- Ecclesiastes 8:2–6—"Obey the king's command, I say, because you took an oath before God. Do not be in a hurry to leave the king's presence. Do not stand up for a bad cause, for he will do whatever he pleases. Since a king's word is supreme, who can say to him, 'What are you doing?' Whoever obeys his command will come to no harm, and the **wise heart** will know the proper time and procedure. For there is a proper time and procedure for every matter, though a man's misery weighs heavily upon him."
- Ecclesiastes 10:4—"If a ruler's anger rises against you, do not leave your post; calmness can lay great errors to rest."

# LEADERSHIP VERSES

- Exodus 3:11–12—"But Moses said to God, 'Who am I, that I should go to Pharaoh and bring the Israelites out of Egypt?' And God said, 'I will be with you. And this will be the sign to you that is I who have sent you: When you have brought the people out of Egypt, you will worship God on this mountain.'"

- Judges 6:14–16—"The Lord turned to him and said, 'Go in the strength you have and save Israel out of Midian's hand. Am I not sending you?' 'But Lord,' Gideon asked, 'how can I save Israel? My clan is the weakest in Manasseh, and I am the least in my family.' The Lord answered, 'I will be with you, and you will strike down all the Midianites together.'"

- 1 Samuel 9:20b–10:9—"'And to whom is all the desire of Israel turned, if not to you and all your father's family?' Saul answered, 'But am I not a Benjamite, from the smallest tribe of Israel, and is not my clan the least of all the clans of the tribe of Benjamin? Why do you say such a thing to me?'...As Saul turned to leave Samuel, God changed Saul's heart, and all these signs were fulfilled that day."

- 1 Samuel 15:22–23—"But Samuel replied: 'Does the Lord delight in burnt offerings and sacrifices as much as in obeying the voice of the Lord? To obey is better than sacrifice, and to heed is better than the fat of rams. For rebellion is like the sin of divination, and arrogance like the evil of idolatry. Because you have rejected the word of the Lord, he has rejected you as king.' "
- Psalm 23:1–6—"The Lord is my shepherd, I shall not be in want. He makes me lie down in green pastures, he leads me beside quiet waters, he restores my soul. He guides me in paths of righteousness for his name's sake. Even though I walk through the valley of the shadow of death, I will fear no evil, for you are with me; your rod and your staff, they comfort me. You prepare a table before me in the presence of my enemies. You anoint my head with oil; my cup overflows. Surely goodness and love will follow me all the days of my life, and I will dwell in the house of the Lord forever."
- Psalm 27:11—"Teach me your way, O Lord; lead me in a straight path because of my oppressors."
- Psalm 143:10—"Teach me to do your will, for you are my God; may your good Spirit lead me on level ground."
- Proverbs 3:3–4—"Let love and faithfulness never leave you; bind them around your neck, write them on the tablet of your heart. Then you will win favor and a good name in the sight of God and man."
- Proverbs 8:14–16—"Counsel and sound judgment are mine; I have understanding and power. By me [wisdom] kings reign and rulers make laws that are just; by me princes govern, and all nobles who rule on earth."
- Proverbs 9:7–9—"Whoever corrects a mocker invites

insult; whoever rebukes a wicked man incurs abuse. Do not rebuke a mocker or he will hate you; rebuke a wise man and he will love you. Instruct a wise man and he will be wiser still; teach a righteous man and he will add to his learning."

- Proverbs 10:17—"He who heeds discipline shows the way to life, but whoever ignores correction leads others astray."
- Proverbs 14:28—"A large population is a king's glory, but without subjects a prince is ruined."
- Proverbs 14:35—"A king delights in a wise servant, but a shameful servant incurs his wrath."
- Proverbs 16:7—"When a man's ways are pleasing to the Lord, he makes even his enemies live at peace with him."
- Proverbs 16:10—"The lips of a king speak as an oracle, and his mouth should not betray justice."
- Proverbs 16:12—"Kings detest wrongdoing, for a throne is established through righteousness."
- Proverbs 16:13—"Kings take pleasure in honest lips; they value a man who speaks the truth."
- Proverbs 16:14—"A king's wrath is a messenger of death, but a wise man will appease it."
- Proverbs 16:15—"When a king's face brightens it means life; his favor is like a rain cloud in spring."
- Proverbs 17:7—"Arrogant lips are unsuited to a fool—how much worse lying lips to a ruler."
- Proverbs 17:26—"It is not good to punish an innocent man, or to flog officials for their integrity."
- Proverbs 18:17—"The first to present his case seems right, till another comes forward and questions him."
- Proverbs 19:2—"It is not good to have zeal without knowledge, nor to be hasty and miss the way."

- Proverbs 19:6—"Many curry favor with a ruler, and everyone is the friend of a man who gives gifts."
- Proverbs 19:10—"It is not fitting for a fool to live in luxury—how much worse for a slave to rule over princes!"
- Proverbs 19:12—"A king's rage is like the roar of a lion, but his favor is like dew on the grass."
- Proverbs 20:2—"A king's wrath is like the roar of a lion; he who angers him forfeits his life."
- Proverbs 20:8—"When a king sits on his throne to judge, he winnows out all evil with his eyes."
- Proverbs 20:26—"A wise king winnows out the wicked; he drives the threshing wheel over them."
- Proverbs 20:28—"Love and faithfulness keep a king safe; through love his throne is made secure."
- Proverbs 21:1—"The king's heart is in the hand of the Lord; he directs it like a watercourse wherever he pleases."
- Proverbs 22:10—"Drive out the mocker and out goes strife; quarrels and insults are ended."
- Proverbs 22:11—"He who loves a pure heart and whose speech is gracious will have the king for his friend."
- Proverbs 22:29—"Do you see a man skilled in his work? He will serve before kings; he will not serve before obscure men."
- Proverbs 24:5–6—"A wise man has great power, and a man of knowledge increases strength; for waging war you need guidance, and for victory many advisors."
- Proverbs 24:21–22—"Fear the Lord and the king, my son, and do not join with the rebellious, for those two will send sudden destruction upon them, and who knows what calamities they can bring?"

- Proverbs 24:23–25—"These are also sayings of the wise: To show partiality in judging is not good: Whoever says to the guilty, 'You are innocent'—peoples will curse him and nations denounce him. But it will go well with those who convict the guilty, and rich blessing will come upon them."
- Proverbs 25:2—"It is the glory of God to conceal a matter; to search out a matter is the glory of kings."
- Proverbs 25:3—"As the heavens are high and the earth is deep, so the hearts of kings are unsearchable."
- Proverbs 25:4–5—"Remove the dross from the silver, and out comes material for the silversmith; remove the wicked from the king's presence, and his throne will be established through righteousness."
- Proverbs 26:8—"Like tying a stone in a sling is the giving of honor to a fool."
- Proverbs 26:10—"Like an archer who wounds at random is he who hires a fool or any passer-by."
- Proverbs 26:24–26—"A malicious man disguises himself with his lips, but in his heart he harbors deceit. Though his speech is charming, do not believe him, for seven abominations fill his heart. His malice may be concealed by deception, but his wickedness will be exposed in the assembly."
- Proverbs 27:3—"Stone is heavy and sand a burden, but provocation by a fool is heavier than both."
- Proverbs 28:2—"When a country is rebellious, it has many rulers, but a man of understanding and knowledge maintains order."
- Proverbs 28:3—"A ruler who oppresses the poor is like a driving rain that leaves no crops."

- Proverbs 28:5—"Evil men do not understand justice, but those who seek the Lord understand it fully."
- Proverbs 28:10—"He who leads the upright along an evil path will fall into his own trap, but the blameless will receive a good inheritance."
- Proverbs 28:15—"Like a roaring lion or a charging bear is a wicked man ruling over a helpless people."
- Proverbs 28:16—"A tyrannical ruler lacks judgment, but he who hates ill-gotten gain will enjoy long life."
- Proverbs 28:28—"When the wicked rise to power, people go into hiding; but when the wicked perish, the righteous thrive."
- Proverbs 29:4—"By justice a king gives a country stability, but one who is greedy tears it down."
- Proverbs 29:12—"If a ruler listens to lies, all his officials become wicked."
- Proverbs 29:14—"If a king judges the poor with fairness, his throne will always be secure."
- Proverbs 29:18—"Where there is no revelation, the people cast off restraint; but blessed is he who keeps the law."
- Proverbs 29:26—"Many seek an audience with a ruler, but it is from the Lord that a man gets justice."
- Proverbs 30:10—"Do not slander a servant to his master, or he will curse you, and you will pay for it."
- Proverbs 30:29–31—"There are three things that are stately in their stride, four that move with stately bearing: a lion, mighty among beasts, a strutting rooster, a he-goat, a king with his army around him."
- Proverbs 31:4–7—"It is not for kings...to drink wine, not for rulers to crave beer, lest they drink and forget what the law decrees, and deprive all the oppressed of their rights.

Give beer to those who are perishing, wine to those who are in anguish; let them drink and forget their poverty and remember their misery no more."

- Proverbs 31:8–9—"Speak up for those who cannot speak for themselves, for the rights of all who are destitute. Speak up and judge fairly; defend the rights of the poor and needy."
- Ecclesiastes 2:18—"I hated all the things I had toiled for under the sun, because I must leave them to one who comes after me."
- Ecclesiastes 2:21—"For a man may do his work with wisdom, knowledge and skill, and then he must leave all he owns to someone who has not worked for it."
- Ecclesiastes 4:13–16—"Better a poor but wise youth than an old but foolish king who no longer knows how to take warning. The youth may have come from prison to the kingship, or he may have been born in poverty within his kingdom. I saw that all who lived and walked under the sun followed the youth, the king's successor. There was no end to all the people who were before them. But those who came later were not pleased with the successor. This too is meaningless, a chasing after the wind."
- Ecclesiastes 7:19—"Wisdom makes one wise man more powerful than ten rulers in a city."
- Ecclesiastes 7:21–22—"Do not pay attention to every word people say, or you may hear your servant cursing you—for you know in your heart that many times you have cursed others."
- Ecclesiastes 8:9b—"There is a time when a man lords it over others to his own hurt."
- Ecclesiastes 10:5–7—"There is an evil I have seen under

the sun, the sort of error that arises from a ruler: Fools are put in many high positions, while the rich occupy the low ones. I have seen slaves on horseback, while princes go on foot like slaves."

- Ecclesiastes 10:16–17—"Woe to you, O land whose king was a servant and whose princes feast in the morning. Blessed are you, O land whose king is of noble birth and whose princes eat at a proper time—for strength and not for drunkenness."
- Isaiah 40:11—"He tends his flock like a shepherd: He gathers the lambs in his arms and carries them close to his heart; he gently leads those that have young."
- Daniel 12:3—"Those who are wise will shine like the brightness of the heavens, and those who lead many to righteousness, like the stars for ever and ever."
- Matthew 15:14—"Leave them; they are blind guides. If a blind man leads a blind man, both will fall into a pit."
- Romans 12:6–8—"We have different gifts according to the grace given us. If a man's gift is prophecy, let him use it in proportion to his faith. If it is serving, let him serve; if it is teaching, let him teach; if it is encouraging, let him encourage; if it is contributing to the needs of others, let him give generously; if it is leadership, let him govern diligently; if it is showing mercy, let him do it cheerfully."
- 1 Corinthians 14:40—"But everything should be done in a fitting and orderly way."
- Ephesians 4:11–12—"It was he who gave some to be apostles, some to be prophets, some to be evangelists, and some to be pastors and teachers, to prepare God's people for works of service, so that the body of Christ may be built up."

- 2 Thessalonians 3:10–12—"For even when we were with you, we gave you this rule: 'If a man will not work, he shall not eat.' We hear that some among you are busybodies. Such people we command and urge in the Lord Jesus Christ to settle down and earn the bread they eat."
- 1 Timothy 3:1–13:

Here is a trustworthy saying: If anyone sets his heart on being an overseer, he desires a noble task. Now the overseer must be above reproach, the husband of one wife, temperate, self-controlled, respectable, hospitable, able to teach, not given to drunkenness, not violent but gentle, not quarrelsome, not a lover of money. He must manage his own family well and see that his children obey him with proper respect. (If anyone does not know how to manage his own family how can he take care of God's church?) He must not be a recent convert, or he may become conceited and fall under the same judgment as the devil. He must also have a good reputation with outsiders, so that he will not fall into disgrace and into the devil's trap. Deacons, likewise, are to be men of worthy of respect, sincere, not indulging in much wine, and not pursuing dishonest gain. They must keep hold of the deep truths of the faith with a clear conscience. The must first be tested and then if there is nothing against them, let them serve as deacons. In the same way, their wives are to be women worthy of respect, not malicious talkers but temperate and trustworthy in everything. A deacon must be the husband of but one wife and must manage his children and his household well. Those who have served well gain an excellent standing and great assurance in their faith in Christ Jesus.

- 1 Timothy 3:17–20—"The elders who direct the affairs of the church are well worthy of double honor, especially those whose work is preaching and teaching. For the Scripture says, 'Do not muzzle the ox while it is treading out the grain,' and 'The worker deserves his wages.' Do not entertain an accusation against an elder unless it is brought by two or three witnesses. Those who sin are to be rebuked publicly, so that the others may take warning."

- Titus 1:6–9—"An elder must be blameless, the husband of but one wife, a man whose children believe and are not open to the charge of being wild and disobedient. Since an overseer is entrusted with God's work, he must be blameless—not overbearing, not quick-tempered, not given to drunkenness, not violent, not pursuing dishonest gain. Rather he must be hospitable, one who loves what is good, who is self-controlled, upright, holy and disciplined. He must hold firmly to the trustworthy message as it has been taught, so that he can encourage others by sound doctrine and refute those who oppose it."

- Titus 3:1–2—"Remind the people to be subject to rulers and authorities, to be obedient, to be ready to do whatever is good, to slander no one, to be peaceable and considerate, and to show true humility toward all men."

- Hebrews 13:7—"Remember your leaders, who spoke the word of God to you."

- Hebrews 13:17—"Obey your leaders and submit to their authority. They keep watch over you as men who must give an account. Obey them so that their work will be a joy, not a burden, for that would be of no advantage to you."

- James 3:1—"Not many of you should presume to be teachers, my brothers, because you know that we who teach will be judged more strictly."
- James 3:16—"For where you have envy and selfish ambition, there you will find disorder and every evil practice."
- 1 John 3:7—"Dear children, do not let anyone lead you astray."

# VERSES ON MANAGING WEALTH (STEWARDSHIP)

- 1 Chronicles 29:11–13—"Yours, O Lord, is the greatness and the power and the glory and the majesty and the splendor, for everything in heaven and earth is yours. Yours, O Lord, is the kingdom; you are exalted as head over all. Wealth and honor come from you; you are the ruler of all things. In your hands are strength and power to exalt and give strength to all. Now, our God, we give you thanks, and praise your glorious name."
- Psalm 127:1–2—"Unless the Lord builds the house, its builders labor in vain. Unless the Lord watches over the city, the watchmen stand guard in vain. In vain you rise early and stay up late, toiling for food to eat—for he grants sleep to those he loves."
- Proverbs 1:19—"Such is the end of all who go after ill-gotten gain; it takes away the lives of those who get it."
- Proverbs 3:1–2—"My son, do not forget my teaching, but keep my commands in your heart, for they will prolong your life many years and bring you prosperity."
- Proverbs 3:9–10—"Honor the Lord with your wealth, with the first fruits of all your crops; then your barns will

be filled to overflowing, and your vats will brim over with new wine."

- Proverbs 3:13–14—"Blessed is the man who finds wisdom, the man who gains understanding, for she is more profitable than silver and yields better returns than gold. She is more precious than rubies; nothing you desire can compare with her."
- Proverbs 3:27–28—"Do not withhold good from those who deserve it, when it is in your power to act. Do not say to your neighbor, 'Come back later; I'll give it tomorrow'—when you now have it with you."
- Proverbs 4:7—"Wisdom is supreme; therefore get wisdom. Though it cost all you have, get understanding."
- Proverbs 6:1–5—"My son, if you have put up security for your neighbor, if you have struck hands in pledge for another, if you have been trapped by what you said, ensnared by the words of your mouth, then do this, my son, to free yourself; press your plea with your neighbor! Allow no sleep to your eyes, no slumber to your eyelids. Free yourself, like a gazelle from the hand of the hunter, like a bird from the snare of the fowler."
- Proverbs 8:10–11—"Choose my instruction instead of silver, knowledge rather than choice gold, for wisdom is more precious than rubies, and nothing you desire can compare with her."
- Proverbs 8:18–21—"With me [wisdom] are riches and honor, enduring wealth and prosperity. My fruit is better than fine gold; what I yield surpasses choice silver. I walk in the way of righteousness, along the paths of justice, bestowing wealth on those who love me and making their treasuries full."

- Proverbs 10:2—"Ill gotten treasures are of no value, but righteousness delivers from death."
- Proverbs 10:4—"Lazy hands make a man poor, but diligent hands bring wealth."
- Proverbs 10:5—"He who gathers crops in summer is a wise son, but he who sleeps during harvest is a disgraceful son."
- Proverbs 10:15—"The wealth of the rich is their fortified city, but poverty is the ruin of the poor."
- Proverbs 10:22—"The blessing of the Lord brings wealth, and he adds no trouble to it."
- Proverbs 11:4—"Wealth is worthless in the day of wrath, but righteousness delivers from death."
- Proverbs 11:18—"The wicked man earns deceptive wages, but he who sows righteousness reaps a sure reward."
- Proverbs 11:24—"One man gives freely, yet gains even more; another withholds unduly, but comes to poverty."
- Proverbs 11:25—"A generous man will prosper; he who refreshes others will himself be refreshed."
- Proverbs 11:26—"People curse the man who hoards grain, but blessing crowns him who is willing to sell."
- Proverbs 11:28—"Whoever trusts in his riches will fall, but the righteous will thrive like a green leaf."
- Proverbs 12:9—"Better to be a nobody and yet have a servant than pretend to be somebody and have no food."
- Proverbs 12:11—"He who works his land will have abundant food, but he who chases fantasies lacks judgment."
- Proverbs 12:14—"From the fruit of his lips a man is filled with good things as surely as the work of his hands rewards him."

- Proverbs 13:7—"One man pretends to be rich, yet has nothing; another pretends to be poor, yet has great wealth."
- Proverbs 13:8—"A man's riches may ransom his life, but a poor man hears no threat."
- Proverbs 13:11—"Dishonest money dwindles away, but he who gathers money little by little makes it grow."
- Proverbs 13:18—"He who ignores discipline comes to poverty and shame, but whoever heeds correction is honored."
- Proverbs 13:21—"Misfortune pursues the sinner, but prosperity is the reward of the righteous."
- Proverbs 13:22—"A good man leaves an inheritance for his children's children, but a sinner's wealth is stored up for the righteous."
- Proverbs 14:4—"Where there are no oxen, the manger is empty, but from the strength of an ox comes an abundant harvest."
- Proverbs 14:20—"The poor are shunned even by their neighbors, but the rich have many friends."
- Proverbs 14:21—"He who despises his neighbor sins, but blessed is he who is kind to the needy."
- Proverbs 14:23—"All hard work brings a profit, but mere talk leads only to poverty."
- Proverbs 14:24—"The wealth of the wise is their crown, but the folly of fools yields folly."
- Proverbs 14:31—"He who oppresses the poor shows contempt for their Maker, but whoever is kind to the needy honors God."
- Proverbs 15:6—"The house of the righteous contains great treasure, but the income of the wicked brings them trouble."

- Proverbs 15:16—"Better a little with the fear of the Lord than great wealth with turmoil."
- Proverbs 15:17—"Better a meal of vegetables where there is love than a fattened calf with hatred."
- Proverbs 16:8—"Better a little with righteousness than much gain with injustice."
- Proverbs 16:16—"How much better to get wisdom than gold, to choose understanding rather than silver."
- Proverbs 16:19—"Better to be lowly in spirit and among the oppressed than to share plunder with the proud."
- Proverbs 17:1—"Better a dry crust with peace and quiet than a house full of feasting with strife."
- Proverbs 17:5—"He who mocks the poor shows contempt for their Maker; whoever gloats over disaster will not go unpunished."
- Proverbs 17:16—"Of what use is money in the hand of a fool, since he has no desire to get wisdom?"
- Proverbs 18:11—"The wealth of the rich is their fortified city; they imagine it an unscalable wall."
- Proverbs 18:23—"A poor man pleads for mercy, but a rich man answers harshly."
- Proverbs 19:1—"Better a poor man whose walk is blameless than a fool whose lips are perverse."
- Proverbs 19:7—"A poor man is shunned by all his relatives—how much more do his friends avoid him! Though he pursues them with pleading, they are nowhere to be found."
- Proverbs 19:8—"He who gets wisdom loves his own soul; he who cherishes understanding prospers."
- Proverbs 19:10—"It is not fitting for a fool to live in luxury—how much worse for a slave to rule over princes!"

- Proverbs 19:17—"He who is kind to the poor lends to the Lord, and he will reward him for what he has done."
- Proverbs 19:22—"What a man desires is unfailing love; better to be poor than a liar."
- Proverbs 20:4—"A sluggard does not plow in season; so at harvest time he looks but finds nothing."
- Proverbs 20:13—"Do not love sleep or you will grow poor; stay awake and you will have food to spare."
- Proverbs 20:21—"An inheritance quickly gained at the beginning will not be blessed at the end."
- Proverbs 21:5—"The plans of the diligent lead to profit as surely as haste leads to poverty."
- Proverbs 21:6—"A fortune made by a lying tongue is a fleeting vapor and a deadly snare."
- Proverbs 21:13—"If a man shuts his ears to the cry of the poor, he too will cry out and not be heard."
- Proverbs 21:17—"He who loves pleasure will become poor; whoever loves wine and oil will never be rich."
- Proverbs 21:20—"In the house of the wise are stores of choice food and oil, but a foolish man devours all he has."
- Proverbs 21:21—"He who pursues righteousness and love finds life, prosperity, and honor."
- Proverbs 22:1—"A good name is more desirable than great riches; to be esteemed is better than silver or gold."
- Proverbs 22:2—"Rich and poor have this in common: The Lord is the Maker of them all."
- Proverbs 22:7—"The rich rule over the poor, and the borrower is servant to the lender."
- Proverbs 22:8—"A generous man will himself be blessed, for he shares his food with the poor."

- Proverbs 22:4—"Humility and the fear of the Lord bring wealth and honor and life."
- Proverbs 22:16—"He who oppresses the poor to increase his wealth and he who gives gifts to the rich—both come to poverty."
- Proverbs 22:22–23—"Do not exploit the poor because they are poor and do not crush the needy in court, for the Lord will take up their case and will plunder those who plunder them."
- Proverbs 22:26–27—"Do not be a man who strikes hands in pledge or puts up security for debts; if you lack the means to pay, your very bed will be snatched from under you."
- Proverbs 23:4–5—"Do not wear yourself out to get rich; have the wisdom to show restraint. Cast but a glance at riches, and they are gone, for they will surely sprout wings and fly off to the sky like an eagle."
- Proverbs 23:19–21—"Listen, my son, and be wise, and keep your heart on the right path. Do not join those who drink too much wine or gorge themselves on meat, for drunkards and gluttons become poor, and drowsiness clothes them in rags."
- Proverbs 24:3–4—"By wisdom a house is built, and through understanding it is established; through knowledge its rooms are filled with rare and beautiful treasures."
- Proverbs 24:30–34—"I went past the field of the sluggard, past the vineyard of the man who lacks judgment; thorns had come up everywhere, the ground was covered with weeds, and the stone wall was in ruins. I applied my heart

to what I observed and learned a lesson from what I saw;
A little sleep, a little slumber, a little folding of the hands
to rest—and poverty will come on you like a bandit and
scarcity like an armed man."

- Proverbs 27:20—"Death and Destruction are never
  satisfied, and neither are the eyes of man."

- Proverbs 27:23–27—"Be sure you know the condition of
  your flocks, give careful attention to your herds; for riches
  do not endure forever, and a crown is not secure for all
  generations. When the hay is removed and new growth
  appears and the grass from the hills is gathered in, the
  lambs will provide you with clothing, and the goats with
  the price of a field. You will have plenty of goat's milk
  to feed you and your family and to nourish your servant
  girls."

- Proverbs 28:6—"Better a poor man whose walk is
  blameless than a rich man whose ways are perverse."

- Proverbs 28:8—"He who increases his wealth by
  exorbitant interest amasses it for another who will be kind
  to the poor."

- Proverbs 28:11—"A rich man may be wise in his own eyes,
  but a poor man who has discernment sees through him."

- Proverbs 28:16—"A tyrannical ruler lacks judgment, but
  he who hates ill-gotten gain will enjoy long life."

- Proverbs 28:19—"He who works his land will have
  abundant food, but the one who chases fantasies will have
  his fill of poverty."

- Proverbs 28:20—"A faithful man will be richly blessed, but
  one eager to get rich will not go unpunished."

- Proverbs 28:22—"A stingy man is eager to get rich and is
  unaware that poverty awaits him."

- Proverbs 28:25—"A greedy man stirs up dissension, but he who trusts in the Lord will prosper."
- Proverbs 28:27—"He who gives to the poor will lack nothing, but he who closes his eyes to them receives many curses."
- Proverbs 29:3—"A man who loves wisdom brings joy to his father, but a companion of prostitutes squanders his wealth."
- Proverbs 29:7—"The righteous care about justice for the poor, but the wicked have no such concern."
- Proverbs 29:13—"The poor man and the oppressor have this in common: The Lord gives sight to the eyes of both."
- Proverbs 30:8–9—"...give me neither poverty nor riches, but give me only my daily bread. Otherwise, I may have too much and disown you and say, 'Who is the Lord?' Or I may become poor and steal, and so dishonor the name of my God."
- Proverbs 31:8–9—"Speak up for those who cannot speak for themselves, for the rights of all who are destitute. Speak up and judge fairly; defend the rights of the poor and needy."
- Ecclesiastes 4:6–8—"Better one handful with tranquility than two handfuls with toil and chasing after the wind. Again I saw something meaningless under the sun: There was a man all alone; he had neither son nor brother. There was no end to his toil, yet his eyes were not content with his wealth. 'For whom am I toiling,' he asked, 'and why am I depriving myself of enjoyment?' This too is meaningless—a miserable business!"
- Ecclesiastes 5:10—"Whoever loves money never has money enough; whoever loves wealth is never satisfied with his income. This too is meaningless."

- Ecclesiastes 5:12—"The sleep of a laborer is sweet, whether he eats little or much, but the abundance of a rich man permits him no sleep."
- Ecclesiastes 5:18–20—"Then I realized that it is good and proper for a man to eat and drink and to find satisfaction in his toilsome labor under the sun during the few days of life God has given him—for this is his lot. Moreover, when God gives any man wealth and possessions, and enables him to enjoy them, to accept his lot and be happy in his work—this is a gift of God. He seldom reflects on the days of his life, because God keeps him occupied with gladness of heart."
- Ecclesiastes 6:2–3—"God gives a man wealth, possessions and honor, so that he lacks nothing his heart desires, but God does not enable him to enjoy them, and a stranger enjoys them instead. A man may have a hundred children and live many years; yet no matter how long he lives, if he cannot enjoy his prosperity and does not receive proper burial, I say that a stillborn child is better off than he."
- Ecclesiastes 6:7—"All man's efforts are for his mouth, yet his appetite is never satisfied."
- Ecclesiastes 7:11–12—"Wisdom, like an inheritance, is a good thing and benefits those who see the sun. Wisdom is a shelter as money is a shelter, but the advantage of knowledge is this: that wisdom preserves the life of its possessor."
- Ecclesiastes 9:16—"Wisdom is better than strength. But the poor man's wisdom is despised, and his words are no longer heeded."
- Ecclesiastes 11:1–2—"Cast your bread upon the waters, for after many days you will find it again. Give portions to

seven, yes to eight, for you do not know what disaster may come upon the land."

- Matthew 6:19–21—"Do not store up for yourselves treasures on earth, where moth and rust destroy, and where thieves break in and steal. But store up for yourselves treasures in heaven, where moth and rust do not destroy, and where thieves do not break in and steal. For where your treasure is, there your heart will be also."

- Matthew 6:24—"No one can serve two masters. Either he will hate the one and love the other, or he will be devoted to the one and despise the other. You cannot serve both God and Money."

- Matthew 19:21—"Jesus answered, 'If you want to be perfect, go, sell your possessions and give to the poor, and you will have treasure in heaven. Then come, follow me.'"

- Matthew 19:23–24—"Then Jesus said to his disciples, 'I tell you the truth, it is hard for a rich man to enter the kingdom of heaven. Again I tell you, it is easier for a camel to go through the eye of a needle than for a rich man to enter the kingdom of God.'"

- Luke 16:15—"He said to them, 'You are the ones who justify yourselves in the eyes of men, but God knows your hearts. What is highly valued among men is detestable in God's sight.'"

- 2 Corinthians 8:14–15—"At the present time your plenty will supply what they need, so that in turn their plenty will supply what you need. Then there will be equality, as it is written: 'He who gathered much did not have too much, and he who gathered little did not have too little.'"

- 2 Corinthians 9:6–7—"Remember this: Whoever sows sparingly will also reap sparingly, and whoever sows generously will also reap generously. Each man should give what he has decided in his heart to give, not reluctantly or under compulsion, for God loves a cheerful giver."

- 1 Timothy 3:2–3—"Now the overseer must be above reproach, the husband of but one wife, temperate, self-controlled, respectable, hospitable, able to teach, not given to drunkenness, not violent but gentle, not quarrelsome, not a lover of money."

- 1 Timothy 6:10—"For the love of money is a root of all kinds of evil. Some people, eager for money, have wandered from the faith and pierced themselves with many griefs."

- Hebrews 13:5—"Keep your lives free from the love of money and be content with what you have, because God has said, 'Never will I leave you; never will I forsake you.'"

- James 1:9–11—"The brother in humble circumstances ought take pride in his high position. But the one who is rich should take pride in his low position, because he will pass away like a wild flower...In the same way, the rich man will fade away even while he goes about his business."

- James 2:5–7—"Listen, my dear brothers: Has not God chosen those who are poor in the eyes of the world to be rich in faith and to inherit the kingdom he promised those who love him? But you have insulted the poor. Is it not the rich who are exploiting you? Are they not the ones who are dragging you into court? Are they not the ones who are slandering the noble name of him to whom you belong?"

- James 2:14–17—"What good is it, my brothers, if a man claims to have faith but has no deeds? Can such faith save him? Suppose a brother or sister is without clothes and daily food. If one of you says to him, 'Go, I wish you well; keep warm and well fed,' but does nothing about his physical needs, what good is it? In the same way, faith by itself, if it is not accompanied by action, is dead."

- James 4:17—"Anyone, then, who knows the good he ought to do and doesn't do it, sins."
- James 5:1–6:

Now listen, you rich people, weep and wail because of the misery that is coming upon you. Your wealth has rotted, and moths have eaten your clothes. Your gold and silver are corroded. Their corrosion will testify against you and eat your flesh like fire. You have hoarded wealth in the last days. Look! The wages you failed to pay the workmen who mowed your fields are crying out against you. The cries of the harvesters have reached the ears of the Lord Almighty. You have lived on earth in luxury and self-indulgence. You have fattened yourselves in the day of slaughter. You have condemned and murdered innocent men, who were not opposing you.